The London Medieval and Renaissance Series

The General Prologue to The Canterbury Tales and The Canon's Yeoman's Prologue and Tale

General Editor A. V. C. Schmidt

Geoffrey Chaucer

The General Prologue to The Canterbury Tales and The Canon's Yeoman's Prologue and Tale

Edited by A. V. C. Schmidt

University of London Press Ltd

ISBN 0 340 18501 5 Boards
ISBN 0 340 09215 7 Paper

First published in this edition 1974

University of London Press Ltd
St Paul's House, Warwick Lane, London EC4P 4AH

Printed and bound in Great Britain by
Hazell Watson & Viney Ltd
Aylesbury, Bucks

Preface

This edition contains *The General Prologue* which introduces the *Canterbury Tales*, and *The Canon's Yeoman's Tale*, which may have been the last of the tales to have been written. Both works are provided with lexical notes printed at the foot of the page to enable the reader to understand the text with the minimum of inconvenience. Fuller discussion of words, historical points, and questions of interpretation are to be found in a very full Commentary at the back of the book, to which the lexical footnotes frequently refer. The Introduction consists of a critical account of both works. *The General Prologue* is treated as a great poem in its own right, an original masterpiece of great inventiveness and subtlety, but also an important guide to the reading of the *Tales* as a whole. Chaucer's realism is examined in terms of his own concepts of 'cheere' 'estat', 'condicioun', etc., which determine the approach to both his methods and his intentions, and there is also a full discussion of 'satire' in the *Prologue* and a section on 'Style and Imagery'.

The Introduction to *The Canon's Yeoman's Tale* places the poem in its background of medieval theories about alchemy, and the Commentary supplies very full explanations of the activities and experiments incidentally described or alluded to in the poem. The main argument is that this tale constitutes an example of Chaucer's 'ironical narratives', of which the *Pardoner's* and *Friar's Tales* are other examples. The Introduction goes on to analyse the tale's polemical purpose, its theme, structure and style.

Acknowledgments

Any editor of Chaucer must be deeply conscious of his debt to earlier editions, in particular to those of Skeat and Robinson. I have also drawn gratefully on the admirable edition of the *General Prologue* by Phyllis Hodgson.

I wish to thank Nicolas Jacobs for some suggestions about the lexical notes, my mother-in-law Mrs Yvonne Jackson for typing part of the text, and my wife for helping me check the proofs.

This book was mainly written during a very enjoyable year spent in Dublin, part of the Introduction being based on lectures given in the English Department of University College. I wish to record my deep appreciation of the friendship and hospitality shown me by the late Fr Thomas Dunning c.m., Professor of Old and Middle English at UCD till his death in 1973. He was not only devoted to medieval literature but also a cause of devotion to it in others, including myself. This edition is a slight tribute to his memory.

Oxford, 1973   A.V.C.S.

Contents

Introduction

The General Prologue

I Chaucer's Poetry

He must have been a man of a most wonderful comprehensive nature, because, as it has been truly observed of him, he has taken into the compass of his *Canterbury Tales* the various manners and humours . . . of the whole English nation in his age. . . . All his pilgrims are severally distinguished from each other. . . . The matter and manner of their tales, and of their telling, are so suited to their different educations, humours, and callings, that each of them would be improper in any other mouth . . . the grave and serious characters are distinguished by their several sorts of gravity. . . . Even the ribaldry of the low characters is different . . . there is such a variety of game springing up before me that I am distracted in my choice. . . . 'Tis sufficient to say . . . *that here is God's plenty.*[1]

This is Dryden's account of the essential nature of Chaucer's genius, and subsequent criticism has done little more than fill in the particulars. Even Matthew Arnold, who found Chaucer's poetry lacking in 'high seriousness' of the Shakespearian or Dantesque kind,[2] acknowledged the exuberant inventiveness of 'the father of English poetry', as Dryden (not quite accurately) called him. *The Canterbury Tales* is not the first great masterpiece of English poetry – *Piers Plowman, Sir Gawain and the Green Knight* and Chaucer's own *Troilus and Criseyde* all preceded it – but it is the culmination of the first phase of the English tradition of which Shakespeare is the centre and the great nineteenth-century novelists and their modern successors the latest development. No individual tale, of course, is a work of the order of *King Lear* or *Macbeth*, but in range and richness Chaucer's total achievement is unrivalled outside that of Shakespeare's plays. *The Merchant's Tale, The Pardoner's Tale* and *The Wife of Bath's Prologue* are amongst the most original as well as most perfect creations in the language – a combination the rareness of which is not commonly recognized. Chaucer's mature poetic style, too, so free from the diffuseness of most medieval and the self-consciousness or complication of much Renaissance and post-Renaissance writing, is easy to take for granted until one realizes how difficult it is to achieve. Once again, as Dryden acutely observed:

As he knew what to say, so he knows also when to leave off; a continence which is practised by few writers.

---

[1] *Preface to the Fables*, pp. 189–90 [see SOURCES AND ABBREVIATIONS, p. 170, for fuller details of this and other sources].
[2] See 'The Study of Poetry', p. 19.

But the temperance which gives Chaucer's style its 'smoothness' does not reflect a lack of depth. It is just that Chaucer's 'depths' are not troubled ones. The great public catastrophes of his age, such as the Black Death, and the great political upheavals, like the Peasants' Revolt, find surprisingly few echoes in *The Canterbury Tales*, for all its deliberately realistic and contemporary framework. And, to judge by the poetry, there were no corresponding tumults *within* the man. Chaucer differs radically from Dante, Shakespeare, Milton and Tolstoy (and perhaps most great writers) in that his work does not seek a resolution or synthesis of discordant energies and conflicting impulses. Not only in a 'comedy' like *The Canterbury Tales* but also in a 'tragedy' (the description is Chaucer's own) like *Troilus*, his attitude is fundamentally calm and detached. This is at once Chaucer's limitation and strength. Chaucer seems not to have been a poet to whom, in Keats's phrase,

> the miseries of the world
> Are misery, and will not let them rest.[3]

The life-enhancing joy of his poetry convinces us, however, that he *is* (again in Keats's phrase), 'a sage' and 'a humanist, physician to all men'.[4]

Chaucer's 'calm' is not due simply to his being a believing Christian. Some of the greatest Christian artists have been tortured by self-doubt and self-despair (one thinks of Donne, Hopkins or Van Gogh). It was much more a matter of what Chaucer himself would have called *temperament* – the balance or blending of qualities in a man's character. The *joy* of his poetry (like that of Bach's music), though reinforced by religious faith, springs from a profound faith in *life* which is different from a facile optimism about human nature or a bland insensitivity to evil and pain. *Troilus and Criseyde* is Chaucer's great study in *pathos*. But in the *Tales*, too, he does not ignore or bypass suffering, grief and cruelty, especially in the form of one human being's exploitation of another. A fine example is the *Clerk's Tale*, in which Grisilde, after the many inhuman tests she is subjected to by her husband, is finally reunited with her children, and faints:

> And in hire swough so sadly holdeth she
> Hire children two, whan she gan hem t'embrace,
> That with greet sleighte and greet difficultee
> The children from hire arm they gonne arace.[5]

---

[3] *The Fall of Hyperion*, Canto I, 148–9.
[4] *Ib.*, 189–90.
[5] D 1100–3.
swough, swoon.   sadly, tightly.
sleighte, effort.   gonne arace, tore away.

The force of these lines comes partly from their reticence and objectivity, partly from the carefully pondered rightness of words like *sleighte*, *sadly*, and *arace* and the labouring rhythm of the third line, which dramatically 'enacts' the efforts of the friends and communicates (without comment) the suppressed intensity of Grisilde's emotion. Again, the tragic death of Arcite in the *Knight's Tale*, and in particular the dying speech, are justly famous. But the simple magnificence of the language at the finale of the scene is less often noticed than the preceding eloquence. It exemplifies the kind of style Wordsworth set out to achieve in *Michael*:

> And with that word his speche faille gan,
> For from his feet up to his brest was come
> *The coold of deeth, that had him overcome,*
>   . . . for in his armes two
> The vital strengthe is lost and al ago.[6]

In focusing on the dying knight's arms, Chaucer reminds us that Arcite's life was dedicated to the god of war, Mars, but that he will now never move and fight again. A powerful response to the '*vital strength*' of man and nature – the energy of life – is a chief source of Chaucer's art and gives it an intensity (and a depth) that are without tension, conflict or strain. To take another example: in the *Franklin's Tale* some apparently straightforward lines of seasonal description communicate with extraordinary force the mood of desolation and despair in which the young squire Aurelius is sunk:

> The bittre frostes, with the sleet and reyn,
> Destroyed hath the grene in every yerd.[7]

The symbolism here (to which the unexpected violence of *destroyed* alerts us) – the green of summer's vegetation suggesting hope and youth – is muted, but all the more poignant for it. Elsewhere Chaucer celebrates the life-bringing return of day in verse of exquisite buoyancy:

> The bisy larke, messager of day,
> Salueth in hir song the morwe gray,
> And firy Phebus riseth up so bright
> That al the orient laugheth of the light,
> And with his stremes dryeth in the greves
> The silver dropes hangynge on the leves.[8]

The idea of 'streams' of sunshine drying 'drops' of water, with its delicately unobtrusive suggestion of paradox, helps to convey a

[6] A 2798–2802.
[7] F 1250–1.
[8] A 1491–6.

subtle sense of oneness in and with the order of things. Chaucer's is a poetry of clear definition and sensuous shapeliness. A more illuminating epithet for it than 'medieval' would be *classical*.

II The Canterbury Tales

No less impressive in Chaucer's mature work than his feel for atmosphere and mood, his rhythmic sensitivity and verbal 'tact', is his sense of *structure*. From the taut, streamlined narrative of the *Pardoner's Tale* to the astonishing twelve-hundred line 'frame-story' which holds the *Tales* together (the story of the Pilgrimage), he reveals a complete control of his material which never degenerates into manipulation. Chaucer's characters have not only vitality but freedom. The Wife of Bath in her *Prologue* threatens to burst the narrative framework almost as Falstaff does that of *Henry IV, Part I*. But the 'threat' is never realized: Chaucer's thematic concerns confine (without frustrating) the Wife's uninhibited self-expression. Her *Prologue* and *Tale* both accordingly take their place in a larger pattern of tales exploring the themes of marriage and true nobility, and Chaucer's creative energies issue not in anarchy but a more complex order.

If the *Tales* throw up a wide range of life-like characters – Dorigen, Simkin, Alison, January (from the Franklin's, Reeve's, Miller's and Merchant's *Tales* respectively) – characters scarcely less real than the pilgrims in whose tales they appear – they are equally varied in their setting, intention and form. The best poems of a Milton, Wordsworth or Pope all bear a generic resemblance to one another – which perhaps suggests the limitations of these undoubtedly great poets. But the emotional range Chaucer spans – from the highly amusing comedy of sex of the *Shipman's Tale* to the subtle exploration of moral crisis in a supposedly ideal marriage of the *Franklin's Tale* – is exceeded only by Shakespeare and equalled by no other English writer. Just as striking as the polar contrasts of literary genre within Chaucer's oeuvre are the varieties of *comedy* in the *Tales*. Nine of these are comedies in the usual modern sense – light-hearted stories which make us laugh (the *medieval* sense of 'comedy' was 'any story which *ended* happily') – and yet only the Reeve's *Tale*, a direct reply to the Miller's, closely resembles the mode or method of any of the others. The variety of Chaucer's treatment of his materials is such that readers are sometimes surprised to discover that a work like the *Merchant's Tale* is at once a handling of the stock *fabliau* theme of the old husband married to a young wife and cuckolded by a young man, and a mirror-image, however distorted, of the *Franklin's Tale*, a deeply serious poem untouched by the slightest levity. The comic tales (with which, in this respect, the *General Prologue* ought to be placed) abound in satire – of knights and squires, alchemists and their dupes, merchants, clerics, students and women. It is usually good-natured and often *dramatic* satire – that is, directed by one pilgrim against another or another's profession, sex or class through the tale he or she tells. (See below, p. 8.) For Chaucer's own attitude we need to turn from the *Tales* to the *Prologue* and the Frame-story.

The General Prologue

The *General Prologue* is at once a great poem in its own right and a perfect introduction to medieval English literature. Chaucer wrote in the East Midland dialect of English, which was spoken at the court in Westminster, in the city of London and in the universities. This dialect, from which the English we speak descends, makes him easier to read than many of his contemporaries, some of them great poets, who wrote in more Northern or Western dialects. Chaucer's English is an earlier form of Shakespeare's, not a foreign tongue requiring 'translation'. We sometimes have to paraphrase to bring out what is compressed or implicit in the original, but much of Chaucer is as clear as if written yesterday, like these lines describing the Summoner:

> A fewe termes hadde he, two or three,
> That he had lerned out of som decree –
> No wonder is, he herde it al the day . . .

In that Chaucer's pronunciation (see *Appendix I*) differed from our own, he *does* resemble a foreign writer; but it is still arguable that for all his (now) obsolete words and idioms, Chaucer's poetry is in some ways actually easier to understand than much of Shakespeare or Milton (see section on *Style* below).

Chaucer probably wrote the *Prologue* in about 1387, before most of the *Tales*. Its length and elaboration indicate that he regarded it as rather more than a mere introduction, like the Prologue to the work of his contemporary William Langland, *Piers Plowman* (*c.* 1362–90). Chaucer's *Prologue* can be read as a self-contained poem, and though it initiates the frame-story, it does not depend on what follows to be understood and appreciated. In this it resembles the *Prologue* to Chaucer's earlier collection of tales (never finished), *The Legend of Good Women* (?1386), a poem of over 550 lines which has an interest independent of and indeed surpassing that of an introduction to the individual legends. Chaucer's purpose seems to have been to create a living portrait-gallery of contemporary humanity as he knew it and to provide a faithful record and interpretation of the colourful and bustling life of his age. In spite of his pervasive moral interest and clear-cut moral standpoint, Chaucer's portraits do not illustrate a moral or philosophical thesis as do those of Pope, say, in his *Moral Essays*. Their contemporariness is as important as their timelessness. The *Prologue* has always been valued for the light it throws on English society in the late fourteenth century. The older critics admired the depth of its human insight, but only more recently has attention focused on the subtleties of its consummate art.

The Frame-Story and the Tales

Chaucer describes the progress of the pilgrims from Southwark to Canterbury in a series of passages known as 'links' which act as a kind of *frame-story* around the individual tales. Because Chaucer died before finishing the poem, some of the links are incomplete or missing, and because of variations between the MSS of the poem, the exact order of the tales is uncertain. All scholars divide them into ten groups, numbered A to I, with the group called B having two parts, B[1] and B[2]. A widely accepted view, based on the internal evidence of the poem rather than on the authority of any MS or group of MSS, places the groups in the order: A, B[1], B[2], D, E, F, C, G, H, I, differing from that of the standard modern edition of Chaucer's *Works* (Robinson's), which follows the ordering of the Ellesmere manuscript.[9]

Two tales are left *unfinished*, the Cook's and the Squire's. The former is a fabliau in type[10] and only about a hundred lines were written. The latter gets further, but Chaucer may have become bored with it or else not known how to finish it. Two other tales are '*fragments*' but not unfinished, the Monk's *Tale* and Chaucer's tale of *Sir Thopas*. These were deliberately designed to be interrupted, the one by the Knight (who finds the Monk's recital of gloomy 'tragedies' too depressing for the occasion) and the other by the Host (on the ostensible grounds that the *rhyming* 'is nat worth a toord'). Of the completed tales two have long 'autobiographical' Prologues (Wife of Bath, Pardoner) and in a third (Canon's Yeoman) Prologue and Tale are scarcely distinguishable (see Introduction and text in this volume). Other tales also have 'autobiographical'

---

[9] See *Pratt* [see Sources and Abbreviations, p. 170], and cf. *Owen*, esp. 201–4, or a different view.

[10] A *fabliau* is a comic tale, often coarse and boisterous, dealing generally with social classes below the aristocratic level. For a guide to criticism of Chaucer's fabliau-tales, see *Brewer*.

passages in their Prologues (e.g. the Reeve's and Merchant's, dealing respectively with the miseries of old age and unhappy marriage). These 'prologues' are in many cases identical with the Links.

The *Tales* cover a wide range of literary types and sum up the poetic achievement of the Middle Ages. This makes them an ideal introduction to medieval literature as a whole (although Chaucerian narrative, it is worth remembering, is always a highly sophisticated development of what is elsewhere a naïve or even crude genre). Of the two least attractive tales, both in prose, the Parson's is a sermon-treatise on the Seven Deadly Sins, and though not dull is mainly of historical interest, while Chaucer's own semi-allegorical tale of *Melibee* again appeals to the specialist rather than the general reader. *Sir Thopas* is a brilliant parody of bad popular romance, the first great parody in English. The Prioress and Second Nun tell tales of Christian martyrs and the Physician a tale of a pre-Christian 'martyr' in the cause of virtue. The Clerk and Man of Law tell tales about women whose patience and endurance are tested under extreme conditions. Together these five tales of *hoolynesse* constitute the least realistic group in the collection. Though very good of their kind, they are not the most accessible of Chaucer's works. The tales of the Manciple and Nun's Priest are both about animals, the one brief and terse, the other (a moral fable) developed with great richness and comic detail. The tales of the Knight, Franklin and Wife of Bath are generally classed as 'courtly romances', though each has a strong philosophical tinge and a moral intensity unusual in romance. The *Wife's Tale* uses a traditional story of the folk-tale type as a peg from which to hang a disquisition on the nature of true nobility (*gentillesse*), while the *Knight's Tale*, a brilliant *tour de force*, is a simultaneous celebration and critique of courtly-chivalric existence. The *Franklin's Tale* is a highly dramatic *nouvelle* about love, marriage and knightly ethics and (once again) the nature of true *gentillesse*, placed in a fantastic romance setting in which magic plays an important part. The Shipman's, Miller's and Reeve's *Tales* are fabliaux of great inventiveness and wit; the *Summoner's Tale* represents the simplest and coarsest variety of the type, while the *Merchant's Tale* can be called without exaggeration the apotheosis of the genre. No less impressive are two other comic works, the *Wife of Bath's Prologue* and the *Canon's Yeoman's Prologue and Tale*, which are wholly original and fit into no category, though they have affinities with the fabliau in mood and tone. Finally, the tales of the Friar and Pardoner are triumphant examples of the type of ironic narrative which is peculiarly Chaucer's own. (On the relations between these and the *Canon's Yeoman's Tale*, see Introduction to the latter below.) The humour of Chaucer's comic tales is by turns sardonic, boisterous and lighthearted, now punctuated by pathos, now by horror. The romances differ from most specimens of the genre and illustrate

Chaucer's tendency to make every literary form he adapts more witty, learned and humane, imbued with the distinctive colouring of his mind and personality. Like Shakespeare with the chronicle-history, revenge-tragedy and comedy of intrigue, Chaucer transforms existing literary types rather than consciously creates new ones.

The *Tales* are generally well-suited to the tellers, though there are a few cases of inconsistency due to lack of final revision. Thus the Man of Law promises a tale in prose but in fact tells (in rhyme royal) the story of Constance, which is not unsuited to him but which may originally have been intended for another pilgrim (the epilogue to the tale does not indicate its teller). Some tales have more than a 'general' appropriateness (i.e. one of tone, content and style) to the teller; they may also be *dramatically motivated*[11] – that is, they may spring out of one pilgrim's reaction to a preceding tale or to the character of the teller. Thus the Miller sets out to 'quyte' (pay back) the Knight's *Tale* with a story which travesties the refined love-situation of the courtly romance. Here we see Chaucer brilliantly contrasting different literary genres, with their widely divergent attitudes and ethos. At the same time, the tale has another function in the whole, for in telling it, the Miller deliberately satirizes an old carpenter, who is cuckolded in the story by an Oxford student. The Reeve, who was 'a wel good wrighte, a carpenter', takes offence and revenges himself by telling an equally gross and violent tale which exposes a *miller* to yet greater discomfort, humiliation and shame. In the same way, a quarrel develops between the Friar and the Summoner that issues in either pilgrim's telling a tale which fiercely attacks the other's profession and character. 'Motivation' is a method which helps Chaucer to make his satire impersonal, and so more effective and convincing. The Summoner and his profession suffer far worse damage at the hands of the Friar than they would if subjected to a direct satirical onslaught from the author (see also section on *Satire* below). Again, in the *Shipman's Tale*, a monk (a very 'manly' one, at that) is shown as insinuating himself into the household of a merchant and seducing his wife; but in this instance Chaucer does not exploit the possibility of motivation, for the tale is neither provoked by the Monk's insulting the Shipman, nor does it provoke the Monk to reply. (Perhaps, considering that the monk in the tale is not in fact *discomfited*, the pilgrim-Monk would have regarded the Shipman's offering as a compliment rather than an insult!) More generally, 'motivation' enlivens the individual tales by giving them a further significance as parts of a dramatic whole, helps to weld together the pilgrims, the frame-story and the separate narratives, and contributes to the creation of areas of local unity

[11] On 'motivation' see *Lumiansky*.

within the total pattern. Thus the Wife of Bath, the Clerk, and the Franklin and Merchant all tell tales which have as their *subject* marriage (and particularly the questions of obedience, 'sovereignty' (or supremacy) in marriage, and adultery) and as their pervasive *theme* the definition of nobility or *gentillesse* in its ambiguous and shifting relations to character and social station. These tales accordingly make up a 'Marriage Group' which is perhaps the most complexly organized 'act' within the whole drama of the tales.[12]

Chaucer does not achieve unity in the *Tales* through forcing a mechanical scheme upon an intractable body of mixed material. The 'unity' is rather something organic that grows from an imaginative absorption in the reality of his creations. Its very appearance of untidy, irregular spontaneousness makes the poem rather like a great medieval cathedral: at first sight so much rich colour, light and shade, and confusingly detailed carving in wood and stone, yet revealing on closer study a structural framework as clear and solid as it is complex and delicate. Yeats's lines about Homer in his poem *Ancestral Houses* apply equally aptly to Chaucer, who

> had not sung
> Had he not found it certain beyond dreams
> That out of life's own self-delight had sprung
> The abounding glittering jet . . .

Life, abundance and *self-delight* are the leading features of Chaucer's art. What is the relationship of this art to the life on which it draws?

III   The Realism of the General Prologue

Chaucer drew widely on literary sources as well as direct observation of life in creating the portraits of the pilgrims (see Commentary on the Prioress and Squire, pp. 131, 129).[13] But although he may distort for the sake of emphasis (as in the caricature of the Miller's portrait) his usual method differs from the medieval *grotesque* of a writer like Langland or a painter like Hieronymus Bosch. Chaucer's avowed aim was to register *his impression* of reality –

> . . . al the condicioun
> Of ech of hem, *so as it semed me* . . . (38–9)

---

[12] See *Kittredge.*
[13] The extent to which he did so is amply documented by Prof. Hodgson (pp. 16–26), who comments: 'How [Chaucer] contrived to endue his most derivative figures with life defies analysis'. The following discussion attempts to show how a prevailing context of realism is built up in the *GP* in which the distinction between literature and life as 'sources' is obliterated.

and even if this 'reality' was a construction of the mind, the poem was intended to seem the record of an actual pilgrimage Chaucer had been on himself. This is why in reporting the pilgrims' appearance and words he was unwilling to

> telle his tale untrewe,
> Or feyne thing, or finde wordes newe (735–6)

or, as he says in the *Miller's Prologue*:

> . . . I moot reherce
> Hir tales alle, be they better or werse,
> Or elles falsen som of my mateere.

Realism is perhaps even harder for a narrative poet to sustain than it is for a dramatist. But Chaucer's realism is not an unselective, 'total' transcription of actuality. He isolates details and varies his method so as to bring out both the individuality and the typicality of his characters, and this means their moral as well as their social representativeness. In the *Tales* themselves the degree of realism fluctuates greatly, but in the *General Prologue* and the Links (which consist of dialogue and action rather than description) there is a fairly uniform level of realism within the given (non-realistic) convention of verse. The portraits move from the minute notation of physical features –

> Upon the cop right of his nose he hade
> A werte, and theron stood a toft of heris . . .

to summarizing comment on moral qualities –

> He was a verray, parfit, gentil knight.

Few of the portraits are composed entirely of physical details, nor are these chosen simply to reveal typifying traits. In this respect Chaucer's method differs from that of seventeenth-century 'character-writers' like John Earle (*Microcosmographie*) or La Bruyère (*Caractères*) but is nearer to that of Dryden in his Achitophel or Zimri (*Absalom and Achitophel*), which are portraits of real people. Whether or not Chaucer drew partly on observation of actual contemporaries, his portraits in the *Prologue* are nearest to those like Pope's portrait of 'Atticus' in his *Epistle to Dr Arbuthnot* (a portrait based on Addison but crystallizing the character and behaviour of the 'literary dictator' as a type). With a few exceptions, they are, as 'types', moral, social and psychological (which for medievals often meant *physio*logical) rather than professional. The exceptions are the Yeoman and Squire, who *are* more 'professional' types than anything else. The Parson and Plowman are embodiments of *ideal* concepts, as are, to a slightly lesser extent, the Knight and the Clerk. In the case of the latter, peculiarly medieval in their single-minded pursuit of one form of excellence (so different from the Renaissance idea of the complete man), it is difficult to disentangle the typical from the ideal, but for all this both men are wholly *credible* as 'people'. The other sixteen pilgrims who are fully described, together with the Canon and Yeoman who arrive towards the end of the journey, make up together the earliest collection of convincingly 'real' characters in English literature – 'earliest' if, that is, we leave aside Pandarus, Criseyde and Diomede in *Troilus and Criseyde* (c. 1383–5).

Troilus and Criseyde provides a convenient point of departure for considering how far Chaucer's realism is a matter of *concreteness* of presentation. These lines describe Criseyde as the Trojan prince Troilus sees her in a temple and falls in love with her:

> She was nat with the leste of hir stature,
> But alle hir lymes so wel answeringe   *limbs*
> Weren to wommanhod, that creature
> Was nevere lasse mannyshe in semynge.   *masculine*
> And ek the pure wise of hire mevynge *very way; moving*
> Shewed wel that men mighte in hire gesse
> Honour, estat, and wommanly noblesse.[14]

Compare lines 151–6 from the Prioress's portrait:

> Ful semely hir wimpel *pinched* was,
> Hir nose tretys, *her eyen greye as glas*,
> Hir mouth ful smal, and thereto *softe and reed*;
> But sikerly she hadde a fair forheed –
> It was almost *a spanne brood*, I trowe –
> For, hardily, she was nat undergrowe!

The first passage relies on generalized assertion. The opening line politely indicates that Criseyde was tall and the remainder tells us that this did not detract from her femininity: she was wholly graceful and elegant as a woman should be. The italicized phrases of the Prioress's description show by contrast how specific the latter is. Even the conventional 'grey as glass' gains a new vitality in the context and becomes as 'real' as the Monk's 'eyen stepe, and rollinge in his heed', while the details of forehead, mouth and wimple concentrate (as the Commentary points out) a wealth of meaning. The *Troilus* passage is not bad writing, but it belongs to an altogether more formal 'courtly' mode. It is not, for that matter, wholly typical

[14] Book I, 281–7.

of the poem, but it does illustrate a type of writing Chaucer in-creasingly abandoned in the latest of his tales (the *Canon's Yeoman's Tale* is an example). The important point is that the heroine's *exact appearance* is left for the reader's imagination to fill in, rather as in the novels of Henry James, for *Troilus and Criseyde* is largely concerned with the inner life of the protagonists. The *General Prologue*, by contrast, exemplifies an intensely *visual* mode of writing, deliberately cultivated as it were in rivalry to the minute realism of the late Gothic painters whose work culminated in the *Très Riches Heures* of the Duc de Berry (cf. also Commentary on 101 ff).

Apart from concreteness, what gives the poem its general air of reality is the *device of the pilgrimage* in which the author claims to have participated. Many medieval poets declare that their story is some-thing they heard or read, and this is often the case. Others, like the authors of dream-vision poems such as *Piers Plowman* or *Pearl*, seem to be relating their own experience – and this is true in that the visions 'took place in' (i.e. were invented by) their imagination rather than being borrowed from a written source. But Chaucer vouches for the truthfulness of his first-person narrative in a way which both obliges him to write realistically and serves to excuse him when doing so leads to possible offences against taste:

> But first I pray yow, of your curteisye,
> That ye n'arette it nat my vileynye,
> Thogh that I pleynly speke in this matere,
> To telle yow hir *wordes* and hir *cheere*,
> Ne thogh I speke hir wordes proprely. (725–9)

The concluding words of this 'Apology' (which is really more of a covert manifesto) are also noteworthy, though not usually quoted as illustrating Chaucer's realism:

> Also I pray yow to foryeve it me,
> Al have I nat set folk *in hir degree*
> Here in this tale, *as that they sholde stonde* . . . (743–5)

For although the *Tales* begin with one told by the pilgrim of highest social rank, they soon proceed without regard to hierarchical decorum. When after the Knight's *Tale* the Host turns to the *Monk* for a story he is rudely interrupted by the drunken *Miller*, who insists on having his way and telling a tale to 'quyte' [answer] that of the Knight. The excuse Chaucer gives (ironically, one need hardly say) for flouting decorum both in his *Prologue* and in the body of the work ('this tale') is his artistic naïveté:

> My wit is short – ye may wel understonde.

What we 'may well understand' is, however, that the Miller's abrupt intrusion makes the movement from the first tale to the second much more graphic and transforms what could have been an awkward transition into a scene of strong dramatic interest. Other writers who used frame-stories before Chaucer failed to exploit their full dramatic potential and left them as somewhat artificial devices for holding together what was virtually an anthology. But Chaucer seizes triumphantly on the opportunity of confronting one who

> nevere yet no vileynye ne sayde
> In al his lyf, unto no maner wight (70–1)

with a 'churl' who

> was a jangler and a goliardeys (560)

Such dynamic oppositions would have been ruled out if his prime concern had been to 'set folk in their degree'. The essence of dramatic realism is to do the unexpected and yet make it seem, once it is done, the inevitable. Chaucer's whole conception in the *General Prologue* enables him to bring together characters with widely divergent attitudes and outlooks who could not have met one another in a work that fitted into any existing medieval literary genre. Part of the *Prologue*'s originality is that it creates a new genre in itself. George Crabbe, in the Preface to his *Tales* (1812), declared that 'to have followed the method of Chaucer might have been of use' but he did not attempt to do so because of its 'great difficulty and hazard'. It is a measure of Chaucer's achievement that he makes us forget the latent improbability of a 'colloquial and travelling intimacy' (in Crabbe's phrase) arising between such different and contrasting personalities. The realism of Chaucer's *art* makes us accept as probable (and therefore realistic) what is at best only possible.

While the Links sustain the general method of the *Prologue*, the tales themselves vary from the rhetorical artifice of the Squire's offering to the down-to-earth directness of the Shipman's. The stylistic conventions of the tale's genre[15] and the character of the teller[16] partly determine the quality of the language and style. The Links are the extension of the *Prologue* into the body of the work, presenting as actors in a living drama what we have hitherto seen as static images. The Links are if anything even more strikingly original than the *Prologue*. The actual idea of a pilgrimage had been previously used in the *Novelle* of Giovanni Sercambi (1385), a work which Chaucer could have known, but the *Canterbury Tales* develop the device in an altogether new and unpredictable way (e.g. in the

[15] See *Muscatine*, and esp. *Payne*, chs. 4 and 5.
[16] See *Hulbert*.

case of the 'Marriage Group' or the tales of the Miller and Reeve, and the Friar and Summoner, the most remarkable examples of a close dramatic relationship between frame-story and individual tales). In the Prologue to *Piers Plowman*, too, Chaucer would have found a visionary panorama of medieval society 'working and wandering as the world asks'; but he has also chosen his characters for the dramatic possibilities they offer as well as their social representativeness. Though Chaucer omits the highest and lowest ranks of society (barons and bishops; hired labourers) he nevertheless manages to include *tales* which deal with the life of the higher classes (e.g. the Knight's, Squire's and Man of Law's *Tales*). At the other extreme, with the exception of characters like the old widows in the *Nun's Priest's Tale* and the *Friar's Tale* or old Janicula in the *Clerk's Tale*, the life of the medieval poor is never presented with the immediacy and power of Langland, say. The sufferings of the poor never enter Chaucer's poetry as material for protest. Even when he is writing satire, his primary aim is to entertain, and when a tale ceases to be entertaining, Chaucer will arrange to have it interrupted – even if it is the tale he has given himself.

The author's own dramatic presence is above all what makes the device of the pilgrimage realistic. In connexion with his own tales of *Sir Thopas* and *Melibee* Chaucer contrives to poke fun at 'himself' by creating a fictional counterpart, 'Chaucer the Pilgrim', as E. T. Donaldson has usefully called him, who must have provided a very amusing contrast (all the funnier for the real similarities) to the self known to his patrons and friends. This character is not a new one, however: Chaucer is dramatically present in nearly every one of his earlier poems, and the main lineaments of the *Canterbury Tales* figure are already present in the 'Geffrey' of the *Hous of Fame*. Nevertheless, even this fact should not make us assume that a *wholly* fictional dramatic mask or *persona* is present in the *General Prologue* from the start, as well as in the body of the poem, in the section where 'Chaucer the Pilgrim' tells his tales. It is quite possible that the idea of exploiting the humour inherent in the discrepancy between his real and fictional selves only occurred to Chaucer after he had written the *Prologue*. At any rate, nothing in the *Prologue* itself demands to be read as coming from Chaucer the Pilgrim. A line like

<blockquote>My wit is short – ye may wel understonde</blockquote>

need not be taken as a 'dramatic' statement coming from a 'naïve' pilgrim-narrator but may be only the conventional medieval expression of modesty used by innumerable writers. In fact, the mode of realism of the Links is rather closer to reportage than that of the *General Prologue* (which reveals, for example, knowledge of the pilgrims' life and characters which could have been acquired only *during* the pilgrimage, not *before* it). There is thus good reason for taking statements by the speaker in the *Prologue* as coming 'straight' from the author. This point becomes important when we attempt to gauge Chaucer's moral standpoint in the *Prologue* and his attitude to the pilgrims he satirizes. It is hard not to be aware of an element of caricature in many of the *Prologue*-portraits, and because Chaucer's satirical intentions often require him to *distort* in the interests of greater vividness his 'portrait-realism' must never be confused with 'historical fact'. The descriptions themselves do not constitute documentary evidence for historical generalization and, indeed, have no value at all as such until they have been analysed and understood as *poetry*. The effect of historical allusions in the portraits is therefore somewhat confusing since they may have revealed to the original audience a level of *intention* (which is a part of *meaning*) not susceptible to modern critical analysis.

References and allusions to real places and people certainly occur in the *Prologue*. Thus two characters who are not actually named until the *Cook's Prologue* appear to have been modelled on living contemporaries – Roger of Ware (the Cook) and Harry Bailly (the Host). Behind the Merchant's portrait may lie the figure of Gilbert Maghfield, a contemporary London merchant, and behind that of the Man of Law the Lincolnshire lawyer Thomas Pynchbeck (see Commentary on line 326). The topical significance of the portraits probably added an extra touch of realism for the original audience but today the allusions are almost an encumbrance, and certainly a distraction. Rather more interesting than the hypothetical contemporary 'source' of the Merchant is the fact that Chaucer abstains from naming him and, further, draws attention to the fact:

> But (soth to seyn) I noot how men him calle (284)

– a line deftly suggesting the man's secretiveness. The fact that the *majority* of the characters are, as it happens, given no name, points to Chaucer's desire to emphasize their typicality as well as their individuality: 'Knight', 'Squire', 'Yeoman', 'Ploughman'. Like the portraits of Titian and Rembrandt, they are, as Blake called them, 'universal'.

'Cheere'

Some portraits may appear more realistic than others, even where this is not just due to greater physical detail. Thus the whole descriptive *mode* of the Squire's portrait strikes us as 'conventional' and designed to evoke the image of the typical young squire. His total appearance (*cheere*) is an *outward expression* of his role in life. By contrast, the other youthful member of the company, the Pardoner, is described in terms which have nothing to do with his profession or social role: the dishevelled hair, beardless face and high-pitched voice express his character as an individual (or, at best, a *physiological* 'type') – although Chaucer no doubt made him physically repulsive because he disliked Pardoners rather than *vice versa*. The amount of physical detail varies according to whether the idea or the image is dominant. Thus the *Manciple* is an embodiment of native 'wit' (as opposed to the kind acquired by learning, like that of his masters). In his portrait no details of looks appear and he is realized solely in 'ethical' terms – only his moral character and way of life are described. At the other extreme is the *Miller*: two lines (558, 564) describe his clothing, nine lines his success at wrestling (547–8) and doorbreaking (550–1), his bawdiness (560–1), his dishonesty (562–3) and his musical abilities (565); the rest of the portrait (ten lines) presents with grotesque precision the colour and shape of his beard, his nose and his mouth. For Chaucer, the Manciple's 'reality' consists in his cunning *mind* (to look at, the man is nondescript, perhaps), whereas the Miller, important as his crookedness and obscenity may be, impresses primarily as grossly *animal*.

Physical details are also expressive of *character*. The Summoner's 'narrow' eyes (for which there are good physical causes) and the glaring hare-like eyes of the Pardoner fitly express the lecherous character of both men. In a more learned and allusive way, the Wife of Bath's widely-spaced teeth 'express' her hyper-active sexuality, for the medieval physiognomists thought such teeth a sign of a bold, lascivious nature – an observation supported by the Wife in her *Prologue* (and cf. Commentary on 445 ff). Elsewhere physical details only *suggest* character, though the role of suggestion is vital in creating the total picture and illuminating particular lines. Thus the description of the Prioress's mouth as 'very small, and also soft and red', by stressing size, feel and colour, reinforces the implications of her name and contributes to the ambiguity of her brooch-motto. Further details strengthen this impression:

> She leet no morsel from hir *lippes* falle . . .
> Hir over *lippe* wyped she so clene . . .
> That of hir *smyling* was ful simple and coy . . .

The epithets 'humble' and 'shy' (*simple and coy*), applied somewhat unexpectedly to her *smiling*, are especially striking. Like the Prioress's *mouth*, the Pardoner's *hair* is emphasized: very long, waxy-yellow, smooth and thin, it suggests effeminacy so strongly as to render Chaucer's explicitness in line 691 otiose. These physical details also support the punning innuendo in line 673:

> This Somnour bar to him a *stif burdoun*

which is further reinforced by the insistence on the *smoothness* of the Pardoner's 'surface'. This quality makes him a fitting compeer to the Summoner, who is so *rough* that he cannot remove his 'whelks' and 'knobs'. These contrasts of surfaces reveal the portrait-artist's feel for *texture* in a surprisingly literal sense for one whose medium is not paint but words.

'Wordes'

Words – those of the pilgrims themselves – also help to create an indelible impression of character. It may be a *Latin tag* unforgettably associated with a pilgrim – the Prioress's *Amor vincit omnia*, or the Friar's *In principio*, or the pathetic *Questio quid iuris* parroted by the Summoner in his cups. Or it may be the name of an *authority* – the Doctor's fifteen physicians, the Franklin's 'Epicurus' (an ironic Chaucerian compliment: the Franklin's 'philosophy' of food is certainly not learnt from books!), the voluminous Aristotle of the Clerk. Elsewhere, the *names of places* illustrate the range of the three most widely-travelled pilgrims – the Knight's sieges and battles – Alisaundre, Algezir, Lyeys, Lettow; the Shipman's havens – from Gotland to Finistere; the Wife of Bath's shrines – in Italy, France, Germany, Spain and the Holy Land. Other names mainly pinpoint the essential interests and concerns of the pilgrim in question – the Merchant's ports of Orwell and Middleburg, the Man of Law's 'Parvys', the Clerk's Oxford, the Ypres and Gaunt whose weavers the Wife surpassed in skill. The 'world' of the pilgrims varies from that of the Knight, who had seen places which were *only* 'names' to Chaucer and his audience, to the Parson's, small enough to traverse on foot in journeys more purposeful than the Wife's 'wandring by the weye' (a phrase which implies triviality as well as street-walking).

'Array'

The variety of the innumerable aspects of contemporary social reality that crowd into the *Prologue* is nowhere better exemplified than in the *clothing* of the pilgrims and their equipment, especially their horses. The Doctor's deep red and blue contrasts with the Shipman's drab 'falding' gown, the Wife's semi-symbolic scarlet contrasts with the sober black the Parson must be imagined as wearing. The Prioress and Monk embody respectively ecclesiastical elegance and ecclesiastical luxury, the one bending her Rule by pleating her wimple, the other contemptuously flinging his out of the window by flaunting the most expensive fur on his sleeves. The two hypocrites, Friar and Merchant, are fittingly juxtaposed, and their clothing manifests their sense of self-importance (*solempnetee*). Contrasting with the portly Friar (who *should* be poor) is the Clerk in his threadbare 'courtepy'. He in turn is placed next to another learned pilgrim, the Man of Law, whose dress ('homely medley') is a compromise between the Clerk's unselfconscious shabbiness and the imposing opulence of the third learned pilgrim, the Doctor. (The Sergeant has spent his money not on books [like the Clerk] but on real property; of the Physician we are told that he was slow to *spend* the gold acquired from 'treating' victims of the plague, but 'kept' it and 'loved' it.) The strongest contrasts in clothing occur in the first group of father, son and servant, who ride together in, respectively, a stained tunic, a flowery robe in the latest style, and a functional costume of woodland green. There is something almost emblematic about these pilgrims, as if we were meant to guess their role in life at a glance.[17] (See also Commentary, p. 131.) Not all the pilgrims' horses (sure indexes of social station) are specifically mentioned, but there is variety enough among those that are: the Clerk's horse resembles its owner in its leanness, the Plowman's mount is the humble mare, the Monk's horse is in 'great estate', as we would expect from one who had 'full many a choice horse' in his stables; the Merchant's way of sitting his mount ('high on horse') reflects his sense of his own dignity, while the Shipman, so skilful in his own element, is not at ease on his nag and rides 'as best he could'. Echoes, parallels and contrasts could be pursued through the complexions, features, attitudes and mannerisms of the pilgrims. Their rich multiplicity is captured no less in the sounds of their conversation and music-making – from the terse, pithy utterance of the logic-trained Clerk ('souning in moral vertu') to the solemn 'resouns' of the money-fixated Merchant ('souninge alwey th' encrees of his winning'). A profound contrast in values is underlined by the use of the same word ('souning'). No less effectively, the graceful, refined existence of the Squire is evoked by his fluting, just as the Miller's bagpipe conjures up the coarse energy of the man.

---

[17] 'In the imagination of the age scarlet and other bright dyes and the smoothness and sheen of fine fur and the softer materials were associated with power and importance, drab colours and coarse fabrics standing for poverty and insignificance' (*Thrupp*, p. 147; and cf. pp. 147–50 generally for the dress of the middle classes and the significance of clothing in the Middle Ages). Compare 391, 456 and *CYT* 79–85.

'Estaat'

The *General Prologue* spans the social world of medieval England –
from the relaxed, leisured milieu of the real and would-be courtiers
to the hard-working existence of the labourers on whose efforts *all*
the estates relied for their bodily needs. The 'fresshe floures, whyte
and rede' cannot grow unless the soil is manured by the 'fother' of
'dong'. The pilgrimage at once asserts the reality of classes and
exposes the irrelevance of class from the standpoint of ultimate
values. But Chaucer seems to say that class-distinctions serve a
useful purpose here and now, even if the enormous middle class
reveals the obsolescence of the old classifications, and there is
comedy in the efforts of the 'fringe' pilgrims such as the Prioress, who

> peyned hire to countrefete chere
> Of court, and been estatlich of manere

and the Monk, who devoted himself to the aristocratic sport of
hunting and

> was a prikasour aright

(like the monk aptly summed up by Langland as riding 'with a heap
of hounds at his arse, *as if he were a lord*' (B, X, 309). *Snobbery* rings
out in the indignant repetitions which seem to record the Friar's own
phrases:

> It is nat honest, it may nat avaunce,
> For to delen with no swich poraille

and appears in the Merchant's attempts to conceal his true position
with an 'estatly governaunce', in the Sergeant's undermining of his
genuine learning, success and efficiency by trying to seem 'bisier than
he was', in the Wife's anger if any woman in her parish took prece-
dence over her at the mass-offering, and, finally, in the uniformly
clothed and wived Gildsmen, the epitome of the new London
bourgeoisie of the day.[18]
    Strongly contrasted with the class-conscious members of the
middle ranks of society are the 'churls' who form a group towards
the end. Three characters who do not fit neatly into any social group
are the Manciple, the Shipman and the Franklin. The first is placed
after the Miller in the churls' group, but by coming next to the
Reeve illustrates a distinction between two kinds of cunning.
Chaucer admires the Manciple but scorns the low and shady
methods of the Reeve. One line

> They were adrad of him as of the deeth

[18] See *Thrupp*, chs. III–VII.

serves to link the latter with the Summoner

> Of [whose] visage children were aferd

but the Reeve merits no softening touch of sympathy even in the midst of repulsion like the line declaring that the Summoner

> was a gentil harlot and a kinde.

The Shipman is another example of cunning (and worse) but he is not included among the churls and takes his place between Cook and Physician (both 'skilful' men, though Chaucer seems surer of the Shipman's maritime and the Cook's culinary than the Doctor's medical expertise – see 401–9, 380–7, 412–14). The Franklin, whose social position at this period would have been at the top of the middle class and just below the Knight, is not a man of skill but, in the full sense of the word, an *amateur*. Critics often note 'autobiographical' touches in this portrait, and was not Chaucer himself an amateur in all he attempted (except, of course, his poetry)? The Franklin's *Tale*, too, with its concern to distinguish the social and ethical meanings of *gentillesse*, coincides with Chaucer's own ideas on the subject as summed up in his Balade on *Gentillesse*.

'Condicioun'

In his attitudes to his characters Chaucer may show whole-hearted respect (Knight, Parson, Plowman), sympathetic delight in a single virtue (the Franklin's hospitality), general admiration for a kind of excellence (Squire, Clerk) tempered by humorous criticism of the excess that may go with it (see lines 97–8, 297–8), plain appreciation of a job well done (Yeoman, Cook – with, in the latter case, a meaningful shudder in lines 385–6), or admiration for the skills of the churls (without this detracting from their 'churlishness'):

> A baggepype *wel* coude he blowe and sowne (Miller)

or

> He was a *wel good* wrighte, a carpenter (Reeve)

In all these cases Chaucer's attitude is *simple*. Complexity enters with the first touch of irony:

> He yaf nat of that text a pulled hen,
> That seith that hunters ben nat holy men . . .
> And I seyde, his opinioun was good (Monk)

or

He was in chirche a noble ecclesiaste (Pardoner)

More subtle are the ironies of the Prioress's portrait, some of which depend on historical information that we do not fully possess (her French and her brooch-motto are discussed in the Commentary). But a larger uncertainty perplexes our understanding. We know what the medieval ideal of a nun was and how Madame Eglentyne falls short of it, but did Chaucer judge her by this standard? Does he judge his characters at all?

While it is a fact that Chaucer never calls any pilgrim 'bad' he does call one of them 'good'. The line

A good man was ther of religioun

is not merely praising the Parson for being 'good of his kind' or 'good at his job', any more than the comparative form in

A bettre preest I trowe ther nowher noon is.

The Parson's portrait is notably explicit: he is 'riche in holy thoght and *werk*' (479), 'holy' and 'vertuous' (515), just as his brother the Plowman is not merely 'a trewe *swinkere*' (531) but *lives* 'in pees and parfit charitee' (532). *Holiness, virtue* and *charity* represented the highest medieval values: they served to set standards, they could not be qualified by reference to higher criteria. From the standard established for *all* the pilgrims (but especially the clerical ones, who had a particular calling to virtue, charity and holiness) by the Parson's portrait, can we see whether Chaucer is judging the Prioress?

Chaucer states that he aimed to tell us

al the condicioun
Of ech of hem . . . (38–9)

as well as

Th'estat, th'array, the nombre, *and eek the cause*
Why that assembled was this compaignye (716–17).

The 'condicioun' of the pilgrims and the 'cause' of their assembling may be connected, if we take *cause* as including not only 'purpose' (to go to Canterbury) but also 'motive' (reason for going). Does each pilgrim's 'total condition' ('*al* the condicioun') include his moral and spiritual state as well as (in the more obvious sense of the word) his appearance, 'image' and social position? If so, each pilgrim's attitude to the pilgrimage itself becomes a relevant consideration. As few as four of the pilgrims (the Parson and Plowman certainly, the Knight and Clerk almost as certainly) seem to be going to the shrine of St Thomas for *religious* reasons (*penitential*, as with the Knight, a man of war seeking to make satisfaction for his sins, or more generally *devotional*, as with the other three). The others have a variety of dubious motives and some are grotesquely out of place. It would seem that Chaucer's concern with realism has resulted in fundamentally undermining his story's credibility – for in choosing a pilgrimage as the means of assembling a varied collection of characters, he has forgotten that some of them would scarcely be there in the first place. The Wife of Bath no doubt found it a good way of meeting a potential sixth husband, but would the *Shipman* choose a pilgrimage as the best way to beguile his time (assuming that *he* is not impelled by devotional urges?) The questions are awkward, but it is the very realism of the poem that is responsible for raising them. And it is here that the realism of the *General Prologue* can be seen as limited and qualified by a further purpose or interest of Chaucer's. This is the symbolic or moral significance of the pilgrimage as an *idea*: that is, to keep before the reader (at however great a distance) the Christian conception of human life and the values on which it is built. We may not be *invited* to judge the pilgrims, but we are certainly given a standard by reference to which they *can* be judged. Interestingly enough, there is one other character who *does* seem to be going on pilgrimage for religious reasons: this is Chaucer himself, who started out 'with ful devout corage' (22) and whose attitude is thus nearest to that of the Parson and the other three.

'Fayrnesse'

This conclusion will appear objectionable only if we base our idea of Chaucer's moral standpoint on the *conclusion* of the *Canterbury Tales* (the heavily didactic treatise on sin which constitutes the *Parson's Tale* and the so-called 'Retractations' that follow, in which the author 'renounces' or 'retracts' all those of his works which are 'conducive to sin' (*sownen unto sin*) – including most of his early works and the bulk of the *Tales*!). But this final or 'deathbed' attitude, which is narrow and negative, is strikingly at variance with the attitude which pervades the *Tales* as a whole – a warm, charitable love of humanity together with an acute sensitivity to moral evil and good. In the *Parson's Tale* and the 'Retractations' we see Chaucer as the *mere* moralist – rather like Tolstoy in his old age, when he denied the worth of much of his greatest work from a standpoint of puritanical harshness. Chaucer's work displays almost everywhere a deep love of human nature in all its richness and poverty, and his creations are (in John Bayley's phrase) 'characters of love', sensed as *real* and *other* in the way we sense the reality and otherness of people we love. This 'love' is an act of the imagination distinct from the minor artist's 'affection' for the whimsical creations of his fancy which resemble aspects of himself. It is as free from sentimentality as the *charitee* of the Parson, who

> was to sinful men nat despitous

but strove

> To drawen folk to hevene *by fayrnesse,*

although

> were any persone obstinat,
> What so he were, of heigh or lough estat,
> Him wolde he snibben sharply . . .

Chaucer avoids the sentimentalist's error of glamorizing vice and the cynic's error of thinking all virtue hypocrisy. There is no sharper critic of vice (especially the vice of hypocrisy) and no warmer advocate of virtue and (for he was a medieval Christian, not an agnostic humanist) *holynesse*. However, Chaucer (and the Parson in the *Prologue*-portrait) lacks the inhuman rigidity of the medieval religious outlook which moderns tend to think typical. The dominant feature of *Chaucer's* outlook is *fayrnesse* – connoting both 'justice' and 'gentleness' (or 'pleasantness'). Like the *charitee* of the Parson and Plowman, Chaucer's 'love' is *parfit* (complete, total). Part of such love is severity towards intransigent or cynically hardened vice, and Chaucer can 'snibben sharply' characters who are not humanly weak but villainously corrupt (cf. p. 20 above). Not all the pilgrims are 'characters of love' in the sense that the author would have liked them had they really existed; but none are 'characters of hate' created solely out of an urge to annihilate them in a destructive rain of satire.

Chaucer, in a word, has the power to endow his creations with a larger life than their function in the narrative strictly requires. His art penetrates more deeply than that of Pope, say, because his love for his characters (that is, his sense of their *reality*) is more intense than his desire to correct their faults. Pope's genius, which created both Sporus and the Man of Ross, might have been able to give us the Friar and the Franklin, but not the Prioress. Yet her portrait is 'complex' without this being due to Chaucer's 'ambivalent' (contradictory) feelings about its subject. The Prioress is, at the same time, more than an 'embodiment' of false courtliness or self-delusion. She exists as a rounded personality because she springs not from the moralizing intellect but the deepest creative imagination, which enables the artist to *realize* a character and also to offer the character for judgment, without actually passing judgment himself. That the achievement should be possible in *non*-dramatic poetry like the *Prologue* is all the greater testimony to Chaucer's wonderful humanity. There is perhaps an element of paradox here: Chaucer is at once not a moralist and yet has a clear and unconfused moral outlook. The presence of bawdy fabliaux in the *Tales* does not of itself mean that Chaucer was 'trying to have it both ways'. Taken in isolation, the fabliaux may seem to be amoral – ebullient and seductive images of 'natural man' which *sownen unto sin*, or, at the very least, fail by the criterion established by Chaucer in his 'Retractations': ' "Al that is writen is writen for oure doctrine [to instruct us]" – and that is myn entente'. But taken in context they can be seen as, morally, the 'partial evil' which contributes to the 'universal good' of the *Tales* as a whole. Chaucer's wish to be true to reality required him to give *harlotries* to the churls, and, to do him justice, he never leaves his stories as the crude, perfunctory things that (to judge by the analogues) they originally were. (The 'justification' of his *realism* is fundamentally the justification of the freedom of the artist and the autonomy of the work of art and cannot be discussed here.) There is nothing cheap, mechanical or sensational about Chaucer's treatment of sex. Whether the fabliaux can be called 'bawdy' but not 'obscene' is a difficult question to be definite about. What *is* certain is the impossibility of dismissing such magnificent works of art as *generically* inferior or worthless. Literary criticism, rather than a 'permissive' attitude to sex, tells us that the fabliaux, from the *Miller's Tale* to the *Merchant's Tale* are, far from being embarrassing, an extraordinary achievement of unselfconscious and completely assured genius, springing from an integrated vision of life the leading feature of which is, in Chaucer's own fine word, *fayrnesse*.

IV Satire in the General Prologue

The foregoing discussion of realism has raised more than once the question of *satire*. In the *General Prologue* Chaucer is less concerned to *attack* folly and vice (the traditional aim of the satirist) than to *expose* it. He does this more or less indirectly and usually by ironic means. Chaucer avoids *invective* like that of his contemporaries Langland and 'moral' Gower. A line like

> But wel I woot he lyed right in dede! (659)

is so rare as to be the exception that proves the rule. Generally the poetry works by implication, suggestion and allusion. This is not to say that the portraits aim at moral neutrality. Chaucer's 'attitude' is no less clear than that of Dryden and Pope. Compare the following passages:

> Next these, a troop of busy spirits press,
> Of little fortunes, and of conscience less;
> With them the tribe, whose luxury had drain'd
> Their banks, in former sequestrations gain'd;
> Who rich and great by past rebellions grew,
> And long to fish the troubled streams anew.
> Some future hopes, some present payment draws,
> To sell their conscience and espouse the cause.
>
> *(Absalom and Achitophel*, Part II, 310–17)

> Each wight who reads not, and but scans and spells,
> Each word-catcher that lives on syllables,
> Ev'n such small critics some regard may claim,
> Preserv'd in *Milton's* or in *Shakespeare's* name.
> Pretty! in amber to observe the forms
> Of hairs, or straws, or dirt, or grubs, or worms;
> The things, we know, are neither rich nor rare,
> But wonder how the Devil they got there?
>
> *(Epistle to Dr Arbuthnot*, 165–72)

> Wel semed ech of hem a fair burgeys
> To sitten in a yeldehalle on a deys.
> Everich, for the wisdom that he can,
> Was shaply for to been an alderman.
> For catel hadde they ynogh and rente –
> And eek hir wyves wolde it wel assente –
> And elles certeyn were they to blame!
>
> *(GP*, 369–75)

It is partly that Dryden and Pope, writing out of stronger feelings, wish to hurt and destroy (although their satire is certainly not invective), while Chaucer is more tolerant and amused. But it is worth noting how *effortlessly* the Chaucerian ironies operate. What he is talking about is the *fitness* of the Gildsmen to hold civic offices, yet he sees this vividly in concrete terms as a matter of 'sitting' on a *deys*, so that *shaply* ('suitable') inevitably acquires comic overtones of a merely *physical* fitness (i.e. they are 'solid' men with broad posteriors!), while the remaining lines at once assert the men's worthiness and deny it by implying that it is their wives' social pretensions that constitute the real driving force behind them. But the greater inexplicitness of Chaucer's method does not reduce the force or blunt the edge of his satiric blows and cuts. The line

> Of *nyce* conscience he took no keep (398)

by saying that the Shipman did not bother about the 'niceties' or 'scruples' of conscience (and then following this immediately with a line which shows that he murdered prisoners captured in sea-battles) devastatingly makes the moral point by *understatement*. We are left with an overwhelmingly cogent impression that, to the Shipman, acts like murder *were* only morally insignificant.

The portraits of the Prioress, Monk and Friar (even without reference to that of the Parson as a model or norm) suffice, when eked out with some knowledge of medieval standards, to enable us to gauge Chaucer's attitude:

> A manly man, to been an abbot able (167)
>
> He was the beste beggere in his hous (252)
>
> And al was conscience and tendre herte (150)

In the first example, no one can fail to see that being virile is scarcely the strongest qualification for being an abbot (the line no doubt aptly expresses the Monk's *own* opinion of the matter!). The irony is of the simplest kind. In the second, what makes the Friar the 'best' of mendicants is his success in picking up money; in the sense of begging in the right spirit and putting the alms received to the right use, he is actually the *worst*. The exploitation of the ambiguity of value-words here makes the irony subtler. In the final example, the word *conscience* (delicate feelings of compassion) is almost certainly *not* intended to evoke admiration, since the implication of the context is that the sympathy felt for animals would not be so readily felt towards suffering *human beings*. But here we have to rely to some extent on reading between the lines. The effect of the whole portrait is to suggest a criticism of Madame Eglentyne as a religious together with sympathy for a woman who should perhaps never have been a nun in the first place. Chaucer's *indignatio*, far less strong, to begin with, than a Langland's, let alone a Swift's, is tempered with humane tolerance throughout. The result is to make the satire more interesting as poetry and more convincing morally, too.

V Style and Imagery

The style of the *Prologue* is as original as the composition of the portraits and the dramatic interchanges of the frame-story. The ten-syllabled rhyming couplet which Chaucer had already used in his first collection of 'framed' tales, *The Legend of Good Women*, acquires a new flexibility and colloquial freshness. The movement of the verse accounts largely for the sense of immediacy and naturalness:

> And shortly, whan the sonne was to reste,
> So hadde I spoken with hem everichon
> That I was of hir felaweshipe anon (30–2).

Not only the vocabulary but also the word-order and tonal quality here are those of conversational *prose*. Yet it is a highly conscious *poetic* skill that has engineered a slight pause after *felaweshipe* and given *anon* a special emphasis through placing it at the end of the line as the rhyme-word. Examples of the *Prologue's* conversational idiom are legion, from the brief interpositions of the author as commentator

> And I seyde his opinioun was good (183)

to the reiteration of phrases which sound like a report of an actual speaker, though not given as direct speech

> What sholde he studie, and make himselven wood,
> Upon a book in cloistre alwey to poure,
> Or swinken with his handes, and laboure
> As Austin bit? How shal the world be served? (184–7)

(See also the lines from the Friar's portrait, 246–8, and the author's apology, 725 ff.)

Chaucer's language is a transparent medium in which words do not draw attention to themselves. Plain statement does much of the work, and where 'ambiguities' arise this is not through lack of clarity but from the inescapable dualities of value-terms (such as *worthy*, 68, 243, etc.) or else from the sheer historical distance between Chaucer and ourselves. Thus, we may remain uncertain about the precise contemporary nuance of *coy* (119) or *countrefete* (139) in the Prioress's portrait, where the degree to which the modern senses of these words had coloured their original meanings is not clear. Or, where the word in question is a proper name, we cannot be sure which association Chaucer wished to be uppermost in our minds (see Commentary on *Seïnt Loy*, 120). But, these limitations apart, the modern reader can find as much or more in the poetry than Chaucer's own contemporaries. Medieval literary theory was academic and artificial and there was no literary criticism in our sense to help the reader. As with Shakespearian drama, it has probably been left to later generations to arrive at an *adequate* appreciation of Chaucer's genius.

The language of the *Prologue* is simple and unadorned. There can be a wealth of suggestion in the very simplicity:

> His woning was ful faire upon an heeth;
> With grene trees yshadwed was his place. (606–7)

Here the 'romantic' associations are partly accidental: *yshadwed* is our 'shaded', not our 'shadowed', a more unusual and poetically suggestive word – but the distinction is hard to bear in mind while reading. At any rate, the word forces us to focus closely on what is being said, and then we realize how appropriate the image of *shadow* (suggesting now furtiveness rather than rustic seclusion) is to the Reeve. The slight oddity of *place*, too (not at all the obvious word), reinforces the sinister overtones by making us think of 'function, place in life' as well as '*dwelling*-place'. Chaucer's style is 'simple' for a negative and two positive reasons: because he avoids tangled, complicated sentences or phrases, and because he uses expressions drawn from common life rather than books, and images which are always sharp and clear. Thus he can both be a learned poet and avoid being a 'difficult' one like Milton (whose *style* is learned) or Shakespeare (whose *thought* is often complicated and full of compressed metaphor). Chaucer's expressions are often of the pithy proverbial type exemplified by the sustained figure (originally Biblical but already part of ordinary speech) of the shepherd and the sheep in lines 502–8 of the Parson's portrait, or by lines like

> Ful prively *a finch eek coude he pulle* (652)

> For she coude of that art *the olde daunce* (476)

> Ther was noon swich from *Hulle to Cartage* (404)

(Cf. further the section on *Style* in the Introduction to the *Canon's Yeoman's Tale*.)

Chaucer's images are mainly similes consisting of a line or half-line: 'as broun as is a bery' (207), 'as swift as fowel in flight' (190), 'as fressh as is the month of May' (92), 'as brood as is a bokeler' (471) – all of them betraying their folk-origin by their alliteration. His colour-comparisons are so traditional as to be virtually proverbial: '*pale* as a forpyned goost' (205; cf. our 'white as a sheet'), '*whyt* . . . as the flour-de-lys' (238) or 'as the morne milk' (358); *red* 'as the bristles of a sowes eres' (556, a variant on the *sow*-image of 552) or 'as blood' (635), *yellow* 'as wex' (675). These comparisons escape triteness by the new aptness they acquire in context: the *bristles* emphasize the Miller's rough animality, just as *wex* suggests the unnatural smoothness of the Pardoner's hair. The dozen-or-so metaphors that occur are again drawn from everyday experience and on the surface there seems a merely formal difference between

> Unto his ordre he *was* a noble post (214)

and

> As leene was his hors *as is* a rake (287)

or

> Ful longe were his legges and ful leene,
> *Ylyk* a staf (591–2)

Post, rake, staf are common, even obvious terms (cf. also 586, 652) but the *context* of 214 suggests an innuendo in the metaphor (cf. Commentary on 238, 257) like those in lines 166 and 191 (Monk) and 673 (Summoner/Pardoner) which might have been lost if the phrase had been formally a simile. Context often helps to make metaphors composed of traditional elements seem witty and new, by comparison with the more static and visual effect of the similes proper. In

> It *snewed* in his hous of mete and drinke (345)

we have at once the ideas of abundance and (paradoxically) cold-ness and discomfort, contrasting strongly with the vividly evoked picture of warmth and lavish hospitality indoors. Other instances are

> And yet he hadde *a thombe of gold*, pardee (563)

> That hadde *a fyr-reed cherubinnes* face (622–3)

> Up roos our Hoste, and was *our aller cok* (824)

Although not boldly exploratory like Shakespeare's, Chaucer's metaphors draw their strength and freshness from their kinship with the down-to-earth traditional simplicity of his similes and proverbs. The precision of the descriptions, in which both simile and metaphor play their part, helps to achieve variety, where it would be all too easy to fall prey to monotony and repetition. Of the Franklin, Chaucer says:

> Whyt was his berd as is the dayesye

(see also Commentary on 332 and Textual Note) and of the Miller:

> His berd as any sowe or fox was reed,
> And therto brood, as though it were a spade.

Chaucer has carefully avoided the possibility of exact repetition by varying the form the similes take, and by word-order and word-choice: 'white was his beard'/'his beard . . . was red'; 'as is . . .'/'as though it were'. The last phrase actually has the effect of suggesting the implement, jutting out aggressively, not 'like' a spade, but almost as if the Miller used his beard to 'dig' (just as he used his 'not-heed' to break down doors)!

The use of key-words like 'eyes', 'mouth', 'beard' in the descrip-tions of the pilgrims unobtrusively establishes a network of echoes and correspondences which acts as an organizing factor in the *Prologue* (cf. also the section on *Style* in the *CYT*):

> No berd hadde he, ne nevere sholde have;
> As smothe it was as it were late shave (689–90)

> His berd was shave as ny as ever he kan (588)

> With many a tempest hadde his berd been shake (406)

These touches resemble the portrait-painter's enrichment of the surface texture of his canvas by the device of laying on the same pigment with strokes of varying thickness. With scrupulous care, Chaucer aims at a controlled but perpetually varying development in his twenty-three full-length portraits, interweaving details of physique, clothing, character and history. At the same time, we have an impression of effortless ease, without contrived 'significances' or obtrusive ingenuities. One example of the detailed working of the imagery must suffice, though many could be found.

Gold is mentioned six[19] times in the *Prologue*, and in five cases the effect is to link one portrait with an earlier one. Of the Clerk, Chaucer writes:

> But al be that he was a philosophre,
> Yet hadde he but litel *gold* in cofre (297–8)

– lines echoed a little later in the portrait of the Physician (another 'learned' pilgrim) –

> For gold in phisyk is a cordial,
> Therefore he loved gold in special (443–4)

The 'echo' creates an implication that there are two ways of employing one's learning; *without regard to* profit (the Clerk) or *as a means to* profit (the Physician). The image of *gold* serves to pinpoint and define the two attitudes, not in the compass of a few lines but at widely separated places in the course of the *Prologue*. What links the two images of 'gold' is their appearance in a *common context* – that of the 'way in which learned men make their living/use their learning' – and what links the two opposed attitudes to 'learning' is the *common image* of 'gold'. The operation of Chaucer's poetry through *images* is subtler (and more effective) than moralizing explicitness. The other example, from two of the ecclesiastical pilgrims, is more straightforward. Chaucer's eye picks out on the Prioress's rosary beads

> a brooch of gold ful sheene (160)

[19] The reference in 563 also involves two connotations of *gold* – 'profit' and 'excellence' ('skill'), but the image does not connect directly with those discussed here.

– echoed in the portrait of the Monk that follows directly –

He hadde of gold ywroght a ful curious pin (196)

'Brooch' and 'pin' are both *ornaments*, one conspicuous by being highly polished (*ful sheene*), the other by its elaborate shape (*A love-knotte in the gretter ende ther was* (197), and both serve to indicate the particular fault of these pilgrims – worldly vanity, with (in both cases) undertones of inappropriate sexual attitudes: the Prioress's brooch has an ambiguous inscription and the Monk's 'love-knot' sharpens suspicions already aroused by other hints scattered throughout the portrait. The metal *gold* here becomes a symbol of *false* values, a paradoxical suggestion reinforced by the image Chaucer later mentions as having been particularly dear to the *Parson*, his model of the good churchman:

And this figure he added eek therto,
That if gold ruste, what shal iren do? (499–500)

Because gold *ought* not to rust like the base metal iron ('because the clergy *ought* not to commit the sins they exhort their parishioners to avoid') an instance of this happening is all the more shocking. By the Parson's standard, the Prioress and Monk come to appear, in their differing degrees, *'rusty* gold', for all the outward beauty and glitter of their ornaments. The image brings to our mind the symbolic (or ethical) meaning of the common saying, 'All that glitters is not gold' (cf. also *CYT*, 409–11 in this volume). The contrast between appearance and reality, physical and spiritual, is achieved with great economy by the use of one and the same image, *gold*.

A proper study of the poetic art of the *Prologue* would require a whole book, not a few pages. The reader must make his own discoveries and comparisons. Analysis serves only to confirm one's initial impression that in its smallest details as much as in its larger architecture the *General Prologue* repays many times over the closest attention we can give it.

The Canon's Yeoman's Tale

The Canon's Yeoman

The background of the pilgrimage to Canterbury can most easily be filled in by reading the *General Prologue* (also printed in this volume). The Canon and his Yeoman are the only characters not included among those who originally set out from Southwark and whose *condicioun* Chaucer described so fully in the *GP*. Their sudden dramatic arrival creates expectations of something unusual, and these are not disappointed. The Canon and the Yeoman do not primarily represent types, professional or social, and the pursuit of alchemy is seen as nearer to a strange addiction or disease than a profession. Of the two, the Yeoman turns out to be the fool, rather than the knave – but he is, even in comparison with morose or embittered characters like the Reeve or Merchant (see their *Prologues*) strikingly joyless and defeated. Any expectations that the Canon, who

> can of murthe and eek of jolitee
> Nat but ynough (47–8)

will tell 'a mery tale or tweye' are, however, not to be fulfilled, and his sudden flight makes him seem a total enigma – except insofar as he remains, permanently trapped, in the Yeoman's virulent *exposé*.

The Yeoman's life, unlike that of the other pilgrims (including 'bad' ones like the Shipman or Summoner) has been a complete failure. The physical effects of his labours are as marked on him as on the lean and hollow Clerk, but he has acquired no valuable knowledge as a compensation. The psychological scars are even deeper, and the Yeoman realizes all too clearly that he is himself one of the dupes he warns the pilgrims against becoming in his solemn finale.[1] Unlike the Physician, he has not won any wealth (the other, and dominant aim of most alchemists) either, but has sacrificed youth and money to the quest of an illusion. His frequent outbursts of spleen against the False Canon of the *Tale* combine to suggest that we are to think of him as having been led astray by the Pilgrim Canon (his ex-master) and as having discovered too late that the latter was a fraud as well as a knave.[2] Coupled with disappointment, the Yeoman feels at the end of his *Tale* that he has been punished for meddling in the hidden secrets of nature. There is more

---

[1] See Commentary on 874 to end.
[2] See Commentary on 520, 535–42, 620, 754.

than an echo in his final words of Pope John XXII's condemnation of alchemists in a decree of the early fourteenth century – although (as Duncan has shown) Chaucer's *whole* criticism of the 'art' is in the orthodox ecclesiastical tradition of anti-alchemical diatribe in the later Middle Ages.[3] The Yeoman himself remains, for all the comic effect of his *Tale*, essentially a figure of pathos.

'That Slyding Scyence'

The story of the growth of alchemy is a fascinating one, but to recapitulate it would not be to the point. The Canon's Yeoman tells us most of what we need to know in order to understand the poem, but the following general considerations might be helpful. In theory, alchemy was simple and rational, but in practice it was complicated, confused and obscure. Deriving from the speculations of Greek scientists, it underwent a characteristic transformation in the Middle Ages. The medieval respect for the authority of the written word made it impossible for all but a few outstanding individuals to test and examine the main presuppositions underlying the whole edifice of speculation. One of these was that all the elements in nature are striving towards a higher state of 'perfection' and that man can discover the principles of this development so as to 'speed up' natural processes and bring about the transformation of the *base* metals into the *noble* (precious) metals, silver and gold. The other main belief, deriving from Aristotle, was that the prime constituents of all material substances were the *Four Elements* (earth, air, water and fire). All of these were to be found in varying proportions in all the metals, and the chief purpose of alchemy was to adjust the proportions of the 'elements' in the base metals so as to make them conform to those of the precious metals, thereby achieving the transmutation of lead, tin, etc., into gold and silver.

Holmyard's historical survey of the subject shows that the by-product of the work of some alchemists was the beginning of a true knowledge of chemistry. But after the work of the great Islamic writers such as Jabir (eighth century) and Rhazes (ninth century) little was added to the sum of chemical knowledge. Western alchemy was largely based on translations of Arabic writings. (The work of that strange [but not untypical] figure Theophrastus Bombastus von Hohenheim [sixteenth century], better known as Paracelsus, shows how little true scientific understanding accompanied familiarity with the minutest details of *werking* or experimentation.) Some of the basic alchemical concepts are fairly clearly set out in the writings which went under the name of *Geber* (i.e. Jabir) and

[3] The decree is printed in *SA*, pp. 691–2; *Duncan*[i], p. 638.

which became the main authorities in early western alchemy. The translation is that of Richard Russell (1678), slightly adapted (printed in *Holmyard*, pp. 135–6):

[Alchemy] treats of the imperfect bodies of minerals, and teaches how to perfect them. . . . We compose this book [*The Investigation of Perfection*] of things perfecting and corrupting . . . because contraries set near each other are the more manifest.

The thing which perfects in minerals is the substance of Argentvive [mercury] and Sulphur proportionably commixed, by long and temperate decoction in the bowels of clean, inspissate [dense] and fixed Earth (with conservation of its Radical Humidity not corrupting) and brought to a solid fusible substance, with due ignition, and rendered malleable. By the definition of this Nature perfecting, we may more easily come to the know-ledge of the thing corrupting . . . which is to be understood in a contrary sense, viz the pure substance of Sulphur and Argentvive, *without* due proportion commixed, etc. . . . having a combustible and corrupting Humidity and being of a rare and porous sub-stance . . . and not . . . malleable.

The first definition I find intruded in . . . Sol and Luna [i.e. gold and silver] according to the perfection of each; but the second in . . . Tin, Lead, Copper and Iron, according to an imperfection of each. And because these imperfect bodies are not reducible to sanity and perfection unless the contrary be operated in them – that is, the manifest be made occult [hidden] and the occult manifest . . . by Preparation, they must be prepared, superfluities in them removed, and what is wanting supplied, and so the known perfection be inserted in them. But perfect bodies need not this preparation; yet they need such Preparation . . . by which their parts may be more subtiliated [rendered finer] and they reduced from their corporality to a fixed spirituality . . . a spiritual fixed body . . . more attenuated and subtiliated than before . . .

. . . Modern artists [alchemists] describe only one *Stone* . . . for the White and the Red [i.e. silver and gold]; for in every *Elixir*, white or red, there is no other thing than Argentvive and Sulphur, of which, one cannot act . . . without the other. Therefore it is called . . . *one Stone*, although it is extracted from many bodies. . . . And because all metallic bodies are compounded of Argentvive and Sulphur, pure or impure, by accident, and not innate in their first nature . . . by convenient preparation it is possible to take away such impurity . . . therefore the end of *Preparation* is to take away superfluity and supply the deficiency of perfect bodies. But Preparation is diversified [varies] . . . for experience has taught us diverse ways of acting – Calcination, Sublimation,

Descension, Solution, Distillation, Coagulation, Fixation and Inceration [solidification into a wax-like substance].

(On all these terms and processes see the *Commentary* on 217–310, 884 esp.)

It is hardly surprising that a 'science' as apparently rational (but as little susceptible to empirical investigation) as this should have appeared to the Yeoman elusive (*slyding*) and illusory – even if, at the end of his tale, he can still maintain that there exists, somewhere, a true knowledge of the secret of secrets which was revealed by God to the original 'philosophers', though it has been buried ever since in cryptic language and symbolism (see 911–22 and *Commentary* on 841–3).

The Tale as Ironic Narrative

In type the *Tale* resembles those of the Merchant, Friar and Pardoner: stories about the duping of men who are the victims of their own lack of insight. References to *blindness* are legion (many are noted in the Commentary). The tale's predominantly comic-satiric mode links it with the fabliaux,[4] but it is unique in that *Prologue* and *Tale* taken together present a significant parallelism: to the False Canon of the *Tale* proper corresponds the pilgrim-Canon and to the deluded Priest corresponds the Yeoman himself. If (as seems unavoidable) we see the False Canon as a portrait, however distorted by resentment and spleen, of the Yeoman's ex-master, then we can see the Yeoman as attacking in the Priest his *own* blindness and folly. In this respect the *CYT* resembles *The Merchant's Tale*, in which the narrator appears to be attacking, in the person of the old knight January, his own folly in marrying a wife much younger than himself. Another tale recalled by the *CYT* is that of the Friar, which tells how the Devil disguised as a yeoman deceives a vicious and boastful summoner into giving his own soul away. The *CYT* also illustrates the type of fabliau in which a clever villain brings about the ruin of a gullible (but by no means necessarily innocent) victim. (The frequent references to the False Canon as a 'fiend' strengthen the impression.) Finally, the tale recalls in its structure that of the Pardoner, who prefaces his moral *exemplum* with a shamelessly frank autobiographical confession of his methods of raising money.[5] The Pardoner is speaking under the influence of drink, and to the freedom that comes from wine can

---

[4] On the *fabliau*, see *GP* Intro. p. 6 n. above.
[5] *The Wife of Bath's Tale* has, at first glance, a similar structure, but in fact the Wife's *Prologue* far outweighs her *Tale* in importance, and the latter is not, like the Pardoner's and Canon's Yeoman's, a moral *exemplum*. (See note 14 below.)

be compared the sudden access of intoxicating liberty experienced by the Canon's Yeoman (who has long brooded over his grievances) on the hasty departure of the Canon. The company of pilgrims provide him with a unique opportunity to 'blow the gaffe' on the arcane and fascinating pursuit with which he has become thoroughly disillusioned. They listen to him as a modern audience might to a spiritualist or freemason (but these parallels are inevitably inexact). The Yeoman brings into the midst of the pilgrims, who are all in their different ways recognizable members of a clearly classified society, the breath of the underworld. At once seductive and repellent, actually squalid if potentially glamorous, it is the world of those who live

> Lurkinge in hernes and in lanes blinde,
> Wheras thise robbours and thise theves by kinde
> Holden hir pryvee fereful residence,
> As they that dar nat shewen hir presence.[6]

The Tale as Polemic

If the real victim is the Yeoman himself, the real villain is perhaps less the Canon than the art of alchemy, with its delusive promise of fulfilling two of mankind's most deep-rooted desires – the desire for wealth and the desire for immortality. Both (all medieval Christians believed) could only be satisfied by God: *true* wealth was virtue, not gold, and true immortality was to be obtained only in heaven, not through the Elixir. Christian alchemists consequently ran the risk of losing their souls as well as their 'body and good' (as the Yeoman puts it).[7] For the 'hard-core' practitioners, however, alchemy had become a god – which replaced the Christian God but remained just as demanding. Combining in various ways the attractions and effects of gambling, financial speculation and drug-addiction, alchemy was for most practitioners a quick way to ruin and disgrace. It was also contagious – because it spread through the contact of alchemists with men who were victims of their own greed and ignorance. This is what the Yeoman has in mind when he claims that the False Canon will 'infecte al a toun,/Though it as greet were as was Ninivee'.[8] It has often been suggested that Chaucer himself may have been duped by an alchemist and wrote the tale to vent his own disappointment and vexation. There is no

---

[6] *CYT*, 105–8.
[7] John XXII's decree, however, notably puts the emphasis on the *social* danger caused by the circulation of 'alchemical [counterfeit] gold'.
[8] *CYT*, 420–1.

proof, only the knowledge of alchemy shown in the tale, which merely indicates an *interest* in the subject. But it is easy to see how even the author of a scientific treatise like the *Astrolabe* could, in an age when 'science' was so much a matter of conjecture, authority and opinion, be deceived by a clever 'philosopher' – especially if he should happen to believe (like Chaucer's friend John Gower) that alchemy *itself* was genuine, even if its practitioners were sometimes not:

> The science of himself is trewe
> Upon the forme as it was founded

although

> now it stant al otherwise;
> Thei speken faste of thilke ston,
> But hou to make it, nou wot non
> After the sothe experience.[9]

On the surface the *CYT* is an exposé of alchemy, buttressed by the uninhibited 'confessions' of an alchemical dupe of seven years' standing, and at the same time of the villainy of one man who used alchemy as a cover for the exercise of fraud. But at a deeper level, it is concerned (like the companion tales told by the Pardoner, Friar and Merchant) with truth and falsehood, deception and self-deception, appearance and reality. Curiously enough, the main story (the gulling of the Priest) does not in itself constitute an indictment of *alchemy*. That is, the claim (as expressed by Gower, say) that alchemy is genuine is not exploded by the example of the Canon's duplicity (any more than the existence of fraudulent mediums undermines the genuine evidence for psychic phenomena). The 'evidence' for alchemy may appear very thin today, and the truth of even so circumstantial an account as Helvetius's[10] is called in question by its *a priori* unlikelihood. But the weight of tradition was such that to a medieval audience the *Tale* might not have appeared a particularly effective debunking of *Alchemy*. (Compare Ben Jonson's play *The Alchemist*, where the absence of any personal animus against alchemists helps to give a general impression that the large-scale confidence-trickster Subtle [the alchemist of the title] is *representative* of the breed as a whole and that the likelihood of there being 'genuine' alchemists is negligible.) The real attack on alchemy comes in the *Prologue*, where the Yeoman recounts his futile seven-year quest for the Stone. But even here it can be said that all he *proves* is that if the ignorant dabble in matters beyond their reach

[9] 'The science itself, in its pristine form, is genuine' (*CA*, IV, 2598–9); 'now things are quite different. Alchemists go on about the Stone, but not one of them has any real, experimental knowledge of how to produce it' (*CA*, IV, 2580–3).
[10] Printed in *Holmyard*, pp. 259–67.

they will usually come to grief and always risk being exploited by clever rogues (canonical or otherwise). If the Yeoman had joined up with a *genuine* 'philosopher' he might have 'thriven' better: *his* case exemplifies a rather trite moral generality. Against this it can be said that the total effect of the *Prologue* is in fact broader, if vaguer, than this account suggests: it not only exposes the Yeoman's folly but also casts serious doubt upon Alchemy as a whole. *Can* a 'science' be 'trewe' if its exponents are capable of such confusion? *Is* there a substratum of truth beneath the errors of the alchemists? The tale thus serves a practical end of warning people against alchemy by showing that the risks are great – whatever the ultimate 'truth' may be. But if the *CYT* were only a 'moral tale' its poetic interest would be relatively slight. The 'moral' depends on the historical situation, which is no longer with us. And yet the tale is an interesting and highly characteristic creation – not one of Chaucer's very best, but nonetheless deftly and at times brilliantly handled. The plot is not, of course, either as tightly constructed or as intrinsically compelling as those of the two brief masterpieces in this genre of ironic narrative, the *Pardoner's* and *Friar's Tales*, or the longer but equally masterly *Merchant's Tale*. The main 'plot' has, in fact, the quality of an anecdote, and only the presence of the narrator, bristling with indignation and smarting with chagrin, suffices to anchor it firmly to the Prologue. What, then, is the prime critical interest of the poem?

Character

It is, in a sense, 'character' – though not 'character isolated by a deed' (in Yeats's phrase)[11] or, for that matter, 'character for its own sake'. Chaucer does not write with a *primarily* psychological interest. With the Yeoman, as with the Pardoner and Wife of Bath, 'character' is the vehicle of a complexly organized thematic purpose. The hollowness and futility of the Yeoman's wasted life has a universal, parabolic significance, which is not obscured by the pathos or the comedy of his situation, and not lessened by the historical remoteness of the setting. All the other pilgrims have an 'occupation', a place and a function in society and a set of relationships, personal as well as social, which help to define their personality and significance. The Yeoman is an outcast and an outsider – a figure more startlingly 'modern' in his rootlessness and 'alienation' than any of

[11] Examples are January, encompassing his ruin by *deliberately* marrying May against good advice, and the gamblers in the *Pardoner's Tale* and the Summoner in the *Friar's Tale*, seeking respectively death and damnation by *conscious acts* the consequences of which they are too blind to see.

the characters depicted in the *General Prologue*, that mirror image of medieval social certainties and social cohesion. The Yeoman has been dislocated from ordinary social living by his strange pursuit and forced to become an obscure and shabby denizen of a London[12] that was already becoming the anonymous metropolis of Dickens's day, to judge by lines 105–8, quoted above. In his membership of an ill-defined 'underworld' the Yeoman, stripped of his pretensions though not of all his hopes, connects more readily with the creations of a Pinter or a Beckett than with any of Chaucer's own.

Theme and Structure

The *Canon's Yeoman's Tale* differs from the majority of the *Canterbury Tales* in that it is not really a 'tale' at all in the sense of a fictional narrative offered as such by the pilgrim telling it. The Yeoman claims that his 'tale' is *fact*:

> There *is* a chanoun of religioun
> *Amonges us* . . .

and, although he denies the identity of the False Canon and his ex-master, he asserts the real danger of the former and offers his tale as a warning against his tricks. In form, the *CYT* is a kind of 'sermon' against alchemy preached by a 'converted sinner' to an audience of 'potential sinners'. All the pilgrims are 'innocents' in the sense that they are ignorant of the facts of alchemy and the duplicity to which alchemists stoop, whether to gain money for their experiments or simply as a form of confidence trickery. The 'sermon' proper is contained in the autobiographical *Prologue*, which vividly exposes the nature of the 'sin'. It is a particular form of avarice, compounded with folly and pride – *avarice* in that the alchemists seek personal wealth, *folly* in that they believe they can achieve it through 'multiplication', and *pride* in that they are attempting to penetrate the hidden secrets of nature.[13] The *Tale* proper is an *exemplum*[14] (of the type common in medieval sermons) which illustrates the argument of the *Prologue*. That it is offered as fact and not merely quoted on authority but given from personal knowledge of the protagonist makes it all the more impressive.

The *implicit theme* of the Sermon is well expressed in a passage from the *Book of Proverbs*:

---

[12] See *Commentary* on line 104.
[13] See esp. *Commentary* on 293–4, 524 and 874 to end.
[14] A narrative illustrating a general moral lesson: *exempla* from everyday life were much used in medieval preaching.

> Happy is the man that findeth wisdom, and the man
> that getteth understanding. For the merchandise of
> it is better than the merchandise of silver, and
> the gain therof than fine gold.[15]

A contrast between true wealth (wisdom) and false wealth (gold and silver) pervades *Proverbs* as it does the *CYT*, and Chaucer may well have had the Biblical sayings in mind as he shaped his meagre anecdotal material into a poem rich in moral significance. The one reference to Solomon (408) contrasts his learning (which taught him that wisdom was more precious than gold) with the pathetic ignorance of the alchemists. In addition to this contrast, the other underlying themes which unify the *CYT* and give it a deeper meaning are ignorance, blindness, folly, greed and pride, false innocence and real villainy, and the relation between lack of scientific knowledge and lack of self-knowledge. Under the rain of curses unleashed by the Yeoman, an image takes shape in our mind of the alchemical laboratory as a kind of miniature hell – hot, sterile and desperate:

> In helle . . .
> Nis ther more wo, ne more rancour ne yre . . .[16]

Yet for all the tale's moral resonances, the dominant impression is one of comic briskness – and if the comedy is not riotously coarse and ebullient like that of the *Miller's Tale* it also lacks the sombre mordancy of the *Merchant's Tale*. (A comparison of Chaucer's treatment of *blindness* in the *CYT* with the blindness of January in the *Merchant's Tale* would bring this out clearly. The dark intensity of the poetry in the latter brings it near to tragedy, but *CYT* never ceases to be comedy, thanks to the Yeoman-narrator, who mingles with his desire to preach the very Chaucerian awareness that 'heer shal aryse game'.)[17] The good wishes and blessings with which the *Merchant's Tale* ends are inescapably ironic in effect –

> Now, goode men, I pray yow to be glad.
> Thus endeth heere my tale of Januarie;
> God blesse us, and his mooder Seinte Marie –

because we have just heard the narrator pour out his own bitterness and self-disgust in the preceding tale. But the Yeoman's last line rings out as fervently sincere: he has drawn his conclusion (that alchemy should be shunned) from the combined evidence of *common-sense* –

> for bet than nevere is late.
> Nevere to thryve were to long a date;

[15] *Proverbs*, iii, 13–14.
[16] *CYT*, 365–6.
[17] In tone, atmosphere and mood, the *CYT* seems to correspond to Jonson's *The Alchemist* rather as *The Merchant's Tale* does to *Volpone*.

experience (both alchemy and alchemists are deceitful); and *authority* –

> . . . this science and this conning . . .
> Is of the secree of secrees, pardee –

which he caps with the grand conclusion that

> whoso maketh God his adversarie . . .
> . . . nevere shal he thryve . . .
> And there a poynt.

This final conclusion may seem too solemn for a comic tale to sustain. But the important point is that it is the right (and inevitable) conclusion for the Yeoman. *His* final wish takes on weight from the evidence the tale has given us of the 'scarsetee' of 'trewthe' nowadays:

> God sende every trewe man boote of his bale!

He is a man who has learnt the lesson at his own cost.

Language and Style

The *CYT* is typically Chaucerian in its use of pithy sayings and proverbs or semi-proverbial expressions (see *Commentary* on 285, 409–12, 414, 514, 854–5, 860). The Yeoman's hard-earned 'wisdom' – such as it is – consists largely of cautionary sayings like 'fire burns', 'all that glitters is not gold', 'fools rush in', all of which spring from a limited but first-hand experience. Vividly original and exploratory metaphor is not a feature of Chaucer's poetry, but the imagery in *CYT* is highly effective for all its unobtrusiveness. Our sense of the identification of the Canon with his dubious art (27–8, 621–2), the mercurial elusiveness of the Stone (309–14) and of the knowledge leading to its attainment (127–30, 179), the ironic reversal of the alchemist's expectations (174–6), the deceiving and blinding effect of his pursuit (177), the pain and disappointment (159–60) which never find the remedy always expected (318–20) and still pathetically prayed for at the end (928), the awareness of a life devoted to alchemy as a delusion (324–5) and an embarrassment (332–3), a disease that infects (335–6, 420) and a danger to life and happiness (870) – all this is achieved in the poem by drawing almost entirely on the associations that arise naturally from the story and setting (see *Commentary* on the passages cited).

Perhaps the most important poetic device in the *Tale* is the use of words which evoke echoes and gather richness of meaning by repetition. A glance at some half-dozen keywords (with synonyms and closely related terms) as they recur in the first two hundred lines of the poem suggests that Chaucer's aim is to fix them in our minds as a means of conveying the ironies implicit in his theme. Thus *wonder* (both as sb./adj. and vb., 7, 16, 50, 76) raises expectations of the marvellous that would be appropriate to an alchemy which *worked* but which are sadly disappointed in the event. Again, the important word *craft* (66, 68, 102, 198, etc.), the root meaning of which was 'power', together with *science, art, conning, wit* (95, 100, 163, 168, 127, 179), all appear in contexts which indicate *mis*use, deficiency or failure. The *craft* ('powers', 'skills') of the Yeoman's Canon is in fact 'impotence' (inability to perfect the 'Work'), where by contrast the *craft* of the False Canon is largely successful (but here it is not 'scientific skill' but 'unscrupulous cunning'). If we take the two Canons to be one and the same man, we have the irony that he is at once 'crafty' and 'not crafty'. The *werk* and *werking* (196, 169) likewise, while not exactly their opposite ('idleness'), turn out to be almost as bad – a waste of time. The *werking* is fruitless, the 'effect' and 'conclusion' are always lacking, alchemy is a maze with no exit, the 'science' slides away from its pursuers like a will o' the wisp. (The image of *sliding* (129, 179) is probably suggested by the behaviour of mercury rather than, as one critic suggests, a serpent.) The 'sliding' motif helps to personify Alchemy, which the Yeoman frequently refers to by the awed and ominous *it* – almost like a savage thinking of his idol. The pursuit of the Stone is furtive and vaguely criminal: terms like *pryvee* and *secree* recur in the poem. But the most potent key-word is, of course, *blinde*. From the *lanes blinde* (105) in which the alchemists 'lurk' (fit symbol of the futility of it all – a 'blind alley') to the *blending* of the Priest in the tale proper, the ideas of deception, delusion, falseness and unreality are kept before our minds. Finally, the word *feend*, recurring in the Yeoman's cries and imprecations, firmly underlines the theme of alchemy as a diabolical pursuit forbidden by God, who punishes those who pry into his secrets unworthily.

Devices of style that enrich the poetry, such as rhetorical figures and similes, are relatively few in the *CYT*, which attempts (in part at least) to mirror the 'lewdness' of the teller. Alliteration occurs for emphasis, not ornament:

His *w*yly *w*renches thou ne mayst nat flee (528)

Now tak heed of this *ch*anouns *c*ursednesse (548)

This *f*als chanoun (the *f*oule *f*eend him *f*ecche!) (606)

A main source of the poem's vitality is its faithfulness to the movement of a particular mind in a definite emotional condition, while remaining within the confines of recognizably patterned verse. The verse may be 'free', compared with that of the *GP* (see text in this volume), but this may be partly due to lack of revision, and it is a mistake to read the lines as if they were a kind of rhythmic prose. In

Chaucer's poetry the *interaction* between freedom and formal pattern is of the essence. The verse is highly *dramatic* in the way it captures from the very first the nervous, agitated tone of the Yeoman, on edge with bottled-up animus towards the Canon:

> Who, sire? My lord? Ye, ye, withouten lye (46)
>
> A, nay! lat be . . . (309)
>
> Nay, nay, God woot, al be he monk or frere (286)

Equally accurate are the expressions of frenzied rage that break from the narrator as he recounts, with mounting excitement, the False Canon's duplicity:

> . . . the devel *out of his skin*
> *Him terve*, I pray to God, for his falshede! –
> For he was ever fals in thoght and dede (720–2)

The movement is marvellously speech-like, and yet the pause after *skin* (which is *dramatically* appropriate in that it prepares for the stinging virulence of the word *terve*) re-asserts the line-structure that is in danger of being submerged by the colloquial speech-pattern. At the same time, the wonderfully lifelike collocation of God and devil in the same act of wishing ('may the devil flay him' . . . 'I pray to God *that* the devil . . .') is achieved as the *result* of the exigencies of verse, and would be impossible in prose. In lines like this, we see Chaucer turning his limitations into strengths: the savage violence of the image has the effect of suggesting both the speaker's powerful feelings and the diabolism of the Canon. Only a devil would be fit to flay a devil.

Even one of the few rhetorical devices used in the tale, *occupatio* (the refusal to tell something followed by a description of the thing) fits in naturally as expressive of the Yeoman's character and state of mind. For in this passage (201–65) what we have is the undigested sensations and experiences of the 'seven yeer' the 'lewed' Yeoman has spent with the Canon, poured forth in superb disarray and vividly evoking his sense of helplessness and simultaneous fascination. It is the earliest study of obsessional neurosis in our literature. Apparatus, ingredients and techniques are bundled together with a dim awareness of the absurdity of some and the incongruity of all:[18]

> Poudres diverse, asshes, dong, pisse, and cley . . .
> Cley maad with hors or mannes heer, and oile
> Of tartre, alum-glas, berm, wort and argoile . . .

---

[18] Duncan [ii] claims that the Yeoman is giving in this passage 'a fair description of some . . . of the operation known as the citrination of silver'. But it is highly doubtful whether the passage is as coherent as Duncan seems to find it.

Organic and inorganic, vegetable and mineral, the whole ensemble is a perfect symbolic image of the intellectual, moral (and, of course, financial) confusion in which alchemists are reduced to living. Their hopes are elastic though in reality as fragile as the pot which 'to-breketh' through their ignorance or bad luck. 'Farewel! al is go' becomes a fitting epitaph on the endeavours of the whole profession, and in context the phrase contains an irony of which the speaker remains totally unaware.

A feature of the poem's style which has often been noticed is the frequent (functionless) repetition of words and phrases, which contributes to the slackening of the verse already produced by the abundance of line-fillers.[19] This must be distinguished sharply from the repetition of key-words discussed above. (For examples, see *Commentary* on 172.)

Conclusion

The main weakness of the poem is not, as has often been stated, its 'lack of unity'. (The thematic unity has been sufficiently demonstrated already; the polemical inadequacy of the *exemplum* may be a weakness, but it is not a sign of lack of unity.) It is rather the intrinsic thinness of the main narrative material – a thinness which becomes pronounced as soon as we compare the tale proper with the work which resembles the *CYT* most closely in structure and conception, the *Pardoner's Tale*. The gulling of the Priest is told convincingly enough, but suffers when placed beside a plot like that of *The Alchemist*, which Coleridge described as 'absolute perfection for necessary entanglement'. If the tale proper is simple, the total handling deserves credit for its originality. The dramatic monologue form (which is virtually what the Yeoman's *Prologue* is) has limitations which full-scale drama escapes; but it also has possibilities which Chaucer is not slow to exploit. His plot may lack 'entanglement', but his main 'character' – not, as some critics remark, the False Canon, but the Yeoman – is a finer and more complex creation than anything in Jonson's play. The moral substance of the poem is no less fully realized, even if the concluding warning may be too 'medieval' a piece of explicitness for most readers.

[19] See *Commentary* on 81.

Biographical Note

Geoffrey Chaucer, the son of John Chaucer, a well-to-do vintner, was born in London about 1343. Little is known about his formal education, but this most well-read of medieval English poets probably got his knowledge of French and Latin at one of the London schools, and he may also have had a general as well as legal education at the Inner Temple during the years from 1361 to 1367. He did not go to either university, though in later life he was in touch with Oxford scholars like Ralph Strode. As a poet he acquired much of his knowlege of men and manners through his experience of court life. He was a page in the household of the Countess of Ulster and then in that of Prince Lionel, from about the age of fourteen to twenty (1357–?63), and a squire of the Royal Household from 1367 to 1378. During these years he became a friend of John of Gaunt, the death of whose wife Blanche was the occasion of Chaucer's first long poem, *The Book of the Duchess* (1369–70). These were formative years for Chaucer: he went on diplomatic missions to France, Flanders and Italy, learnt Italian and read the works of Dante and Boccaccio, which deeply influenced his own poems written after about 1380. As a very young man he had served in the English army in France, where he was captured and ransomed (1360), and he took part in Gaunt's French expedition nine years later. In 1366 he married Philippa, one of the Queen's ladies; but nothing is known of their life together. They may have had two sons, Thomas and Lewis, and a daughter Elizabeth, who became a nun, but the evidence is not certain that these Chaucers (of whom we have historical records) were the poet's children.

In the last twenty-five years of his life, Chaucer held a succession of administrative appointments which brought him into contact with businessmen and merchants. Between 1374 and 1386 he was the King's senior customs official for wools, skins and hides in the port of London, and in 1382 he took over the Petty Customs for wine, etc. In his later years he was Clerk of the King's Works (1389–91), a post which included responsibility for the upkeep of the royal palaces, and in 1391 he became Deputy Forester of the King's Somersetshire forest of North Petherton. He eked out the income from these offices with exchequer grants received from his royal masters Edward III, Richard II and Henry IV. During the politically disturbed later years of the fourteenth century, Chaucer managed to avoid making enemies in high places and, while never becoming a rich man (like Shakespeare in his last years), he avoided poverty. His poetry, written for and circulated among the court circle and his friends, was highly successful but did not bring him much financial reward. After 1385 Chaucer left London and lived in Kent, where he was justice of the peace for four years and, in 1386, knight of the shire (member of Parliament) for Kent. In 1399 he leased a house in the garden of Westminster Abbey. He died in 1400, and tradition has it that he was buried in the Abbey.

During his years as a customs official Chaucer was hard-worked and had little leisure for poetry, though one of his finest earlier poems *The Parliament of Fowls* (and possibly also the unfinished comic fantasy *The House of Fame*) belong to this period. But after 1382 he had the help of deputies, and in the 1380s he translated Boethius's *Consolation of Philosophy* and wrote his great narrative poem *Troilus and Criseyde*. The increase of leisure which came with his move to Kent may have stimulated him to begin the *Canterbury Tales*, the crowning work of his maturity and the greatest work of medieval English literature. The *General Prologue* is dated about 1387. Between this work and *Troilus* he wrote the (unfinished) collection of tales called *The Legend of Good Women*. The *Prologue* of this is an exquisite semi-autobiographical love-vision in which the heroic couplet is used for the first time. The *Tales* (some of which Chaucer had written years before) occupied the remaining years of his life and were left unfinished at his death in 1400.

The later fourteenth century is now seen as the first great age of English literature and Chaucer as the 'representative' writer of that age. His reputation reached its height in the fifteenth century and he was read and admired from the time of Spenser to that of Wordsworth, in spite of the increasing difficulties presented by his language and the lack of knowledge of the principles of his metre. But the later nineteenth century failed to appreciate Chaucer's subtle comic art, his psychological profundity and dramatic realism, and Matthew Arnold's judgment that his poetry 'lacks high seriousness' is not untypical of the time. Ironically, this was the period in which Chaucer's work was first systematically studied and edited, in spite of the offence which his frankness caused to the Victorian sense of propriety. However it is only in this century that the fervent appreciation Chaucer's art and genius drew from poet-critics like Dryden, Blake and Crabbe has been fully recaptured. The study of Chaucer and his contemporaries grows and flourishes and *The Canterbury Tales* may soon become again, in its original form, a living classic.

Some Suggestions for Further Reading

Of the many books on Chaucer's life and times the best still remains G. G. Coulton's pungently-written *Chaucer and his England* (Methuen, University Paperback edn., 1963). D. S. Brewer's *Chaucer in his Time* (Nelson, 1963, reprinted 1974) is also very helpful. There are many pictorial companions and guides of varying quality. The court culture which provided the background for much of Chaucer's work is well studied in the opening chapters of Gervase Mathew's *The Court of Richard II* (John Murray, 1968) and there is much entertaining background information on medieval popular life in J. J. Jusserand's *English Wayfaring Life in the Middle Ages* (Benn, 1950). Useful introductions to the poetry are John Speirs's *Chaucer the Maker* (Faber pbk. 1964) and the Pelican *Age of Chaucer* (edited by Boris Ford). The classic introduction to Chaucer's earlier work (including *Troilus*) is C. S. Lewis's *The Allegory of Love* (Galaxy pbk. 1958) and the best single study of the *Tales* is W. W. Lawrence's *Chaucer and the Canterbury Tales* (Columbia University Press, repr. 1969). The standard edition of the complete works is F. N. Robinson's (Oxford University Press, 2nd edn. 1957), but other useful texts are the 'Everyman' editions of the *Tales*, edited by A. C. Cawley and of *Troilus and Criseyde*, edited by John Warrington, both of which are widely available. These have marginal glosses and footnote-paraphrases of difficult lines, which make for easier reading.

The General Prologue to
The Canterbury Tales

Whan that Aprill with his shoures sote
The droghte of March hath perced to the rote
And bathed every veyne in swich licour,
Of which vertu engendred is the flour;
Whan Zephirus eek with his swete breeth   5
Inspyred hath in every holt and heeth
The tendre croppes, and the yonge sonne
Hath in the Ram his half(e) cours yronne,
And smale fowles maken melodye
That slepen al the night with open ȳe   10
(So priketh hem nature in hir corages) –
Than longen folk to goon on pilgrimages
And palmers for to seken straunge strondes,
To ferne halwes, couthe in sondry londes;
And specially, from every shyres ende   15
Of Engelond, to Caunterbury they wende,
The holy blisful martir for to seke,
That hem hath holpen whan that they were seeke.
   Bifil that in that seson on a day,
In Southwerk at the Tabard as I lay   20
Redy to wenden on my pilgrimage

The abbreviation (c) *means 'See Commentary at the back of the book for further discussion'.*
[1] *Whan that* = simply 'when' (also 18, below).   *sote*, sweet.
[2] *droghte*, dryness.   *perced*, pierced.   *rote*, root.
[3] *veyne*, vein (of a leaf).   *licour*, liquid, moisture.   *swich*, such.
[4] *vertu*, 'potency', 'generating force'.   *Of which vertu*, 'by means of which generating power . . .'.   *engendred*, generated, produced.
[5] *Whan*, when.   *Zephirus*, the balmy west wind (zephyr).   *eek*, also.
[6] *Inspyred*, both 'blown upon' (Lat. *inspirare*) and 'filled with the breath or spirit (*sc.* of spring)'.   *holt*, wood.
[7] *croppes*, shoots or tops of plants.   *yonge sonne*, young sun.
[8] 'Has run his half-course in the sign of the Ram' (c).
[9] *fowles*, birds (c).   *maken*, make (c).
[10] *slepen*, sleep.   *ȳe*, eye (c).
[11] *priketh*, stimulates.   *hem*, them.   *nature*, here perh. a personification is intended, the Goddess Nature (c).   *hir corages*, their instincts, hearts (cf. 22).
[12] *Than*, then (cf. *whan* above, 5).   *longen*, long, wish earnestly.   *goon*, go.
[13] *palmers*, pilgrims (c).   *for to seken*, to seek.   *straunge strondes*, foreign shores.
[14] *To.* Understand '(and to go) to'.   *ferne halwes*, distant shrines (lit. 'far-off saints').   *couthe*, (well-)known.   *sondry londes*, various countries.
[15] *shyres*, shire's.
[16] *wende*, go, set out.
[17] i.e. St Thomas Becket of Canterbury (c).   *blisful*, blessed.
[18] *holpen*, helped.   *seeke*, sick.
[19] *Bifil*, it happened.   *seson*, time.   *on a day*, one day.
[20] A *tabard* was a short jacket.   *lay*, lodged, was staying.

To Caunterbury with ful devout corage,
At night were come into that hostelrye
Wel nyne and twenty in a compaignye
Of sondry folk, by aventure yfalle   25
In felaweshipe, and pilgrims were they alle,
That toward Caunterbury wolden ryde.
The chambres and the stables weren wyde,
And wel we weren esed atte beste.
And shortly, when the sonne was to reste,   30
So hadde I spoken with hem everichon
That I was of hir felaweshipe anon,
And made forward erly for to ryse,
To take our wey, ther as I yow devyse.
   But natheles, whyl I have tyme and space,   35
Er that I ferther in this tale pace,
Me thinketh it acordaunt to resoun
To telle yow al the condicioun
Of ech of hem, so as it semed me,
And whiche they weren, and of what degree,   40
And eek in what array that they were inne:
And at a knight than wol I first biginne.
   A KNIGHT ther was, and that a worthy man,
That fro the tyme that he first bigan
To ryden out, he loved chivalrye –   45

---

²² *ful*, very (Chaucer's usual word).　*corage*, spirit, feeling (cf. 11).
²³ *hostelrye*, inn.
²⁴ *Wel nyne*, etc., 'a good twenty-nine'.
²⁵⁻⁶ 'Various kinds of people, fallen together in company by chance.'
²⁷ *wolden ryde*, wished to ride.
²⁹ *weren*, were.　*esed atte beste*, given the best possible accommodation and treatment.　*atte* = at the.
³⁰ *to reste*, i.e. *gone* to rest, set.
³¹ *everichon*, every one (lit. 'ever-each-one').
³¹⁻² 'I had spoken to each one of them in such a way that I became a member of their company without ado (*or*, "soon got to know them well")'.
³³ *forward*, agreement. (A subject of *made*, 'we', is understood from 31–2.)
³⁴ *ther as I yow devyse*, to that place I (shall) describe to you, (*ther as* is ME for 'where') or perhaps, here, 'in the way that'.
³⁵ *natheles*, nevertheless.
³⁶ *pace*, proceed.
³⁷ *Me thinketh*, it seems to me (cf. 'methinks') (c).　*acordaunt to resoun*, reasonable; a rational or sensible thing (to do). On the implications of this phrase, see Commentary.
³⁸⁻⁴¹ 'To tell you in full what impression I had of the appearance of each of them – what sort of people they were, their social position, the clothes they were wearing.'
⁴² *wol I*, will I (with sense of intention) – 'I am going to . . .'.
⁴³ *worthy*, 'distinguished' (cf. 47, 50 below).
⁴⁵ *chivalrye*, the knightly way of life (c), martial deeds.

Trouthe and honour, fredom and curteisye.
Ful worthy was he in his lordes werre,
And therto hadde he riden – no man ferre –
As wel in Cristendom as in hethenesse,
And evere honoured for his worthinesse.   50
At Alisaundre he was, whan it was wonne.
Ful ofte tyme he hadde the bord bigonne
Aboven alle naciouns in Pruce.
In Lettow hadde he reysed, and in Ruce,
No Cristen man so ofte of his degree.   55
In Gernade at the seege eek hadde he be
Of Algezir, and riden in Belmarye.
At Lyeys was he, and at Satalye,
Whan they were wonne; and in the Grete See
At many a noble armee hadde he be.   60
At mortal batailles hadde he been fiftene,
And foughten for our feith at Tramissene
In listes thryes, and ay slayn his foo.
This ilke worthy knight hadde been also
Somtyme with the lord of Palatye   65
Agayn another hethen in Turkye –
And evermore he hadde a sovereyn prys.
And though that he were worthy, he was wys,

46 *Trouthe*, truth, truthfulness (esp. 'fidelity to one's oath or pledged word'). *fredom*, noble generosity (c).

47 *his lordes werre*, possibly the King's wars in France (1345–60) (c).

48 *therto*, thither (to these wars).   *ferre*, further (comparative of *fer*, far).

49 'In heathen as much as in Christian lands'.

50 'And (was) ever', etc.   *worthinesse*, excellence, esp. as a soldier.

51 *Alisaundre*, Alexandria.

52 'Many a time he had sat at the head of the table' ('bord').   *bigonne*, lit. begun.

53 *naciouns*, (knights of other) nationalities.   *Pruce*, Prussia.

54 *Lettow*, Lithuania.   *reysed*, been in military expeditions.   *Ruce*, Russia.

56–7 *Gernade*, Granada.   *Algezir*, modern Algeciras.   *Belmarye*, now Benmarin, in Morocco.

58 *Lyeys*, Lyas in Armenia.   *Satalye*, Attalia (Antalya), in Asia Minor.

59 *the Grete See*, probably the Mediterranean.

60 *armee*, armada, armed expedition (and see textual note on this line).

62 *foughten*, (and he had) fought.   *Tramissene*, Tremezen (Tlemcen) in Algeria.

62–3 'He had fought three times in the lists' (i.e. in response to a challenge from a Saracen).   *ay*, every time.   *foo*, foe (c).

64 *ilke*, same.

65 *Palatye*, Palatia in Anatolia, modern Turkish Balat.   *somtyme*, at one time, on one occasion (not 'sometimes').

66 *Agayn*, against (on this and all the Knight's campaigns, see Commentary).

67 *a sovereyn prys*, the highest esteem, the highest honours.

68 'Though a distinguished man, he showed his wisdom in being humble' (see next line).   *were* is subjunctive, 'though he might be *worthy*, he was, nonetheless, wise also'.

And of his port as meeke as is a mayde.
He nevere yet no vileinye ne sayde   70
In al his lyf, unto no maner wight.
He was a verray, parfit gentil knight.
But, for to tellen yow of his array –
His hors were goode, but he was nat gay.
Of fustian he wered a gipoun   75
Al bismotered with his habergeoun;
For he was late ycome from his viage,
And wente for to doon his pilgrimage.
  With him ther was his sone, a yong SQUYER,
A lovyere, and a lusty bacheler,   80
With lokkes crulle as they were leyd in presse.
Of twenty yeer of age he was, I gesse.
Of his stature he was of evene lengthe,
And wonderly delivere, and of greet strengthe.
And he had been somtyme in chivachye   85
In Flaundres, in Artoys, and Picardye,
And born him wel, as of so litel space,
In hope to stonden in his lady grace.
Embrouded was he, as it were a mede
Al ful of fresshe floures, whyte and rede.   90
Singinge he was, or floytinge, al the day;
He was as fressh as is the month of May.

---

⁶⁹ *port*, bearing, demeanour.   *meeke*, etc., as mild-mannered as a girl.
⁷⁰⁻¹ *never . . . no . . . ne . . . no . . .* = never . . . any . . . any (C).   *vileinye*,
any insulting or rude utterance thought unworthy of a knight.   *no maner wight*,
any kind of person, anyone whatsoever (note omission of genitival 'of').
⁷² *verray*, real, genuine.   *parfit*, perfect, complete.   *gentil*, noble.
⁷⁴ *hors*, horses (uninflected plural).   *gay*, dressed in bright clothes.
⁷⁵ *fustian*, fustian, a thick cotton fabric.   *wered*, was wearing.   *gipoun*, tunic.
⁷⁶ *bismotered*, dirtied, soiled ('besmutted').   *with his habergeoun, by* his hauberk
(the coat of chain-mail he wore when campaigning) (C).
⁷⁷ 'He was just back from his travels.'
⁷⁸ *wente*, was going.   *for to doon*, to make.
⁷⁹ Pronounce SQUYÉR.
⁸⁰ *lovyere*, lover (C).   *lusty*, lusty, vigorous.   *bacheler*, bachelor (C).
⁸¹ *lokkes crulle*, locks of hair curled (as if with some kind of curling-instrument).
⁸² *I gesse*, I should imagine.
⁸³ 'He was of medium height.' Pronounce *statúre*.
⁸⁴ *wonderly delivere*, remarkably agile (or nimble).
⁸⁵ *chivachye*, in small military expeditions involving cavalry (cf. French *cheval*).
⁸⁶ See Commentary.
⁸⁷ 'And he had acquitted himself well, considering the short time he had served.'
⁸⁸ 'In the hope of winning his lady's favour'.   *lady* is an old genitive case
without 's'.   *stonden*, stand.
⁸⁹ *embrouded*, embroidered. See Commentary on 79 ff.   *mede*, meadow.
⁹¹ *floytinge*, playing the flute.
⁹² *May* (C).

Short was his gowne, with sleves longe and wyde.
Wel coude he sitte on hors, and faire ryde.
He coude songes make and wel endyte,   95
Juste, and eek daunce, and wel purtreye and wryte.
So hote he lovede that by nightertale
He slepte namore than dooth a nightingale.
Curteys he was, lowely and servisable,
And carf biforn his fader at the table.   100
    A YEMAN hadde he and servaunts namo
At that tyme – for him liste ryde so –
And he was clad in cote and hood of grene.
A sheef of pecok arwes, bright and kene,
Under his belt he bar ful thriftily;   105
(Wel coude he dresse his takel yemanly –
His arwes drouped noght with fetheres lowe)
And in his hand he bar a mighty bowe.
A not-heed hadde he, with a broun visage.
Of wodecraft wel coude he al the usage.   110
Upon his arm he bar a gay bracer,
And by his syde a swerd and a bokeler,
And on that other syde a gay daggere,
Harneised wel and sharp as point of spere;
A cristofre on his brest of silver shene.   115

[94] 'He knew well (*coude*) how to sit a horse, and could ride excellently' (*faire* is an adverb).

[95] *endyte*, compose (music and poetry); cf. 325.

[96] *Juste*, joust.   *purtreye*, draw.   *wryte*, write (noting not his *literacy* but rather the elegance of his handwriting).

[97] *hote*, hotly, ardently.   *by nightertale*, during the night-time.

[98] *namore*, no more; cf. 10 (c).

[99] *Curteys*, courteous.   *lowely*, modest, diffident, unassuming. *servisable*, willing.

[100] *carf*, carved (strong preterite of *kerven*, to cut/carve).   *biforn*, before ('in presence of') (c).

[101] YEMAN, yeoman, here a serving-man of rank above *groom*.   *namo*, no more (cf. *namore* 98 above). The 'he' in this line refers to the Knight, as does the 'him' in 102.

[102] '. . . for that is how he wished to ride' (lit. 'for so it pleased him to ride'). An impersonal construction, frequent in ME (cf. 37, note).

[104] *pecok arwes*, peacock-feathered arrows.   *kene*, sharp.

[105] *bar*, carried.   *thriftily*, properly, well.

[106] 'He knew how to arrange his equipment as a good yeoman should' (lit. 'in a yeomanlike manner', or *yemanly* may be an adj.)

[107] See Commentary.

[109] *not-heed*, close-cropped head.

[110] 'He had a thorough knowledge of the practice of woodcraft.'

[111] *bracer*, the archer's protective arm-covering.

[112] *swerd and bokeler*, sword and buckler (small shield).

[114] *Harneised*, mounted (which is why the dagger looked *gay*, 'splendid').

[115] *cristofre*, an image of St Christopher, patron saint of foresters (cf. *vernicle*, 685).

An horn he bar, the bawdrik was of grene;
A forster was he, soothly, as I gesse.
Ther was also a Nonne, a PRIORESSE,
That of hir smyling was ful simple and coy;
(Hir gretteste ooth was but by Seïnt Loy)   120
And she was cleped Madame Eglentyne.
Ful wel she song the servyce divyne,
Entuned in hir nose ful semely;
And Frenssh she spak ful faire and fetisly,
After the scole of Stratford atte Bowe –   125
For Frenssh of Paris was to hir unknowe.
At mete wel ytaught was she withalle:
She leet no morsel from hir lippes falle,
Ne wette hir fingres in hir sauce depe.
Wel coude she carie a morsel and wel kepe   130
That no drope ne fille upon hir brest.
In curteisye was set ful muchel hir lest.
Hir over lippe wyped she so clene
That in hir coppe was no ferthing sene
Of grece, whan she dronken had hir draughte.   135
Ful semely after hir mete she raughte –
And, sikerly, she was of greet desport,
And ful plesaunt and amiable of port,
And peyned hir to countrefete chere
Of court, and been estatlich of manere,   140

116 *bawdrik*, baldric, the belt or strap by which the horn was fastened.
117 *forster*, forester (whence the names 'Forster', 'Foster').   *soothly*, truly.
119 *coy*, quiet, demure (rather than 'coy').
120 *Seïnt Loy*, St Eligius (c).
121 *cleped*, called.   *Eglentyne*, 'Sweetbriar' (c).
122 *song*, sang.
123 *entuned*, intoned (c).   *semely*, in a seemly or proper manner (cf. 136).
124 *spak*, spoke.   *faire and fetisly*, well and choicely.
125 'As they taught it at the Benedictine nunnery near Stratford-at-Bow' (c).
126 *unknowe*, unknown. (cf. 56, *be* for 'been').
127 'Her table-manners were good, moreover.'   *mete*, food.
129 *wette*, wetted.   *depe*, deeply.
130–1 *wel kepe/That* . . . either 'hold it well, so that' or 'ensure that'; the latter is preferable since the sense runs on from line 130 to 131.
131 'That no drop should fall' (*fille* is subjunctive).
132 *curteisye*, courtly manners or behaviour.   *lest*, pleasure (variant of *list*, *lust*).
133 *over*, upper.   *clene*, cleanly.
134 *coppe*, cup.   *ferthing*, small round spot shaped like a farthing.
136 *mete*, food (the modern meaning is a specialization – Chaucer's word being 'flesh').   *raughte*, reached (c).
137 *sikerly*, certainly she was, etc., 'she was an amusing (entertaining) person'.
139–41 'And she went out of her way to imitate court-manners, to maintain a dignified air and to be thought worthy of respectful treatment.'

And to been holden digne of reverence.
But, for to speken of hir conscience –
She was so charitable, and so pitous,
She wolde wepe, if that she saugh a mous
Caught in a trappe, if it were deed or bledde.   145
Of smale houndes hadde she, that she fedde
With rosted flessh, or milk and wastel-breed.
But sore wepte she if oon of hem were deed,
Or if men smoot it with a yerde smerte;
And al was conscience and tendre herte.   150
Ful semely hir wimpul pinched was,
Hir nose tretys, hir eyen greye as glas,
Hir mouth ful smal, and therto softe and reed;
But sikerly she hadde a fair forheed –
It was almost a spanne brood, I trowe –   155
For, hardily, she was nat undergrowe!
Ful fetys was hir cloke, as I was war.
Of smal coral aboute hir arm she bar
A peire of bedes, gauded al with grene,
And theron heng a broche of gold ful shene,   160
On which ther was first write a crowned A,
And after – *Amor vincit omnia.*
  Another NONNE with hir hadde she,
That was hir chapeleyne, and PREESTES three.
  A MONK ther was, a fair for the maistrye,   165

---

[142] *conscience* here means 'sensitivity', 'delicate susceptibilities', not our 'con-science'. Cf. 398 (the modern meaning) and 526 (something nearer to 'con-scientiousness').

[143] *pitous*, compassionate, full of feelings of pity.

[144] *saugh*, saw (cf. 193, *seigh*).

[146] *of smale houndes*, some little dogs (cf. the construction with *de*, *des* in French).

[147] *wastel-breed*, cake-bread, made of fine flour (*wastel*, cf. Fr. *gâteau*, also Eng. war, wardrobe, Fr. *guerre*, *garderobe*).

[149] 'Or if anyone should strike it sharply with a stick' (*men*, or its contracted form *me* was ME for 'one' (cf. Ger. *man*); *smerte* is adv. – 'smartly'; note the -e ending (adverbial).

[150] *conscience*, see 142n above.

[151] *wimpul*, wimple, a covering for head and neck.   *pinched*, pleated.

[152] *tretys*, well-formed.   *eyen*, eyes (for the -en pl. cf. oxen, children).

[156] *hardily*, 'if I may make bold to say . . .'.   *undergrowe*, stunted.

[157] *fetys*, neat, elegant.   *war*, aware ('as I observed').

[159] *a peire of bedes*, a set (lit. 'pair') of beads (i.e. a rosary).   *gauded al with grene*, the large beads (called 'gaudes') being green in colour (c).

[160] *heng*, hung.   *shene*, bright.

[161] *write*, written, inscribed.

[162] *Amor vincit omnia*, 'love conquers all things'; from Vergil's Eclogue x, 69; 'omnia vincit Amor: et nos cedamus Amori', the phrase was proverbial (c).

[164] *chapeleyne*, personal assistant ('capellana') (c).

[165] *a fair for the maistrye*, fit to wield authority (cf. 167, 'to been an abbot able').

An out-rydere, that lovede venerye –
A manly man, to been an abbot able.
Ful many a deyntee hors hadde he in stable,
And whan he rood, men mighte his brydel here
Ginglen in a whistling wind as clere   170
An eek as loude as dooth the chapel belle,
Ther as this lord was keper of the celle.
The reule of Seynt Maure or of Seynt Beneit –
(By cause that it was old and somdel streit) –
This ilke Monk leet olde thinges pace,   175
And heeld after the newe world the space.
He yaf nat of that text a pulled hen,
That seith that hunters been nat holy men,
Ne that a monk, whan he is recchelees,
Is lykned til a fissh that is waterlees,   180
(This is to seyn, a monk out of his cloistre) –
But thilke text heeld he nat worth an oistre;
And I seyde, his opinioun was good.
What sholde he studie, and make himselven wood,
Upon a book in cloistre alwey to poure,   185
Or swinken with his handes, and laboure
As Austin bit? How shal the world be served?
Lat Austin have his swink to him reserved!
Therfore he was a prikasour aright:
Grehoundes he hadde, as swift as fowel in flight;   190
Of priking and of hunting for the hare

---

¹⁶⁶ *an out-rydere*, an outrider, who looked after the monastic estates.   *venerye*,
hunting.
¹⁶⁷ *able*, fit, capable (of).
¹⁶⁸ *deyntee*, choice, valuable (c).
¹⁷⁰ *Ginglen*, jingle.
¹⁷² *celle*, subsidiary monastic house, 'cell'.
¹⁷³ *reule*, (monastic) rule, the *regula* or code of discipline of a religious order.
Seynt Maure, Seynt Beneit, St Maurus, St Benedict (c).
¹⁷⁴ *somdel streit*, somewhat strict (from Fr. *estreit*, a different word from Eng.
straight).
¹⁷³⁻⁶ The syntax is difficult (c).
¹⁷⁷ 'He didn't give a plucked hen' (i.e. 'cared nothing for . . .').   *text*, (c).
¹⁷⁹ *recchelees*, 'reckless', neglectful (*sc.* of his rule). See textual note on this read-
ing.
¹⁸² *thilke*, that same (= 'the ilke').   *heeld*, considered.
¹⁸⁴ *What*, for what reason, why.   *wood*, mad.
¹⁸⁵ *poure . . . upon*, pore over.
¹⁸⁶ *swinken*, toil.
¹⁸⁷ *As Austin bit*, as (St) Augustine commands (*bit* = *biddeth*) (c).
¹⁸⁹ *a prikasour aright*, a real hard-riding man.
¹⁹¹ *priking*, riding, or perhaps, 'tracking the hare by its "pricks" or footprints'
(which wd. make the rest of the line tautological) (c).

Was al his lust – for no cost wolde he spare.
I seigh his sleves purfiled at the hond
With grys, and that the fyneste of a lond;
And, for to festne his hood under his chin,   195
He hadde of gold ywroght a ful curious pin:
A love-knotte in the gretter ende ther was.
His heed was balled, that shoon as any glas,
And eek his face, as he had been anoint.
He was a lord ful fat and in good point,   200
His eyen stepe, and rollinge in his heed,
That stemed as a forneys of a leed,
His bootes souple, his hors in greet estat –
Now certainly he was a fair prelat.
He was nat pale as a forpyned goost.   205
A fat swan loved he best of any roost.
His palfrey was as broun as is a berye.
   A FRERE ther was, a wantown and a merye,
A limitour, a ful solempne man.
In alle the ordres foure is noon that can   210
So muchel of daliaunce and fair langage.
He hadde maad ful many a mariage
Of yonge wommen, at his owne cost.
Unto his ordre he was a noble post.
Ful wel biloved and famulier was he   215

<hr>

¹⁹² *lust*, pleasure (cf. *lest*, 132).   *for no cost*, etc., he would spare no expense (at it); '*for* he would spare . . .' is possible but unlikely.
   ¹⁹³ *seigh*, saw (cf. *saugh*, 144).   *purfiled*, edged, trimmed.   *hond*, hand.
   ¹⁹⁴ *grys*, grey fur (Fr. *gris*).   *of a lond*, in the land.
   ¹⁹⁵ *festne*, fasten.
   ¹⁹⁶ *ywroght*, made, fashioned.   *a ful curious pin*, a most skilfully designed pin (cf. the Horatian phrase '*curiosa felicitas*').
   ¹⁹⁷ *love-knotte*, an elaborately looped knot.   *gretter*, bigger.
   ¹⁹⁸ *balled*, bald.   *shoon*, shone.
   ¹⁹⁹ 'as if he had been anointed (with oil).'
   ²⁰⁰ *in good point*, in good condition (cf. Fr. *embonpoint*).
   ^{201–2} *stepe*, bright (rather than 'prominent', 'protuberant').   *stemed*, glowed (*not* 'steamed').   *That* (202) may refer to his eyes or his head, almost certainly the former (otherwise Chaucer would be repeating l.198; and cf. also the construction in that line: '*His heed . . . that shoon . . .*').   *forneys of a leed*, furnace under a cauldron (*leed*).
   ²⁰³ *souple*, supple, pliable (made of soft leather; cf. 457).   *in greet estat*, in excellent condition.
   ²⁰⁵ *a forpyned goost*, a spirit in torment.
   ²⁰⁸ FRERE, friar.   *wantown*, high-spirited.   *merye*, pleasant, jovial.
   ²⁰⁹ *limitour*, 'limiter' (c).   *solempne*, dignified, imposing (c); cf. 274, 364.
   ²¹⁰ *the ordres foure*, the four orders (of friars) (c).   *can*, knows.
   ²¹¹ *daliaunce and fair langage*, flirtation and winning language.
   ²¹⁴ *post*, pillar (support).
   ^{215–16} *famulier . . ./With . . .*, intimate with.

With frankeleyns overal in his contree,
And eek with worthy wommen of the toun;
For he hadde power of confessioun
(As seyde himself) more than a curat –
For of his ordre he was licenciat.   220
Ful swetely herde he confessioun,
And plesaunt was his absolucioun.
He was an esy man to yeve penaunce
Ther as he wiste to han a good pitaunce.
For unto a povre ordre for to yive   225
Is signe that a man is wel yshrive:
For 'if he yaf', he dorste make avaunt,
'He wiste that a man was repentaunt';
(For many a man so hard is of his herte,
He may nat wepe, althogh him sore smerte;   230
Therfore, in stede of weping and preyeres,
Men moot yeve silver to the povre freres).
His tipet was ay farsed ful of knyves
And pinnes, for to yeven faire wyves.
And certeinly he hadde a murye note: 235
Wel coude he singe and pleyen on a rote;
Of yeddinges he bar outrely the prys.
His nekke whyt was as the flour-de-lys;
Therto he strong was as a champioun.
He knew the tavernes wel in every toun,   240

---

²¹⁶ *frankeleyns*, franklins (See 331n).
²¹⁷ *worthy*, 'wealthy', or 'respectable' or both (cf. 243n).
²¹⁹ *curat*, parish priest.
²²⁰ *licenciat*, 'licensed' (c).   *of his ordre*, perhaps 'in status' (Hodgson).
²²⁴ 'In cases where he knew it would be made worth his while.' (*pitaunce*, which here = 'gift', was originally a donation to buy extra provisions for a religious order. The meaning of 'a scant allowance, remuneration' is a later development.)
²²⁵ 'For making donations to a poor order (is a sign) . . .'
²²⁶ *wel yshrive*, has made a good confession (lit. 'is well shriven').
²²⁷ 'For "if a man gave" – he dared avow – "he could know (for sure) that he was repentant" ' (c).
²³⁰ 'He is unable to weep, even if he should feel sharp remorse.'
²³² *men moot yeve*, people ought to give.
²³³ *tipet*, hood (often used as a pocket).   *farsed*, stuffed.
²³⁴ *wyves*, women generally (though it could mean 'wives').
²³⁵ *murye note*, i.e. an agreeable voice.
²³⁶ *rote*, fiddle.
²³⁷ 'He was the best of ballad-singers' (*yeddinges* were stories set to music). *outrely*, utterly, absolutely.
²³⁸ *flour-de-lys*, lily-flower (c).
²³⁹ *champioun*, either one who fights on behalf of another (e.g. in a judicial combat) or else a professional prizefighter (a likelier meaning, given the generally mercenary context of the Friar's activities).

And everich hostiler and tappestere
Bet than a lazar or a beggestere;
For unto swich a worthy man as he
Acorded nat, as by his facultee,
To have with sike lazars aqueyntaunce.   245
(It is nat honest, it may nat avaunce,
For to delen with no swich poraille,
But al with riche and sellers of vitaille.)
And overal, ther as profit sholde aryse,
Curteys he was and lowely of servyse –   250
Ther nas no man nowher so vertuous.
He was the beste beggere in his hous;
(And yaf a certayn ferme for the graunt –
Noon of his brethren cam ther in his haunt!) –
For thogh a widwe hadde noght a sho,
So plesaunt was his 'In principio',
Yet wolde he have a ferthing, er he wente.   255
His purchas was wel bettre than his rente.
And rage he coude, as it were right a whelp.
In love-days, ther coude he muchel help –
For ther he was nat lyk a cloisterer
With a thredbar cope, as is a povre scoler;   260
But he was lyk a maister or a pope:

241 *hostiler*, innkeeper.   *tappestere*, barmaid, (female) tapster. The *-ster* ending denotes femininity (cf. 'spinster', and note below).
242 *Bet*, better (adv.; cf. the adj. at 524 and – used advbly. – at 342).   *lazar*, leper (from the leper Lazarus in the parable, Luke, xvi, 20).   *beggestere*, beggar-woman.
243 *worthy*, distinguished, respectable (cf. 217n, 43n and (c)).
244 'It was not fitting (*acorded nat*), considering his position (*facultee*).'
246-7 'It is not becoming (*honest*) or profitable to have anything to do with such poor wretches (*poraille*).'
248 *But al with riche*, etc., 'But wholly (or exclusively) with rich people and with food-merchants.'
249 *overal, ther as*, everywhere that.
250 'He was courteous, and offered his services humbly' (c).
251 *vertuous*, either ironic, or 'energetic, efficient' (Skeat); cf. Ital. *virtù*.
252a-252b 'And he gave a certain fixed sum (*ferme*) for the grant (of a licence to beg, so that) none of his fellow-friars trespassed on his territory.'   *ferme*, cf. modern 'farm (out)'. See Textual Notes, 5, iii.
253 *widwe*, widow.   *sho*, shoe.
254 '*In principio*', 'in the beginning', the opening words of St John's Gospel, which he quoted as he went begging from house to house. Chaucer may intend a play on words: 'So pleasant were his *opening words* . . .'.
255 'He would still manage to obtain a farthing before leaving.'
256 *purchas*, what he picked up by begging.   *rente*, income. A difficult line (c).
257 *rage*, frisk about (c).   *as it were right a whelp*, exactly like a puppy-dog.
258 *love-days*, days of settlement (*dies amoris*).   *muchel*, much.
260 *cope*, cloak (worn by priests).
261 *maister*, Master (of Arts, or Theology).

Of double worsted was his semicope,
That rounded as a belle out of the presse.
Somwhat he lipsed, for his wantownesse,
To make his Englissh swete upon his tonge;   265
And in his harping, whan that he had songe,
His eyen twinkled in his heed aright,
As doon the sterres in the frosty night.
This worthy limitour was cleped Huberd.
   A MARCHANT was ther with a forked berd,   270
In mottelee, and hye on horse he sat;
Upon his heed a Flaundrissh bever hat,
His bootes clasped faire and fetisly.
His resons he spak ful solempnely,
Souninge alwey th' encrees of his winning.   275
He wolde the see were kept for any thing
Bitwixe Middelburgh and Orewelle.
Wel coude he in eschaunge sheeldes selle.
This worthy man ful wel his wit bisette:
Ther wiste no wight that he was in dette,   280
So estatly was he of his governaunce,
With his bargaynes, and with his chevisaunce.
For sothe he was a worthy man withalle,
But (soth to seyn) I noot how men him calle.
   A CLERK ther was of Oxenford also,   285
That unto logik hadde longe ygo.
As leene was his hors as is a rake,
And he nas nat right fat, I undertake,

---

262 *double worsted*, a heavy woollen cloth.   *semicope*, half-cope (short cloak).
263 *rounded*, fell into a round shape (c).   *presse*, mould.
264 *lipsed*, lisped.   *for his wantownesse*, as a 'playful' affectation. (But again there is a sinister implication.)
271 *in mottelee*, dressed in motley (cloth with figuring, often of mixed colour).
272 *a Flaundrissh bever hat*, a Flemish beaver-skin hat.
273 *clasped*, etc., fastened elegantly with a clasp.
274 'He uttered his opinions (*resons*) in a (pompously) grave and dignified tone of voice (*solempnely*).'
275 'Always harping upon (*souninge*) his profits.' (Contrast 'sowning *in*', 307).
276 'He wanted the sea between Middelburg and Orwell to be guarded (*kept*) at all costs (*for any thing*)' (c).
278 *eschaunge*, exchange.   *sheeldes*, 'shields', French *écus*.
279 *ful wel his wit bisette*, employed his mind (or knowledge) very shrewdly.
280 *Ther wiste no wight*, not a soul knew.
281-2 'So impressively did he go about arranging his bargains and his loan-raising schemes' (*chevisaunce*). (Cf. *Piers Plowman*, B, V, 245).
284 *I noot*, (= *ne woot*), I do not know.   *how men him calle*, what his name is (c).
285 CLERK, a university student. Translate 'clerk'.   *Oxenford*, Oxford.
286 'Who had long been a student of logic' (c).
288 'And you can be sure *he* was not particularly fat, either.'

But loked holwe, and therto sobrely.
Ful thredbar was his overest courtepy;   290
For he had geten him yet no benefyce,
Ne was so worldly for to have offyce.
For him was lever have at his beddes heed
Twenty bokes, clad in blak or reed,
Of Aristotle and his philosophye,   295
Than robes riche, or fithele, or gay sautrye.
But al be that he was a philosophre,
Yet hadde he but litel gold in cofre;
But al that he mighte of his freendes hente,
On bokes and on lerninge he it spente,   300
And bisily gan for the soules preye
Of hem that yaf him wherwith to scoleye.
Of studie took he most cure and most hede.
Noght o word spak he more than was nede,
And that was seyd in forme and reverence,   305
And short and quik and ful of hy sentence,
Sowning in moral vertu was his speche,
And gladly wolde he lerne, and gladly teche.
    A SERGEANT OF THE LAWE, war and wys,
That often hadde been at the Parvys,   310
Ther was also, ful riche of excellence.
Discreet he was, and of greet reverence –
He semed swich, his wordes weren so wyse.
Justyce he was ful often in assyse,

289 *holwe*, hollow (cf. *widwe*, wid*ow*).   *and therto sobrely*, and serious, to boot.
290 *overest courtepy*, short outer coat.
291 'For he had not yet obtained a benefice for himself.'
292 *to have offyce*, to hold a secular post.
293 *him was lever*, he preferred. (Another impersonal construction; cf. notes to 37 and 102.)
296 *fithele*, fiddle.   *sautrye*, psaltery.
297 *philosophre*, a pun on 'philosopher' and the cant meaning of 'alchemist'. The Clerk is clearly a 'philosophre' only in the first sense. (On the activities of alchemists, see the *Canon's Yeoman's Tale* [also in this volume] and Commentary, *passim*; for the rhyme, cf. *CYT* 283–4.)
298 *hadde*, possessed (emphatic; hence the final -e is not elided).   *cofre*, coffer.
299 *of his freendes hente*, obtain from his friends.
301 *gan . . . preye*, prayed.
302 *to scoleye*, to be a university student.   *wherwith*, the means ('the wherewithal').
303 'His main care and attention were devoted to his studies.'
304 *o*, one.
305 *in forme and reverence*, in a decorous and respectful way.
306 'Briefly, pithily, and edifyingly.'
307 *sowning in*, tending towards, 'such as to inculcate'. (Cf. *souninge*, trans., at 275.)
309 *war and wys*, cautious and prudent.
310 *the Parvys*, the portico of St Paul's, where lawyers congregated.

By patente and by pleyn commissioun.   315
For his science, and for his heigh renoun,
Of fees and robes hadde he many oon.
So greet a purchasour was nowher noon:
Al was fee simple to him in effect –
His purchasing mighte nat been infect.   320
Nowher so bisy a man as he ther nas –
And yet he semed bisier than he was.
In termes hadde he caas and domes alle
That from the tyme of King William were falle.
Therto he coude endyte, and make a thing,   325
(Ther coude no wight pinche at his wryting)
And every statut coude he pleyn by rote.
He rood but hoomly in a medlee cote
Girt with a ceint of silk, with barres smale;
Of his array telle I no lenger tale.   330
   A FRANKELEYN was in his compaignye.
Whyt was his berd as is the dayesye;
Of his complexioun he was sangwyn.
Wel loved he by the morwe a sop in wyn.
To liven in delyt was ever his wone,   335
For he was Epicurus' owne sone,
That heeld opinioun that pleyn delyt

³¹⁵ *patente*, letters patent (from the King).   *pleyn commissioun*, letters granting full jurisdiction over all cases.
³¹⁶ *science*, learning.   *renoun*, reputation.
³¹⁷ *fees*, rewards (in the form of property). The fees and robes were gifts (and bribes?) from clients.
³¹⁸ *purchasour*, purchaser (of land).
³¹⁹⁻²⁰ 'He always bought property outright – there was no weak spot in his land-purchasing activities.'   *fee simple*, a technical phrase for a type of tenure granting unrestricted possession to the owner.
³²³ *in termes hadde he*, he had at his fingertips (c).   *caas and domes alle*, all the legal cases and decisions.
³²⁴ *were falle*, had occurred, been made.
³²⁵ *endyte*, compose (cf. 95).   *make a thing*, draw up a document (or brief).
³²⁶ *pinche at*, find fault with (c).
³²⁷ 'He knew (*coude*) every statute in full (*pleyn*) by rote (by heart).'
³²⁸ *hoomly*, simply, unostentatiously, or perhaps 'informally' (Hodgson). *medlee*, motley (see l. 271).
³²⁹ *ceint*, girdle.   *barres smale*, narrow stripes.
³³¹ A 'FRANKLIN' was generally a free man possessing considerable property, the antecedent of the better-known country 'squire' of later days.
³³² *dayesye* (four syllables), daisy (= 'day's eye', i.e. the sun).
³³³ 'He was sanguine of temperament' (c).
³³⁴ *by the morwe*, in the morning, for breakfast.   *a sop in wyn*, bread or cake dipped in wine.
³³⁵ *wone*, practice or custom ('wont').   *delyt*, pleasure.
³³⁶ *Epicurus*, the Greek philosopher (3rd–4th cents. B.C.) who taught that pleasure was the highest good (c).
³³⁷ *pleyn delyt*, pleasure in the highest degree.

Was verray felicitee parfyt.
An housholdere, and that a greet, was he;
Seynt Julian he was in his contree.   340
His breed, his ale, was alweys after oon;
A bettre envyned man was nowher noon.
Withoute bake mete was nevere his hous,
Of fissh and flessh – and that so plentevous,
It snewed in his hous of mete and drinke,   345
Of alle deyntees that men coude thinke.
After the sondry sesons of the yeer,
So chaunged he his mete and his soper.
Ful many a fat partrich hadde he in muwe,
And many a breem and many a luce in stuwe.   350
Wo was his cook but if his sauce were
Poynaunt and sharp, and redy al his gere.
His table dormant in his halle alway
Stood redy covered al the longe day.
At sessiouns, ther was he lord and syre;   355
Ful ofte tyme he was knight of the shyre.
An anlaas and a gipser al of silk
Heng at his girdel, whyt as morne milk.
A shirreve hadde he been, and a countour;
Was nowher swich a worthy vavasour.   360
　　An HABERDASSHER and a CARPENTER,
A WEBBE, a DYER, and a TAPICER –
And they were clothed alle in o liveree,

338 'Constituted true and perfect happiness.'
340 St Julian was the patron of hospitality.　　*his contree*, his part of the world.
341 *after oon*, according to one (standard) – hence, uniformly excellent.
342 *envyned*, provided with wine.
343 *bake mete*, baked meats (i.e. probably baked in *pies*).
344 *plentevous*, plentiful, abundant.
345 *snewed*, snowed.　　*mete*, food (cf. l. 136).
347 *after*, according to.
349 *muwe*, mew – the place where fowl were kept for fattening. (cf. Mod. E. 'mews').
350 *breem*, bream.　　*luce*, pike.　　*stuwe*, fishpond.
351 *Wo*, (adj.) miserable.　　*but if*, unless.
352 *Poynaunt*, piquant.
353 *table dormant*, fixed table (contrasted with the usual trestle-table or *bord*, (cf. l. 52), which was moveable).
355 'He would preside at sessions' (i.e. meetings of the Justices of the Peace).
356 *knight of the shyre*, member of Parliament for his county.
357 *anlaas*, anlace – a short two-edged knife.　*gipser*, purse.
358 *morne milk*, morning-milk.
359 *shirreve*, the sheriff or reve of a shire.　*countour*, accountant.
360 *vavasour*, '(member) of the landed gentry' (Hodgson); lit. 'sub-vass al' – one who held land as tenant of a vassal or baron.
362 WEBBE, weaver.　　TAPICER, tapestry-maker.
363 *o liveree*, one (single) livery.

Of a solempne and a greet fraternitee.
Ful fressh and newe hir gere apyked was: 365
Hir knyves were chaped noght with bras,
But al with silver wroght ful clene and weel –
Hir girdles and hir pouches, every deel.
Wel semed ech of hem a fair burgeys
To sitten in a yeldehalle on a deys.   370
Everich, for the wisdom that he can,
Was shaply for to been an alderman.
For catel hadde they ynogh and rente –
And eek hir wyves wolde it wel assente –
And elles certeyn were they to blame!   375
It is ful fair to been ycleped 'madame',
And goon to vigilyes al bifore,
And have a mantel royalliche ybore.
  A COOK they hadde with hem for the nones
To boille the chiknes with the marybones,   380
And poudre-marchant tart, and galingale.
Wel coude he knowe a draughte of London ale.
He coude rooste, and sethe, and broille, and frye,
Maken mortreux, and wel bake a pye.
But greet harm was it (as it thoughte me)   385
That on his shine a mormal hadde he –
For blankmanger, that made he with the beste.

---

³⁶⁴ *solempne*, highly respectable.   *fraternitee*, gild.
³⁶⁵ *gere*, apparel.   *apyked*, trimmed.
³⁶⁶ *chaped*, provided with *chapes* (i.e. metal plates mounted on the point of the sheath).
³⁶⁹ *burgeys*, burgess.
³⁷⁰ *yeldehalle*, gildhall.   *deys*, dais or raised platform, high table.
³⁷¹ *the wisdom that he can*, the wisdom at his disposal (lit. that he knows).
³⁷² *shaply*, fit.
³⁷³ *catel*, property.   *rente*, income.
³⁷⁴ *wolde it wel assente*, would have been willing enough.
³⁷⁶ *ycleped*, called (cf. l. 269).
³⁷⁷ 'And take precedence at vigils' (i.e. the celebrations on the eve of religious feast-days).
³⁷⁸ *royalliche ybore*, carried like a queen's.
³⁷⁹ *for the nones*, (here, probably) for the occasion.
³⁸⁰ *marybones*, marrow-bones.
³⁸¹ *poudre-marchant*, a flavouring-powder.   *tart*, sharp, tart.   *galingale*, a flavouring made from sweet cyperus root.
³⁸² *knowe*, distinguish.
³⁸³ *sethe*, boil (Mod. E. 'seethe').
³⁸⁴ *mortrëux* (three syllables), 'mortrews', a thick soup.
³⁸⁵ *harm*, misfortune.   *thoughte me*, seemed to me.
³⁸⁶ *shine*, shin.   *mormal*, a sore.
³⁸⁷ *blankmanger*, chicken stew, cooked in milk (hence the white colour from which its name derives).

A SHIPMAN was ther, woning fer by weste:
For aught I woot, he was of Dertemouthe.
He rood upon a rouncy, as he couthe,   390
In a gowne of falding to the knee.
A daggere hanging on a laas hadde he
Aboute his nekke, under his arm adoun.
The hote somer had maad his hewe al broun;
And certeinly, he was a good felawe.   395
Ful many a draughte of wyn had he ydrawe
Fro Burdeux-ward, whyl that the chapman sleep.
Of nyce conscience took he no keep:
If that he faught, and hadde the hyer hond,
By water he sente hem hoom to every lond.   400
But of his craft to rekene wel his tydes,
His stremes, and his daungers him bisydes,
His herberwe, and his moone, his lodemenage –
Ther nas noon swich from Hulle to Cartage.
Hardy he was, and wys to undertake;   405
With many a tempest hadde his berd been shake.
He knew alle the havenes, as they were,
From Gootland to the cape of Finistere,
And every cryke in Britayne and in Spayne;
His barge ycleped was the Maudelayne.   410

388 SHIPMAN, sailor, seaman.   *woning*, dwelling.   *fer by weste*, far in the west.
389 *Dertemouthe*, Dartmouth, once a great port.
390 *rouncy*, nag.   *as he couthe*, as (best) he could (c).
391 *falding*, frieze, a rough cloth.
392 *laas*, cord.
394 *hewe*, complexion.
395 *good felawe*, boon companion (but the phrase, which contains a hint of rascality, acts as an ironically light comment on the Shipman's villainy (c) (cf. 650).
396 *ydrawe*, drawn (i.e. tapped from the wine-casks).
397 *Fro Burdeux-ward*, while sailing from Bordeaux (c).   *chapman*, merchant.   *sleep*, slept (another form of the preterite; cf. 148).
398 'He cared nothing (*took he no keep*) for scruples of conscience (*nyce conscience*)' (cf. notes on 142, 150, 526).
399 *hyer hond*, upper hand.
400 'He sent them home by water to whichever land they came from' – i.e. made them 'walk the plank'.
401 *of his craft*, as for his professional skill, in . . . .
402 *stremes*, currents.   *him bisydes*, near at hand.
403 *herberwe*, harbour.   *moone*, (position of the) moon.   *lodemenage*, pilotage.
404 *Cartage*, possibly Spanish Cartagena rather than Carthage.
405 *wys to undertake*, prudent (or skilful) in his ventures.
408 *Gootland*, Gotland, an island in the Baltic.   *Finistere*, either Finisterre in Brittany or Cape Finisterra in Spain.
409 *cryke*, inlet ('creek').   *Britayne*, Brittany.
410 *barge*, ship.   *Maudelayne*, Magdalen (c).

With us ther was a DOCTOUR OF PHISYK:
In al this world ne was ther noon him lyk
To speke of phisik and of surgerye –
For he was grounded in astronomye.
He kepte his pacient a ful greet deel   415
In houres, by his magik natureel.
Wel coude he fortunen the ascendent
Of his images for his pacient.
He knew the cause of everich maladye,
Were it of hote, or cold, or moiste, or drye,   420
And wher they engendred, and of what humour –
He was a verray, parfit practisour.
The cause yknowe, and of his harm the rote,
Anon he yaf the seke man his bote.
Ful redy hadde he his apothecaries.   425
To sende him drogges and his letuaries,
For ech of hem made other for to winne –
Hir frendshipe nas nat newe to biginne.
Wel knew he th'olde Esculapius,
And Deiscorides, and eek Rufus;   430
Olde Ypocras, Haly, and Galyen;
Serapion, Razis, and Avicen;
Averrois, Damascien, and Constantyn,
Bernard, and Gatesden, and Gilbertyn.
Of his diete mesurable was he,   435
For it was of no superfluitee,

411 PHISYK, medicine ('physic').
413 *To speke of*, either 'when it comes to physic . . .' or 'as one who could *talk*
about physic, etc., but not *perform*'. The second is likelier.
414 *astronomye*, here 'astrology' (C).
415 *kepte*, watched.
416 *houres*, astrological hours (C).   *magik natureel*, natural (as opposed to
'black') magic (C).
417 *fortunen*, find or place in a favourable ('fortunate') position.   *ascendént*,
ascendant (C).
418 *images*, (C).
420 These were the four elementary qualities (C).
421 'Where they were generated and from what "humour" they arose' (C).
422 *practisour*, practitioner.
423 'Once the cause and the source of the man's sickness were known.'
424 *bote*, remedy.
426 *drogges*, drugs.   *letuaries*, electuaries (medicines in syrup form).
428 'Their friendship (i.e. collusion) was a long-established thing.'
429 ff. The physicians named wrote the chief medical textbooks in use during the
Middle Ages (C).
430 Pronounce *Déiscóridés*.
431 *Ypocras*, Hippocrates.   *Galyen*, Galen.
432 *Avicen*, Avicenna.
435 *mesurable*, moderate.
436 *of no superfluitee*, not excessive.

But of greet norissing, and digestible.
His studie was but litel on the Bible.
In sangwin and in pers he clad was al,
Lyned with taffata and with sendal.   440
And yet he was but esy of dispence –
He kepte that he wan in pestilence.
For gold in phisik is a cordial,
Therfore, he lovede gold in special.
A good-WYF was ther of bisyde BATHE,   445
But she was somdeel deef – and that was scathe.
Of cloth-making she hadde swich an haunt,
She passed hem of Ypres and of Gaunt.
In al the parisshe wyf ne was ther noon
That to the offring bifore hire sholde goon;   450
And if ther dide, certeyn, so wrooth was she,
That she was out of alle charitee.
Hir coverchiefs ful fyne were of ground;
I dorste swere they weyeden ten pound
That on a Sonday were upon hir heed.   455
Hir hosen weren of fyn scarlet reed,
Ful streyt yteyd, and shoes ful moiste and newe.
Bold was hir face, and fair, and reed of hewe.
She was a worthy womman al hir lyve:
Housbondes at chirche-dore she hadde fyve,   460
(Withouten other companye in youthe) –
But therof nedeth nat to speke as nouthe.
And thryes hadde she been at Jerusalem;

[437] 'But very nourishing and digestible.'
[439] *sangwin*, scarlet (cloth).   *pers*, Persian blue (blue-grey).
[440] *taffata*, taffeta.   *sendal*, thin silk or linen (both lining-materials).
[441] *esy of dispence*, moderate in his spending.
[442] 'He kept what he acquired in time of plague' (C).
[443] 'Because gold is used as a cordial in medicine . . . .'
[445] *good*-WYF (C).   *of bisyde* BATHE, from the environs of Bath (C).
[446] 'But she was somewhat deaf, and that was a pity' (cf. l. 385).
[447] 'She had such skill (*haunt* = practice) in cloth-making, that . . . .'
[448] *passed*, surpassed.   *Gaunt*, Ghent, in Flanders (C).
[450] *the offring*, the point in the Mass at which the people would bring to the priest their offerings of bread and wine.   *sholde goon*, might (be permitted to) go.
[451] *wrooth*, angry.
[453] *coverchiefs*, head-coverings, kerchiefs (*chief* is French *chef*, head).   *ground*, texture.
[454-5] *they weyeden . . . that . . . were*, we would say 'The ones that were on her head on Sundays weighed . . .'. A comic exaggeration.
[456] *hosen*, stockings (note the plural in -n).
[457] *streyt yteyd*, closely fastened.   *moiste*, soft, flexible.
[461] *Withouten*, apart from.   *other companye*, other lovers.
[462] 'But there's no need to speak about that for the moment.'
[463] *Jerusalem*, pronounce 'Jér'salém'.

She hadde passed many a straunge streem;
At Rome she hadde been, and at Boloigne,   465
In Galice at Seint Jame, and at Coloigne:
She coude muche of wandring by the weye.
Gat-tothed was she, soothly for to seye.
Upon an amblere esily she sat,
Ywimpled wel, and on hir heed an hat   470
As brood as is a bokeler or a targe;
A foot-mantel aboute hir hipes large,
And on hir feet a paire of spores sharpe.
In felawship wel coude she laughe and carpe.
Of remedyes of love she knew, perchaunce,   475
For she coude of that art the olde daunce.
   A good man was ther of religioun,
And was a povre PERSOUN of a toun;
But riche he was of holy thoght and werk.
He was also a lerned man, a clerk,   480
That Cristes gospel trewely wolde preche;
His parisshens devoutly wolde he teche.
Benygne he was, and wonder diligent,
And in adversitee ful pacient;
And swich he was ypreved ofte sythes.   485
Ful looth were him to cursen for his tythes,
But rather wolde he yeven, out of doute,
Unto his povre parisshens aboute
Of his offring, and eek of his substaunce:
He coude in litel thing han suffisaunce.   490

---

[465] *Boloigne*, Boulogne, where there was an image of the Virgin Mary sought by pilgrims.
[466] *Galice*, Galicia.   *Seint Jame*, the shrine of St James at Compostella. *Coloigne*, Cologne, where the shrine of the Three Kings was situated.
[468] *Gat-tothed*, gap-toothed, i.e. with teeth set wide apart (*gat* is an opening; cf. gate) (C) on 445 ff.
[469] *amblere*, an ambling horse.
[470] *Ywimpled wel*, covered with a wimple. (Cf. l. 151 and note).
[471] *targe*, targe or shield.
[472] *foot-mantel*, an outer riding-skirt, to protect her gown.
[473] *spores*, spurs.
[474] *felawship*, company.   *carpe*, chat, talk.
[475] *remedyes of love*, love-cures.   *perchaunce*, doubtless.
[476] 'For she was well-versed in all the rules of that time-honoured game.'
[478] PERSOUN, parson, parish priest.
[482] *parisshens*, parishioners.
[485] 'And such he had been proved (to be) many times.'
[486] 'He was very reluctant to use excommunication (*to cursen*) in order to procure the tithes (due to him)' (C).
[487] *rather*, sooner.   *yeven*, give.   *out of doute*, to be sure.
[489] 'Out of the offerings (he received from his parishioners) and out of his own income (from his benefice).'
[490] *suffisaunce*, enough.

Wyd was his parisshe, and houses fer asonder,
But he ne lefte nat, for reyn ne thonder,
In sikness nor in meschief to visyte
The ferreste in his parisshe, muche and lyte,
Upon his feet, and in his hand a staf. 495
This noble ensample to his sheep he yaf –
That first he wroghte, and afterward he taughte.
Out of the gospel he tho wordes caughte,
And this figure he added eek therto –
That if gold ruste, what shal iren do? 500
For if a preest be foul, on whom we truste,
No wonder is a lewed man to ruste;
And shame it is, if a preest take keep –
A shiten shepherde and a clene sheep.
Wel oghte a preest ensample for to yive, 505
By his clennesse, how that his sheep sholde live.
He sette nat his benefyce to hyre
And leet his sheep encombred in the myre,
And ran to London unto Seïnt Poules
To seken him a chauntrye for soules, 510
Or with a bretherhed to been withholde;
But dwelte at hoom, and kepte wel his folde,
So that the wolf ne made it nat miscarie:
He was a shepherde, and noght a mercenarie.
And though he holy were and vertuous, 515
He was to sinful man nat despitous,
Ne of his speche daungerous ne dygne,

492 *ne lefte nat*, did not cease.
493 *meschief*, misfortune.
494 *ferreste*, farthest.   *muche and lyte*, great and small.
496 *ensample*, example.   *yaf*, gave.
497 *wroghte*, acted.
498 *tho*, those.
499 *figúre*, metaphor, figure of speech (C).
502 'It is no wonder if a layman should rust.'
503 *if a preest*, etc. 'if priests will but take heed of it . . . .'
504 *shiten*, dirty (C).
507 'He did not hire out his benefice' (i.e. to a stranger, in return for money).
507-9 We should say, 'He did not hire out . . . nor did he leave (*leet*) . . . or run . . .'.
510 *chauntrye*, chantry (C). Metrically awkward; perhaps we should read *chaunterie*.
511 'Or to be retained (*withholde*) by a gild (*bretherhed*)' – i.e. as the chaplain of a gild-church.
514 *mercenarie*, hireling.
515 *were*, might be, was.
516 *despitous*, contemptuous towards.
517 *daungerous ne dygne*, aloof or unapproachable (C).

But in his teching discreet and benygne.
To drawen folk to heven by fayrnesse,
By good ensample, this was his bisinesse,   520
But it were any persone obstinat:
What-so he were, of heigh or lowe estat
Him wolde he snibben sharply for the nones.
A bettre preest I trowe that nowher noon is.
He waited after no pompe and reverence,   525
Ne maked him a spyced conscience;
But Cristes lore and his apostles twelve
He taughte – but first he folwed it himselve.
     With him ther was a PLOWMAN, was his brother,
That hadde ylad of dong ful many a fother.   530
A trewe swinker and a good was he,
Livinge in pees and parfit charitee.
God loved he best with al his hole herte,
At alle tymes, thogh him gamed or smerte,
And thanne his neighebour right as himselve.   535
He wolde thresshe, and therto dyke and delve
For Cristes sake, for every povre wight,
Withouten hyre, if it lay in his might.
His tythes payde he ful faire and wel,
Bothe of his propre swink and his catel.   540
In a tabard he rood upon a mere.
     Ther was also a Reve and a Millere,
A Somnour and a Pardoner also,
A Maunciple, and myself – ther were namo.
     The MILLER was a stout carl for the nones –   545

---

[518] *discreet*, civil.
[519] *fayrnesse*, goodness (i.e. his own). See Intro. p. 21.
[521] *persone*, here 'person' (cf. *persoun*, 477 above).
[522] *What-so he were*, (but) whoever *he* might be . . . .
[523] *snibben*, reprimand.   *for the nones*, to be sure, indeed.
[525] 'He did not expect (*or* "look for") reverential treatment.'
[526] *spyced*, seasoned (and so, 'over-refined', 'over-particular'). In dealing with his people, he did not pay too much attention to small matters at the expense of large (c).
[527] 'The teaching (*lore*) of Christ and that of his twelve apostles.'
[529] *a* PLOWMAN, *was*, a Plowman, who was.
[530] *ylad*, carted.   *fother*, load.
[531] *A trewe swinker*, an honest labourer.
[534] *thogh him gamed or smerte*, whether (to do so) – i.e. love God – should cause him pleasure or pain.
[536] *dyke*, make ditches.   *delve*, dig.
[538] *hyre*, payment.
[540] *his propre swink*, his own labour.   *his catel*, his property.
[541] *tabard*, see note on l. 20.   *mere*, mare (a humble horse to ride).
[545] *carl*, fellow.

Ful big he was of brawn, and eek of bones.
That proved wel, for overal ther he cam,
At wrastling he wolde have alwey the ram.
He was short-sholdred, brood, a thikke knarre;
Ther nas no dore that he nolde heve of harre,   550
Or breke it at a renning with his heed.
His berd as any sowe or fox was reed,
And therto brood, as though it were a spade.
Upon the cop right of his nose he hade
A werte, and theron stood a tuft of heres   555
Reed as the bristles of a sowes eres;
His nosethirles blake were and wyde.
A swerd and bokeler bar he by his syde.
His mouth as greet was as a greet forneys.
He was a jangler and a goliardeys,   560
And that was most of sinne and harlotryes.
Wel coude he stelen corn, and tollen thryes;
And yet he hadde a thombe of gold, pardee.
A whyt cote and a blew hood wered he.
A baggepype wel coude he blowe and sowne,   565
And therwithal he broghte us out of towne.
   A gentil MAUNCIPLE was ther of a temple,
Of which achatours mighte take exemple
For to be wyse in byinge of vitaille:
For whether that he payde, or took by taille,   570
Algate he wayted so in his achat,

---

⁵⁴⁶ *brawn*, muscle.
⁵⁴⁷ 'That certainly proved (to be true) – for wherever he came.'
⁵⁴⁸ A ram was the usual prize in wrestling-matches.
⁵⁴⁹ *a thikke knarre*, a muscular fellow (*knarre*, a knot in wood, referring here to the miller's knotted muscles).
⁵⁵⁰ *nolde* (= *ne wolde*), would not (we should say, '*could* not').   *heve of harre*, heave off its hinge(s).
⁵⁵¹ *at a renning*, by running (straight) at it.
⁵⁵⁴ *cop right of*, very top of.
⁵⁵⁵ *werte*, wart.
⁵⁵⁷ *nosethirles*, nostrils.
⁵⁵⁹ *greet forneys*, a huge furnace.
⁵⁶⁰ *jangler*, noisy talker.   *goliardeys*, ribald joker on bawdy matters (C).
⁵⁶¹ *that*, i.e. what he said.   *harlotryes*, scurrilous matters, obscenity.
⁵⁶² *tollen thryes*, toll three times (C).
⁵⁶³ 'And yet he was honest, as millers go' (i.e. not honest at all) (C).
⁵⁶⁵ *sowne*, sound, play.
⁵⁶⁶ *therwithal*, with it (the bagpipe).
⁵⁶⁷ *gentil*, worthy (or perhaps 'mild, gentle'). (Cf. 72 (C).)   MAUNCIPLE, manciple, an officer who bought provisions for a college or inn of court (*temple*).
⁵⁶⁸ *of which*, from whom.   *achatours*, purchasers.
⁵⁶⁹ 'As to how best they should buy provisions.'
⁵⁷⁰ 'Whether he paid cash or bought on credit' (*taille*, tally).
⁵⁷¹ 'He was in every way (*algate*) so watchful when out purchasing.'

That he was ay biforn and in good stat.
Now is nat that of God a ful fair grace
That swich a lewed mannes wit shal pace
The wisdom of an heep of lerned men? 575
Of maistres hadde he more than thryes ten,
That were of lawe expert and curious,
Of which ther were a doseyn in that hous
Worthy to been stiwardes of rente and lond
Of any lord that is in Engelond, 580
To make him live by his propre good,
In honour detteleees (but if he were wood),
Or live as scarsly as him list desyre;
And able for to helpen al a shyre
In any cas that mighte falle or happe. 585
And yet this maunciple set hir aller cappe.
    The REVE was a sclendre colerik man.
His berd was shave as ny as ever he can;
His heer was by his eres ful round yshorn;
His top was dokked lyk a preest biforn. 590
Ful longe were his legges and ful lene,
Ylyk a staf – ther was no calf ysene.
Wel coude he kepe a gerner and a binne;
Ther was noon auditour coude on him winne.
Wel wiste he, by the droghte and by the reyn, 595
The yelding of his seed and of his greyn.
His lordes sheep, his neet, his dayerye,
His swyn, his hors, his stoor, and his pultrye

---

[572] *ay biforn*, always before (others).   *in good stat*, successful in his purchasing (because he always made a bargain), or perhaps 'solvent' (because he did not overspend).
[574] *pace*, surpass, exceed.   *lewed*, uneducated.
[575] *heep*, heap (i.e. crowd).
[577] *of lawe expert and curious*, experienced and skilled in the law.
[581] 'to make him live within his means' (lit. by his own income).
[582] 'In honour, without debts – unless he were mad.'
[583] *as scarsly, &c.* 'as economically as he should wish to'.
[584] *al a shyre*, a whole county.
[586] 'And yet this manciple could run rings round them' (lit. 'set all their caps', *hir aller cappe*.) The phrase often implies dishonest dealing, but not necessarily here (*aller* is the old genitive plural of *al*, all).
[587] *colerik*, of choleric disposition (C).
[588] *as ny*, as closely.
[590] *dokked . . . biforn*, cut close . . . in front.
[592] *Ylyk*, like.   *ysene*, visible.
[593] *kepe*, look after.   *gerner*, granary.   *binne*, bin.
[594] *on him winne*, get the better of him.
[597] *neet*, cattle.   *dayerye*, dairy (produce).
[598] *hors*, horses.   *stoor*, livestock.   *pultrye*, poultry.

Was hoolly in this reves governinge,
And by his covenaunt yaf the rekeninge   600
Sin that his lord was twenty yeer of age.
Ther coude no man bringe him in arrerage.
Ther nas baillif, ne herde, nor other hyne,
That he ne knew his sleighte and his covyne.
They were adrad of him as of the deeth!   605
His woning was ful faire upon a heeth;
With grene trees yshadwed was the place.
He coude bettre than his lord purchace.
Ful riche he was astored prively;
His lord wel coude he plesen subtilly,   610
To yeve and lene him of his owne good,
And have a thank, and yet a cote and hood.
In youthe he lerned hadde a good mister –
He was a ful good wrighte, a carpenter.
This Reve sat upon a ful good stot,   615
That was al pomely gray, and highte Scot.
A long surcote of pers upon he hade,
And by his syde he bar a rusty blade.
Of Northfolk was this Reve of which I telle,
Bisyde a toun men clepen Baldeswelle.   620
Tukked he was, as is a frere, aboute,
And evere he rood the hyndreste of our route.
  A SOMONOUR was ther with us in that place,

---

⁵⁹⁹ *governinge*, control.
⁶⁰⁰⁻¹ 'And by the terms of his contract he had given (*yaf*) account (of his dealings since (*sin that*). . . .'
⁶⁰² 'No one could show him to be in arrears.'
⁶⁰³⁻⁴ 'There was no bailiff, &c., whose crafty practices and deceit he (i.e. the Reve) did not know.'
⁶⁰⁵ 'They were mortally afraid of him' (c).
⁶⁰⁶ *woning*, dwelling-place.   *ful faire upon*, pleasantly situated on.
⁶⁰⁹ 'He had richly provided himself with property on the quiet' (*prively*).
⁶¹⁰⁻¹² 'He knew how to please his lord in a subtle way – by giving and lending him some of his own (i.e. the lord's own) possessions, and so obtaining thanks and a coat and hood besides.'
⁶¹³ *mister*, craft ('mystery').
⁶¹⁴ *wrighte*, craftsman.
⁶¹⁵ *stot*, stallion.
⁶¹⁶ *pomely gray*, dappled with round apple-shaped spots of grey.   *Scot*, a common name for horses in Norfolk, where the Reeve lived. (A horse in the *Friar's Tale* is also called *Scot*.)
⁶¹⁷ *surcote*, outer coat.
⁶¹⁹ *Northfolk*, Norfolk.
⁶²⁰ *men clepen Baldeswelle*, called Bawdeswell (in Norfolk).
⁶²¹ *Tukked . . . aboute . . .* tucked up with a girdle (round his middle).
⁶²² *hyndreste*, hindermost.   *route*, company.
⁶²³ SOMONOUR, Summoner.

That hadde a fyr-reed cherubinnes face –
For sawcefleem he was, with eyen narwe.   625
As hoot he was and lecherous as a sparwe
With scalled browes blake and piled berd:
Of his visage children were aferd!
Ther nas quiksilver, litarge, ne brimstoon,
Boras, ceruce, ne oille of tartre noon,   630
Ne oynement that wolde clense and byte,
That him mighte helpen of his whelkes whyte,
Nor of the knobbes sittinge on his chekes.
Wel loved he garleek, oynons, and eek lekes,
And for to drinken strong wyn, reed as blood –   635
Thanne wolde he speke and crye as he were wood.
And whan that he wel dronken hadde the wyn,
Thanne wolde he speke no word but Latyn.
A fewe termes hadde he, two or three,
That he had lerned out of som decree –   640
(No wonder is, he herde it al the day!) –
And eek ye knowen wel, how that a jay
Can clepen 'Watte' as wel as can the pope.
But whoso coude in other thing him grope,
Thanne hadde he spent al his philosophye: 645
Ay '*Questio quid iuris*' wolde he crye.
He was a gentil harlot and a kynde;
A bettre felawe sholde men noght fynde.
He wolde suffre, for a quart of wyn,

[624] 'A fire-red face, like that of one of the cherubim' (c).
[625] *sawcefleem*, with a red pimpled face (thought to be caused by too much salt phlegm, *salsum phlegma*, in the constitution). ((c) on ll. 420–1 and cf. 333, 458, 587). *eyen narwe*, narrow, slitted eyes.
[626] *sparwe*, sparrow.
[627] *scalled*, scabby.   *piled*, scanty (with the hair falling out).
[629] *litarge*, litharge, lead oxide.
[630] *Boras*, borax.   *ceruce*, ceruse, white lead.   *oille of tartre*, cream of tartar (cf. *CYT*, 237, 259).
[631] *oynement*, ointment.
[632] 'That might help him (to remove) his white pimples (*whelkes*).'
[634] 'garlic, onions, leeks.'
[642] *jay*, jackdaw.
[643] *clepen*, call out *Watte*, Wat (short for 'Walter').
[644] *in other thing him grope*, examine him in any other matter (involving a knowledge of Latin or law).
[646] *Questio quid iuris*, a stock legal phrase meaning 'The question is, what is the law on this matter?'
[647] *gentil harlot*, 'a nice fellow (though a rogue)'.   *harlot* meant 'low fellow' in Chaucer's day and came to mean 'prostitute' only in later ME (cf. the Miller's *harlotryes*, 561). On *gentil*, see 72 (c).
[648] *felawe*, companion (perhaps implying rascality, as in 650 below).
[649–51] 'In return for a quart of wine he was willing to allow any of his cronies to keep his concubine for a year, and let him off scot-free.'

A good felawe to have his concubyn   650
A twelf-month, and excuse him atte fulle;
Ful prively a finch eek coude he pulle.
And if he foond owher a good felawe,
He wolde techen him to have noon awe,
In swich cas, of the erchedeknes curs,   655
But if a mannes soule were in his purs –
For in his purs he sholde ypunisshed be.
'Purs is the erchedeknes helle', seyde he.
But wel I woot he lyed right in dede!
Of cursing oghte ech gilty man him drede –   660
For curs wol slee, right as assoilling savith –
And also war him of a *Significavit*.
In daunger hadde he at his owne gyse
The yonge girles of the diocyse,
And knew hir counseil, and was al hir reed.   665
A gerland hadde he set upon his heed,
As greet as it were for an ale-stake;
A bokeler hadde he maad him of a cake.
      With him ther rood a gentil PARDONER
Of Rouncival, his freend and his compeer,   670
That streight was comen fro the court of Rome.
Ful loude he song 'Com hider, love, to me!'
This Somnour bar to him a stif burdoun –
Was never trompe of half so greet a soun!
This Pardoner hadde heer as yelow as wex,   675
But smothe it heng, as dooth a stryke of flex;

---

652 *pulle*, pluck – i.e. the Summoner himself was an adept at bedding a woman on the sly (*Ful prively*).
653 *owher*, anywhere.
654–5 'He would teach him not to stand in awe of the archdeacon's excommunication (*curs*) if he was keeping a concubine (*in swich cas*, lit. in such circumstances).'
656–8 The Summoner maintained that there was no need to fear excommunication unless a man's soul resided in his purse, because that was where he would suffer – i.e. by having to pay a fine to be released.
661 'Excommunication will slay, just as absolution will save.'
662 'And he should also beware a writ of excommunication' (of which the opening word was *Significavit*).
663 'He had within his control (*daunger*), just where he wanted them (*at his owne gyse*), the young people (*girles*) of the diocese.'
665 *was al hir reed*, 'was wholly their adviser' (Skeat).
667 *ale-stake*, the support for a garland outside an ale-house.
669 *gentil*, worthy. See 72 (c).
670 *Rouncival*, the hospital of the Blessed Mary of Rouncivalle, at Charing in London, a 'cell' (subsidiary convent) of the Priory at Roncesvalles, in Navarre.
671 *the court*, i.e. the Papal Court.
672 *hider*, hither. The opening line or refrain of a popular song.
673 *bar to him a stif burdoun*, accompanied him with a strong (*stif*) ground bass (c).
675 *wex*, wax.
676 *stryke of flex*, hank (or bunch) of flax.

By ounces heng his lokkes that he hadde,
And therwith he his shuldres overspradde;
But thinne it lay, by colpons oon and oon.
But hood, for jolitee, wered he noon,   680
For it was trussed up in his walet.
Him thoughte he rood al of the newe jet –
Dischevelee, save his cappe, he rood al bare.
Swiche glaringe eyen hadde he as an hare.
A vernicle hadde he sowed upon his cappe;   685
His walet lay biforn him in his lappe,
Bretful of pardoun comen from Rome al hoot.
A voys he hadde as smal as hath a goot.
No berd hadde he, ne never sholde have –
As smothe it was as it were late yshave.   690
I trowe he were a gelding or a mare!
But of his craft, fro Berwik into Ware,
Ne was ther swich another pardoner:
For in his male he hadde a pilwe-beer,
Which that he seyde was Oure Lady veyl;   695
He seyde he hadde a gobet of the seyl
That Seÿnt Peter hadde whan that he wente
Upon the see, til Jesu Crist him hente.
He hadde a croys of latoun ful of stones,
And in a glas he hadde pigges bones.   700
But with thise relikes, whan that he fond
A povre person dwelling upon lond,
Upon a day he gat him more moneye
Than that the person gat in monthes tweye;

677 *ounces*, thin clusters.
679 *colpons*, portions.   *oon and oon*, one by one, singly.
680 *for jolitee*, 'for the fun of it.' (The Pardoner is in holiday mood).
681 *trussed*, wrapped.   *walet*, wallet, bag.
682 *al of the newe jet*, in the very latest fashion.
683 *Dischevelee*, with hair hanging loose (cf. French *cheveux*).
685 *vernicle*, a little 'veronica' ('*Veronike*') (c).
687 *Bretful of pardon*, brim-full of pardons (indulgences).
688 *smal*, high-pitched.   *goot*, goat.
692 *But of his craft*, but as regards his profession . . . .   *fro Berwik unto Ware*, a way of saying 'from North to South of England, the whole length of the country.'
694 *male*, bag.   *pilwe-beer*, pillow-case.
695 'Our Lady's veil.' For the genitive case without -s, compare l. 88.
696 *gobet*, a gobbet or small piece.
698 *him hente*, caught hold of him (i.e. summoned Peter to follow him). See Matt., xiv, 29.
699 *a croys of latoun*, a cross made of latten (an alloy of copper and zinc).
702 'A poor country parish-priest.'
703 *a day*, one day.
704 *tweye*, two.

And thus, with feyned flaterye and japes,   705
He made the person and the peple his apes.
But trewely to tellen, atte laste,
He was in chirche a noble ecclesiaste.
Wel coude he rede a lessoun or a storie,
But alderbest he song an offertorie;   710
For wel he wiste, whan that song was songe,
He moste preche, and wel affyle his tonge,
To winne silver, as he ful wel coude.
Therfore he song the murierly and loude.
  Now have I told you shortly, in a clause,   715
Th'estate, th'array, the nombre, and eek the cause
Why that assembled was this compaignye
In Southwerk, at this gentil hostelrye,
That highte the Tabard, faste by the Belle.
But now is tyme to yow for to telle   720
How that we baren us that ilke night,
Whan we were in that hostelrye alight;
And after wol I telle of our viage,
And al the remenaunt of our pilgrimage.
But first I pray yow, of your curteisye,   725
That ye n'arette it nat my vileynye,
Thogh that I pleynly speke in this matere,
To telle yow hir wordes and hir cheere,
Ne thogh I speke hir wordes proprely.
For this ye knowen al so wel as I –   730
Whoso shal telle a tale after a man,
He moot reherce as ny as ever he can
Everich a word, if it be in his charge,
Al speke he never so rudeliche and large;

---

⁷⁰⁵ *japes*, deceitful tricks.
⁷⁰⁶ *He made . . . his apes*, 'he made monkeys of them'.
⁷⁰⁸ *ecclesiaste*, churchman.
⁷⁰⁹ lesson, storie (c).
⁷¹⁰ *alderbest*, best of all (*alder* = *aller*; cf. l. 586 and note).   *offertorie*, the Offertory of the Mass, beginning after the Creed, which would be said or sung (i.e. *intoned*).
⁷¹² *affyle*, file down (i.e. speak smoothly or plausibly).
⁷¹³ *as he, &c.* as he well knew how to.
⁷¹⁴ *the murierly and loude*, the more merrily and (the more) loudly, (*murierly* = lit. 'merrierly').
⁷¹⁵ *in a clause*, briefly.
⁷¹⁹ *highte*, was called.   *faste by*, just near.
⁷²¹ *we baren us*, we spent.   *ilke*, same.
⁷²⁶ 'Not to ascribe it (*n'arette it nat*) to lack of good breeding on my part (*m vileynye*) if I should. . . .'
⁷²⁹ *hir wordes proprely*, paraphrase, 'the words they actually used'.
⁷³³ *charge*, power.
⁷³⁴ *Al speke he*, though he should have to speak.   *large*, bluntly.

Or elles he moot telle his tale untrewe,   735
Or feyne thing, or fynde wordes newe.
He may nat spare, althogh he were his brother;
He moot as wel seye o word as another.
Crist spak himself ful brode in holy writ –
And wel ye woot no vileynye is it.   740
Eek Plato seïth (whoso can him rede),
The wordes moote be cosin to the dede.
Also I pray yow to foryeve it me,
Al have I nat set folk in hir degree
Here in this tale, as that they sholde stonde: 745
My wit is short – ye may wel understonde.
    Greet cheere made our Hoste us everichon,
And to the soper sette he us anon,
And served us with vitaille at the beste.
Strong was the wyn, and wel to drinke us leste.   750
A semely man OUR HOOSTE was withalle
For to han been a marshal in an halle.
A large man he was with eyen stepe,
(A fairer burgeys is ther noon in Chepe),
Bold of his speche, and wys, and wel ytaught –   755
And of manhood him lakkede right naught.
Eek therto he was right a myrie man,
And after soper pleyen he bigan,
And spak of myrthe amonges othere thinges,
Whan that we hadde maad our rekeninges,   760
And seyde thus: 'Now, lordinges, trewely,
Ye been to me right welcome, hertely;
For by my trouthe, if that I shal nat lye,
I saugh nat this yeer so myrie a compaignye
At ones in this herberwe as is now.   765
Fayn wolde I doon yow myrthe – wiste I how!
And of a myrthe I am right now bithoght,

737 *althogh he were*, i.e. even if the person whose 'broad' speech the speaker is
reporting should be his own brother.
738 *moot*, must.   *o*, one.
739 *ful brode*, in direct, down-to-earth language.
742 *cosin*, cousin (i.e. closely related to).
743 *foryeve*, forgive.
744 'If I have not placed the pilgrims in an order determined by their rank.'
752 *marshal*, marshal – a kind of master of ceremonies at public feasts.
753 *stepe*, see note on line 201.
754 *Chepe*, Cheapside, in London.
756 *him lakkede*, he was lacking (in).
758 *pleyen*, make merry.
760 'When we had paid our bills.'
765 *At ones*, at one time.   *herberwe*, inn.
767 *I am . . . bithoght*, I have thought (of).

To doon yow ese – and it shal coste noght.
Ye goon to Caunterbury – God yow spede,
The blisful martir quyte yow your mede! 770
And wel I woot, as ye goon by the weye,
Ye shapen yow to talen and to pleye;
(For trewely, confort ne myrthe is noon
To ryde by the weye doumb as a stoon);
And therfore wol I maken yow disport, 775
As I seyde erst, and doon yow som confort.
And if yow lyketh alle by oon assent
Now for to stonden at my juggement,
And for to werken as I shal yow seye,
Tomorwe, whan ye ryden by the weye, 780
Now (by my fader soule that is deed),
But ye be myrie, I wol yeve yow myn heed!
Hold up your hondes, withouten more speche.'
  Our counseil was nat longe for to seche:
Us thoughte it was noght worth to make it wys, 785
And graunted him withouten more avys,
And bad him seye his verdit as him leste.
  'Lordinges,' quod he, 'now herkneth for the beste –
But tak it not, I pray yow, in desdeyn.
This is the poynt, to speken short and pleyn – 790
That ech of yow, to shorte with our weye,
In this viage shal telle tales tweye
To Caunterbury-ward (I mene it so),
And homward he shal tellen othere two,
Of aventures that whylom han bifalle. 795
And which of yow that bereth him best of alle –

770 'May the blessed martyr reward you for it!'
772 *Ye shapen yow*, you intend.   *talen*, tell stories, make conversation.
773,776 *confort*, pleasure.
777–8 'And if you are willing unanimously to stand by (or 'submit to'), my judgment.'
779 *werken*, do.
781 'By the soul of my father, who is dead.'
785 'It did not seem worth our while to make it a matter for (lengthy) deliberation.'
786 *withouten more avys*, without further ado (lit. consideration).
787 *verdit*, verdict.   *as him leste*, as he liked.
788 *herkneth*, listen. (When there is no pronoun with the verb, the -eth ending signifies the imperative plural.)
789 'Do not turn up your noses (at my suggestion).'
791 *to shorte with*, as a means of shortening (more literally, 'with which to shorten').
793 *To Caunterbury-ward*, on the way to Canterbury (cf. l. 397).
794 *othere two*, two more, another two.
795 *whylom*, once upon a time.

That is to seyn, that telleth in this cas
Tales of best sentence and most solas –
Shal have a soper at our aller cost
Here in this place, sitting by this post,   800
Whan that we come agayn fro Caunterbury.
And for to make yow the more mury,
I wol myselven goodly with yow ryde,
Right at myn owne cost, and be your gyde.
And whoso wol my juggement withseye   805
Shal paye al that we spenden by the weye.
And if ye vouchesauf that it be so,
Tel me anon, withouten wordes mo,
And I wol erly shape me therfore.'
    This thing was graunted, and our othes swore   810
With ful glad herte, and preyden him also
That he wolde vouchesauf for to do so,
And that he wolde been our governour,
And of our tales juge and reportour,
And sette a soper at a certeyn prys,   815
And we wolde reuled been at his devys
In heigh and lowe – and thus, by oon assent,
We been acorded to his juggement.
And therupon the wyn was fet anon;
We dronken, and to reste wente echon,   820
Withouten any lenger taryinge.
    Amorwe, whan that day bigan to springe,
Up roos our Hoste, and was our aller cok,
And gadrede us togidre alle in a flok,
And forth we riden, a litel more than pas,   825

---

⁷⁹⁸ *sentence*, meaning, content.   *solas*, pleasure, amusement. We might
paraphrase, 'Tales which give you food for thought as well as being entertaining'.
    ⁷⁹⁹ *at our aller cost*, at our joint expense.
⁸⁰³ *goodly*, willingly (though the word is little more than a line-filler here).
⁸⁰⁵ *withseye*, oppose, resist.
⁸⁰⁸ *mo*, more.
⁸⁰⁹ *shape me therfore*, get ready for (it).
⁸¹⁰ *swore*, we swore (see line below).
⁸¹¹ *preyden* (= we *preyden*), we asked.
⁸¹⁴ *reportour*, umpire.
⁸¹⁶ *devys*, direction. ('We were happy to be governed by his suggestions.')
⁸¹⁷ *in heigh and lowe*, in all matters, under all circumstances.
⁸¹⁸ *been acorded to*, accepted.
⁸¹⁹ *fet*, fetched.
⁸²² *Amorwe*, the next morning.   *springe*, dawn (cf. 'day-spring').
⁸²³ *our aller cok*, cock to awake all of us (lit. 'cock of us all').
⁸²⁴ *gadrede*, gathered.
⁸²⁵ *riden*, rode.   *pas*, walking-pace.

Unto the watering of Seynt Thomas;
And ther our Host bigan his hors areste
And seyde, 'Lordinges, herkneth, if yow leste!
Ye woot your forward, and I it yow recorde.
If evensong and morwesong acorde,   830
Lat se now who shal telle the firste tale.
As ever moot I drinke wyn or ale –
Whoso be rebel to my juggement
Shal paye for al that by the weye is spent.
Now draweth cut, er that we ferrer twinne;   835
He which that hath the shortest shal biginne.
Sire Knight,' quod he,' my maister and my lord,
Now draweth cut, for that is myn acord,
Cometh neer,' quod he, 'my lady Prioresse;
And ye, sir Clerk, lat be your shamefastnesse,   840
Ne studieth noght! Ley hond to, every man!'
   Anon to drawen every wight bigan,
And shortly for to tellen, as it was,
Were it by aventure, or sort, or cas –
The sothe is this, the cut fil to the Knight,   845
Of which ful blythe and glad was every wight;
And telle he moste his tale, as was resoun,
By forward and by composicioun,
As ye han herd; what nedeth wordes mo?

   826 *the watering*, the watering-place (a brook near the second milestone on the
way to St Thomas's shrine at Canterbury).
   827 *areste*, stop, rein in.
   828 *if yow leste*, please.
   829 *woot*, know.   *forward*, agreement (cf. l. 33).   *I it yow recorde*, I (will)
remind you (of) it.
   830 'If evensong and matins agree' – i.e. 'if what you said yesterday is what you
still feel today'.
   832 Paraphrase, 'As surely as I ever hope to be able' (Skeat) or 'May I never
drink . . . *unless* rebels against my judgment be compelled to pay . . .'.
   835 *Draweth cut*, draw lots (note the -eth ending of the plural imperative form).
er that we ferrer twinne, before we go any further (*twinne*, lit. sunder, depart).
   838 *draweth cut*, the plural form again, here used out of politeness to the Knight
(cf. modern French usage).
   839 *Cometh* (pronounce 'com'th'), see above note.   *neer*, nearer, the comparative
form of *ny* (near).
   840 *lat*, let. This may be a contracted form of the plural imperative, as suggested
by the pronoun *ye* and *studieth* in the next line.   *shamefastnesse*, bashfulness,
modesty.
   841 *Ley hond to*, take your pick.
   842 *every wight*, everybody.
   844 'chance, lot or destiny' (the terms are not rigorously distinguished).
   845 *the cut fil*, the lot fell.
   847 *as was resoun*, as was right or proper.
   848 *composicoun* (from the French) is virtually a synonym for the native word
forward.

And whan this goode man saugh that it was so,   850
As he that wys was and obedient
To kepe his forward by his free assent,
He seyde, 'Sin I shal biginne the game,
What, welcome be the cut, a Goddes name!
Now lat us ryde, and herkneth what I seye.'   855
    And with that word we riden forth our weye,
And he bigan with right a myrie cheere
His tale anon, and seyde as ye may here.

[853] *Sin*, since.   *shal*, must, am to.
[854] *What*, why!   *a*, in.
[856] *riden*, rode (cf. l. 825).
[857] *with right a myrie cheere*, 'with cheerful good-will' (*cheere* = originally 'face', 'expression', whence 'cheer*ful*' 'with a (glad) expression').

The Canon's Yeoman's Prologue and Tale

Introduction

Whan ended was the lyf of Seint Cecyle,
Er we had riden fully fyve myle,
At Boghton under Blee us gan atake
A man that clothed was in clothes blake,
And undernethe he hadde a whyt surplys.　　　　　5
His hakeney, that was al pomely grys,
So swatte that it wonder was to see:
It semed he had priked myles three.
The hors eek that his yeman rood upon
So swatte that unnethe mighte it gon:　　　　　10
Aboute the peytrel stood the foom ful hye;
He was of foom al flekked as a pye.
A male tweyfold on his croper lay;
It semed that he caried lyte array.
Al light for somer rood this worthy man,　　　　　15
And in myn herte wondren I bigan
What that he was, til that I understood

---

¹ *lyf*, life.　　*Seynt Cecyle*, St Cecilia (c).
² *Er*, before ('ere').　　*fully*, a full.　　*myle*, miles.
³ *Boghton under Blee*, Boughton under Blean (c).　　*us gan atake*, there overtook
us (c).
⁴ *blake*, black.
⁵ *whyt surplys*, white surplice.
⁶ *hakeney*, hackney-horse ('hack'; a middle-sized half-bred horse).　　*pomely
grys*, dapple-grey (*gris pommelé*, with grey *apple*-shaped markings) cf. *GP*, 616.
⁷ *swatte*, sweated (pret. of *sweten*).　　*wonder was to see*, was an extraordinary
sight (c).
⁸ *semed*, seemed.　　*priked myles three*, galloped for three miles (lit. spurred –
'pricked' – his horse) (cf. *GP*, 189, 191).
⁹ *yeman*, yeoman. (On his social rank see *GP*, 101–17 (c).)
¹⁰ *unnethe mighte it gon*, it could scarcely move (advb. f. adj. *eathe*, easy 'un').
gon, go (c).
¹¹ *peytrel*, collar ('poitrel', orig. f. Lat. *pectorale*, the breast-armour protecting a
war-horse).　　*foom*, foam.　　*hye*, thickly ('high').
¹² *of*, with.　　*flekked*, spotted ('flecked').　　*pye*, magpie (c).
¹³ *male tweyfold*, double ('twofold') bag (cf. 'mail', Fr. *malle*) (c).　　*croper*,
crupper.
¹⁴ 'he was lightly clothed'.　　*lyte*, little.　　*array*, clothing. (With 'carry' in
sense of 'wear', cf. Fr. *porter*.)
¹⁵ *Al light for somer*, very lightly (clad), because of the summer weather.　　*rood*,
rode.
¹⁶ *herte*, heart.　　*wondren*, wonder, speculate.
¹⁷ 'What sort of person he was, until I noticed. . . .'

How that his cloke was sowed to his hood;
For which, when I had longe avysed me,
I demed him som chanon for to be.   20
His hat heng at his bak doun by a laas,
For he had riden more than trot or paas;
He had ay priked lyk as he were wood.
A clote-leef he hadde under his hood
For swoot and for to kepe his heed from hete.   25
But it was joye for to seen him swete!
His forheed dropped as a stillatorie
Were ful of plantain and of paritorie.
And whan that he was come he gan to crye,
'God save', quod he, 'this joly compaignye!   30
Faste have I priked,' quod he, 'for your sake,
Bycause that I wolde yow atake,
To ryden in this mery companye.'
His yeman eek was ful of curteisye,
And seyde, 'Sires, now in the morwetyde   35
Out of your hostelrye I saugh you ryde,
And warned heer my lord and my soverayn,
Which that to ryden with yow is ful fayn,
For his desport – he loveth daliaunce.'
'Freend, for thy warning God yeve thee good chaunce!'   40

¹⁸ *How that,* how (on this use of *that* see 29 (c)).
¹⁹ 'For which reason, when I had mulled it over a while' (cf. Fr. *s'aviser*).
²⁰ 'I concluded that he was some sort of canon' (c).
²¹ *heng,* hung.   *bak,* back.   *laas,* strap.
²² *more than trot or pass,* faster than at a trot or walking-pace.
²³ 'He had been galloping hell-for-leather all the way' (lit. as if he were mad, *wood*).   *ay,* always, throughout.
²⁴ *clote-leef,* burdock leaf.
²⁵ 'To prevent himself from sweating and to protect his head from the heat'. (Note use of *for* to mean 'to prevent, avoid'.)
²⁶ *joye,* a joy.   *for to seen,* to see.
²⁷ *dropped,* dripped.   *stillatorie,* '(dis)tillatory', still (c).
²⁸ *Were ful,* that might (happen to) be full. (*Were* is subjunctive and the rel. pron. is omitted.)   *paritorie,* pellitory of the wall (c).
²⁹ *Whan that,* when (c).
³⁰ *quod,* said ('quoth').   *joly,* merry.
³¹ *For your sake,* on your account.
^{32–3} 'Because I wished to overtake you, in order to ride. . . .'
³⁴ *eek,* too.
³⁵ *seyde,* said.   *Sires,* etc., Gentlemen, early this morning. . . .
³⁶ *hostelrye,* inn (c).   *saugh,* saw.
³⁷ *warned,* informed.   *soverayn,* master.
^{38–9} 'Who would be very glad to ride with you for his amusement. He (is a man who) loves chatting with people' (cf. 'dalliance', in which the specialized sense *'amorous* conversation' has prevailed, and also *GP,* 211).
⁴⁰ *warning,* information (see 37n above).   *yeve,* give.   *good chaunce,* good luck (cf. Fr. *bonne chance*).

Than seyde our Host, 'for certein, it wolde seme
Thy lord were wys, and so I may wel deme.
He is ful jocund also, dar I leye.
Can he oght telle a mery tale or tweye
With which he glade may this compaignye?'   45
'Who, sire? My lord? Ye, ye, withouten lye –
He can of murthe and eek of jolitee
Nat but ynough; also sir, trusteth me,
And ye him knewe as wel as do I,
Ye wolde wondre how wel and craftily   50
He coude werke, and that in sondry wyse.
He hath take on him many a greet empryse
Which were ful hard for any that is here
To bringe aboute, but they of him it lere.
As homely as he rit amonges yow,   55
If ye him knewe it wolde be for your prow.
Ye wolde nat forgoon his aqueyntaunce
For mochel good, I dar leye in balaunce
Al that I have in my possessioun:
He is a man of heigh discrecioun,   60
I warne you wel, he is a passing man.'
'Wel,' quod our Host, 'I pray thee tel me than –
Is he a clerk or noon? Tel what he is.'

---

[41] *than*, then.
[41-2] 'To be sure, your master would appear to be a wise man, I'd be right in thinking.'
[43] 'He's a very sprightly soul, too, I bet!' *leye*, lay (down – *sc.* a pledge or wager).
[44] *oght*, at all ('aught'). *mery*, entertaining. *tweye*, two.
[45] *he glade may*, he may amuse, cheer.
[46] *Ye, ye*, etc., yes, yes, believe me (lit. without a lie).
[47] *can*, knows. *murthe . . . jolitee*, amusement . . . entertainment.
[48] *Nat but ynough*, more than enough. *trusteth*, trust (c).
[49] 'If *you* knew him as well as *I* do'. *And*, if. *knewe* is subj. (c).
[50] *craftily*, skilfully.
[51] *in sondry wyse*, in various ways (c).
[52] *take on him*, undertaken (c). *empryse*, enterprise.
[53] *were*, would be. *ful*, very.
[54] *bringe aboute*, achieve. *but they*, etc., 'unless they were to learn it from him'.
[55] 'However undistinguished he (may appear as he) rides among you' (c). *homely*, simply, plainly ('homely'; and cf. *GP*, 328 (c)). *rit*, rides.
[56] *for your prow*, to your advantage (Lat. *prodesse*; cf. 'prowess').
[57-9] 'You wouldn't miss getting to know him for anything – I'll bet you everything I've got!' *forgoon*, forgo. *aqueyntaunce*, acquaintance. *mochel*, much. *good*, property (c). *I dar leye*, see 43n.
[60] *heigh discrecioun*, great knowledge (rather than 'discretion'; cf. also *prudence*, 77 below).
[61] *warne*, assure. *a passing man*, a quite exceptional person ('surpassing').
[63] *clerk*, a man of learning (c). (cf. *GP*, 285–308) (c)). *or noon*, or not.

'Nay, he is gretter than a clerk, ywis!'
Seyde this yeman, 'and, in wordes fewe   65
Host, of his craft somwhat I wol yow shewe.
I seye, my lord can swich subtilitee –
(But al his craft ye may nat wite at me,
And som what helpe I yet to his werking) –
That al this ground on which we been ryding,   70
Til that we come to Caunterbury toun,
He coude al clene turne it up-so-doun
And pave it al of silver and of gold.'
And whan this yeman hadde thus ytold
Unto our Host, he seyde, 'Benedicite!   75
This thing is wonder mervaillous to me –
(Sin that thy lord is of so heigh prudence,
By-cause of which men sholde him reverence)
That of his worship rekketh he so lyte.
His oversloppe nis nat worth a myte,   80
As in effect, to him, so mote I go!
It is al baudy and to-tore also.
Why is thy lord so sluttish, I thee preye,
And is of power better cloth to beye –
If that his dede accorde with thy speche?   85

64 *gretter*, greater.   *ywis*, to be sure.
66 *craft*, skill (with something of root sense, 'power').   *I wol*, I intend.
67 *can*, knows, 'is versed in'.   *swich*, such.   *subtilitee*, subtle arts.
68 Either 'But you won't learn everything (*al*) he knows from me' (*wite*, lit. 'know' *at me*, from me) – i.e. because the Canon's Yeoman does not possess his master's learning – or else 'I cannot divulge all his cunning devices to you' – i.e. because this would be to betray the Canon's secrets. The first alternative is preferable in the light of 69.
69 'And I, moreover, (actually) assist him in his operations' (c).   *werking*, working.
70 *we been*, we are (c).
71 *til that . . . to*, from here . . . right up to. See 29n.
73 *al*, entirely.   *of . . . of*, with.
74 *ytold*, spoken.
75 *he*, i.e. the Host.   *Benedicite*, bless me! (pronounce *ben'cite*; see 81 (c)).
76 *wonder*, exceedingly (cf. 7n).   *This thing*, see 79 below.
77 *Sin that*, since (cf. 29 (c)).
78 *men sholde*, etc., he deserves to be treated with respect (c).
79 *worship*, dignity, honour (i.e. as reflected in his outward looks).   *rekketh he so lyte*, he cares so little ('reck' as in 'reckless').
80 *oversloppe*, upper or outer garment.   *nis nat*, is not (*nis = ne is*) (c).   *myte*, a brass farthing ('mite').
81 *in effect, to him*, in reality as far as a man like him is concerned.   *so moot I go*, as I may have the power to walk (c).
82 *baudy*, dirty.   *to-tore*, tattered (the *to-* is intensive).
83 *sluttish*, slovenly.
84 *And is of power*, when he has the means.   *beye*, buy.
85 'If he's really capable of what you say.'

Telle me that, and that I thee biseche.'
'Why,' quod this yeman, 'wherto axe ye me?
God help me so, for he shal never thee!
But I wol nat avowe that I seye,
And therfor, kepe it secree, I yow preye.   90
He is to wys, in feith, as I bileve:
That that is overdoon, it wol nat preve
Aright, as clerkes seyn; it is a vyce.
Wherfor in that I holde him lewed and nyce.
For whan a man hath over greet a wit,   95
Ful oft him happeth to misusen it;
So dooth my lord, and that me greveth sore.
God it amende, I can sey yow namore.'
'Therof no fors, good yeman,' quod our Host,
'Sin of the conning of thy lord thou wost,   100
Tel how he dooth, I pray thee hertely,
Sin that he is so crafty and so sly.
Wher dwellen ye, if it to telle be?'
'In the suburbes of a toun,' quod he,
'Lurkinge in hernes and in lanes blinde,   105
Wheras thise robbours and thise theves by kinde
Holden hir pryvee fereful residence,
As they that dar nat shewen hir presence;
So faren we, if I shal seye the sothe.'
'Now,' quod our Host, 'yit lat me talke to the.   110
Why artow so discoloured of thy face?'

---

[87] *whereto*, why.   *axe*, ask.
[88] *for*, because.   *thee*, prosper, succeed.
[89] 'But I don't wish to have what I say made public.'
[90] *secree*, secret, quiet.
[92-3] *that that*, that which.   *overdoon*, overdone.   *preve/Aright*, turn out
succesfully.
[94] *holde*, consider.   *lewed and nyce*, a stupid ass (*lewed*, lit. 'ignorant' and see 63
(c))   *nyce*, foolish, ult. f. Lat. *nescius*, 'ignorant').
[95] *over-greet*, too great.   *wit*, intellect.
[96] *him happeth*, it befalls him.
[99] *Therof no fors*, never mind about that.   *quod*, see 30n.
[100] *conning*, 'scientific know-how'.   *wost . . . of*, know about.
[102] *crafty, sly*, skilful (but with a hint of the modern meanings). See Intro. p. 41.
[103] *if it to telle be*, if you're allowed to tell us.
[104] *suburbes*, suburbs.   *toun* (c).
[105] *hernes*, corners.   *lanes blinde*, blind alleys.
[106] *by kinde*, either 'by their very nature' or 'naturally'.   *thise* (c).
[107] *Holden*, keep.   *pryvee*, secret.   *fereful*, fearful (active *and* passive: they
both cause fear and feel it).
[108] *As they*, etc., like men who don't dare (to).   *shewen*, show.
[109] *faren*, fare.   *sothe*, truth.
[110] *yit*, yet, further.
[111] *artow*, = 'art thou'.

'Peter!' quod he, 'God yeve it harde grace!
I am so used in the fyr to blowe
That it hath chaunged my colour, I trowe.
I am nat wont in no mirour to prye,   115
But swinke sore and lerne multiplye.
We blondren ever and pouren in the fyr,
And, for al that, we fayle of our desyr –
For ever we lakken our conclusioun.
To muchel folk we doon illusioun   120
And borwe gold, be it a pound or two,
Or ten or twelve, or many sommes mo,
And make hem wenen, at the leeste weye,
That of a pound we coude make tweye.
Yet is it fals, but ay we han good hope   125
It for to doon, and after it we grope.
But that science is so fer us biforn
We mowen nat (al though we hadde it sworn)
It overtake, it slit awey so faste!
It wol us maken beggers atte laste.'   130
Whyl this yeman was thus in his talking,
This chanoun drough him neer and herde al thing
Which this yeman spak, for suspecioun
Of mennes speche ever hadde this chanoun:
For Catoun seith that he that gilty is   135

112 *Peter*, by St Peter (c).   *God*, etc., God damn it.
113 *used*, accustomed.   *fyr*, fire.
114 *I trowe*, I daresay.
115 *mirour*, mirror.   *prye*, look closely ('pry').
116 *swinke sore*, work hard.   *lerne multiplye*, learn transmutation (c).
117 *blondren*, stumble about (with sense of 'blunder', too; cf. 861).   *pouren*,
pore over (cf. *GP*, 185).
118 *fayle of*, fail to get, fall short of.
119 *lakken our conclusioun*, fail to achieve the end (we are aiming at).
120 *muchel folk*, many people.   *doon illusioun*, deceive.
121 *borwe*, borrow.   *pound*, pound (weight).
122 *sommes*, sums.   *mo*, more.
123 *hem*, them.   *wenen*, etc., imagine, at the very least.
124 *of*, (out) of.   *a*, one.   *tweye*, two.
125 *Yet*, up to the present time.   *ay*, always.   *han*, have.
125-6 *The* 'it' in each case refers to the 'science' of 'multiplying' gold.
127 *that science*, the knowledge of how to do that.   *so fer us biforn*, so far beyond
us.
128 *mowen nat*, cannot.
129 *slit*, slides (see 55 (c)).
130 *atte*, at the (cf. *GP*, 29).
132 *drough him neer*, drew nearer (*him* is refl. and *neer* the comp. of *ny*, near; see
137n below).   *herde al thing*, heard everything.   *spak*, spoke.
134 *Of mennes speche*, of what people said.
135 *Catoun*, Cato (c).   *seith*, says.

Demeth al thing be spoke of him, ywis.
That was the cause he gan so ny him drawe
To his yeman, to herknen al his sawe.
And thus he seyde unto his yeman tho,
'Hold thou thy pees, and spek no wordes mo – 140
For if thou do, thou shalt it dere abye!
Thou sclaundrest me heer in this companye
And eek discoverest that thou sholdest hyde.'
'Ye,' quod our Host, 'telle on, what so bityde:
Of al his threting rekke nat a myte!' 145
'In feith,' quod he, 'namore I do but lyte.'
And whan this chanon saugh it wolde nat be
But his yeman wolde telle his privetee,
He fledde awey for verray sorwe and shame.
'A!' quod the yeman, 'heer shal aryse game. 150
Al that I can, anon now wol I telle.
Sin he is goon, the foule feend him quelle!
For never herafter wol I with him mete
For peny ne for pound, I yow bihete.
He that me broghte first unto that game, 155
Er that he dye, sorwe have he and shame!
For it is ernest to me, by my feith –
That fele I wel, what so any man seith.
And yet for al my smert and al my grief,
For al my sorwe, labour and meschief, 160

[136] *Demeth*, see 20n. *spoke*, spoken. *ywis*, you can be sure.
[137] *gan . . . drawe*, drew. On *gan* see 3 (c).
[138] *herknen*, listen to ('hearken'). *sawe*, his words (cf. 'saw', sb.).
[139] *tho*, then.
[141] *it dere abye*, pay for it dearly (lit. 'buy').
[142] *thou sclaundrest*, you are slandering.
[143] *discoverest*, are revealing. *that*, that (which).
[144] *what so bityde*, whatever may come of it.
[145] *threting*, threats. *rekke nat a myte*, don't give a hang (cf. 8on).
[146] 'I *don't* particularly, as it happens.'
[148] *But*, but that. *wolde*, etc., was going to reveal his private affairs.
[149] *for verray sorwe and shame*, out of sheer vexation and embarrassment (cf. 156 below).
[150] 'Now we're going to have some fun!'
[151] *can*, know. *anon*, right away. *wol I*, I'm going to.
[152] *foule feend*, foul fiend. *quelle*, destroy.
[153] *mete*, see his face.
[154] *bihete*, promise (cf. 'behest').
[155] *game*, game (*sc.* alchemy; cf. *ernest* (c) below).
[156] *dye*, die.
[157] *ernest*, a serious matter (c).
[158] *fele*, feel. *what so*, whatever.
[159] *smert*, pain, injury.
[160] *meschief*, bad luck.

I coude never leve it in no wyse
Now wolde God my wit mighte suffyse
To tellen al that longeth to that art!
But natheles yow wol I tellen part
Sin that my lord is gon, I wol nat spare: 165
Swich thing as that I knowe I wol declare.'

Prologue

'With this chanoun I dwelt have seven yeer
And of his science am I never the neer.
Al that I hadde I have ylost therby –
And God wot so hath many mo than I!   170
Ther I was wont to be right fresh and gay
Of clothing, and of other good array,
Now may I were an hose upon myn heed,
And wher my colour was bothe fresh and reed,
Now is it wan and of a leden hewe   175
(Who so it useth sore shal he rewe!)
And of my swink yet blered is myn ÿe:
Lo which avantage is to multiplye!
That slyding scyence hath me maad so bare
That I have no good wher that ever I fare,   180
And yet I am endetted so therby
Of gold that I have borwed, trewely,

---

161 *leve it,* abandon (alchemy).
162 *suffyse,* be adequate.
163 *longeth,* belongs, pertains.   *that art,* i.e. alchemy.
164 *natheles,* nonetheless.
165 *spare,* refrain, hold back.
166 *swich thing as that,* whatever.
168 *never the neer . . . of,* no nearer to.   *his science,* what he knows.
169 *ylost,* lost (C).
171 *ther,* where, whereas.
172 *array,* attire (C).
173 *were,* wear.   *hose,* hose, stocking.   *heed,* head.
174 *colour,* complexion.
175 *leden,* leaden (C).
176 'Whoever practises alchemy will regret it bitterly!'
177 *of my swink,* as a result of my labours.   *blered,* dimmed ('bleared').   *ÿe,* eye (C).
178 *which avantage,* what profit.   *multiplye,* see 116n (C).
179 *slydinge,* sliding, elusive (cf. 129).
180 *good,* possessions (also 190, 192).   *that,* see 18n above.
181–2 'As a result of practising alchemy I am so deeply in debt for gold I have borrowed, truly. . . .'

That whyl I live I shal it quyte never.
Lat every man be war by me for ever:
What manner man that casteth him therto   185
If he continue I holde his thrift ydo.
So helpe me God, ther by shal he nat winne,
But empte his purs and make his wittes thinne;
And whan he thurgh his madnes and folye
Hath lost his owene good thurgh jupartye,   190
Thanne he excyteth other folk therto
To lese hir good as he himself hath do;
For unto shrewes joye it is and ese
To have hir felawes in peyne and disese.
Thus was I ones lerned of a clerk;   195
Of that, no charge; I wol speke of our werk.
Whan we been ther as we shul exercyse
Our elvish craft we semen wonder wyse –
Our termes been so clergial and so queynte.
I blowe the fyr, til that myn herte feynte.   200
What sholde I tellen ech proporcioun
Of thinges whiche that we werche upon
(As on fyve or sixe ounces, may wel be,
Of silver, or som other quantite)
And bisie me to telle yow the names   205
Of orpiment, brent bones, yren squames,
That into poudre grounden been ful smal,

[183] *quyte*, make good, pay back.
[184] *Lat*, let.   *by me*, by (taking example from) me.
[185] *casteth him thereto*, decides to devote himself to it.
[186] *his thrift*, 'his happy days' (lit. profit, success).   *ydo*, at an end ('*ydone*'; cf. 346).
[188] 'But empty his purse and drive himself crazy.'
[189] *thurgh*, through.   *folye*, folly.
[190] *owene*, own.   *thurgh jupartye*, by taking risks, on hazard (c).
[191] *excyteth*, incites, entices.
[192] *lese*, lose.   *do*, done.
[193] *shrewes*, wicked people.   *ese*, pleasure.
[194] 'To have other people (lit. their companions) in trouble and distress (along with them)' (c).
[195] *ones*, once.   *lerned of a clerk*, taught by a learned man (cf. 63).
[196] *no charge*, no matter.
[197] *ther as*, where.   *shul*, are to.
[198] *elvish*, strange, weird.   *semen*, seem.   *wonder*, see 7 (c).
[199] *termes*, terms.   *clergial*, technical.   *queynte*, abstruse.
[200] *feynte*, is collapsing (*feynte* is subj.).
[201] *What*, why, to what purpose.
[202] *thinges*, materials.   *werche*, work.
[205] *bisie me*, go to trouble.
[206] *orpiment*, trisulphide of arsenic ('orpiment', f. Lat. *auripigmentum*).   *brent*, burnt.   *yren squames*, iron flakes.
[207] *poudre*, powder.   *ful smal*, very finely.

And in an erthen pot how put is al,
And salt yput in, and also papeer,
Biforn thise poudres that I speke of heer,   210
And wel ycovered with a lampe of glas;
And mochel other thing which that ther was,
And of the pot and glasses enluting,
That of the eyre might passen out no thing;
And of the esy fyr and smart also   215
Which that was maad, and of the care and wo
That we hadde in our materes sublyming,
And in amalgaming and calcening
Of quiksilver, yclept Mercurie crude?
For alle our sleightes we can nat conclude.   220
Our orpiment and sublymed Mercurie,
Our grounden litarge eek on the porphurie,
Of ech of thise of ounces a certeyn –
Nought helpeth us, our labour is in veyn;
Ne eek our spirites ascencioun,   225
Ne our materes that lyen al fixe adoun,
Mowe in our werking no thing us avayle,
For lost is al our labour and travayle,
And al the cost – a twenty devel weye! –
Is lost also, which we upon it leye.   230
Ther is also ful many another thing

208 *erthen,* earthenware.
209 *papeer,* paper.
210 *Biforn,* before.   *heer,* here.
211 *lampe,* plate (OF *lame,* Lat. *lamina*).
213 'and about closing with clay the pot and the glass' (i.e. where they join; Lat. *lutum,* clay).
214 *eyre,* air.   *passen out,* escape.
215 *esy . . . smart,* gentle, fierce (C).
216 *maad,* made.   *wo,* trouble.
217 *materes sublyming,* the sublimation of our materials (C).
218 *amalgaming, calcening,* amalgamation, calcination (C).
219 *yclept,* called.   *Mercúrie crude,* crude mercury or common quicksilver (as distinguished from the purely hypothetical substance the alchemists believed in).
220 *sleightes,* stratagems.   *conclude,* achieve the results we are seeking.
221 *orpiment,* see 206n above.   *súblyméd,* see 217n above.
222 *grounden,* ground.   *litarge,* white monoxide of lead ('litharge').   *porphurie,* porphyry, a hard crystalline rock used as a slab.
223 *a certeyn,* a certain quantity (cf. 471).
224 *veyn,* vain.
225 *oure spirites ascencioun,* rising of our vapours (C).
226 *materes,* substances.   *lyen,* etc., lie fixed at the bottom (C).
226–7 *Ne . . ./Mowe . . . avayle,* Nor can (they) be of any use . . .   *werking,* operation, experiment.
228 *travayle,* effort.
229 *cost,* expense.   *a twenty,* etc., 'twenty devils take it!'
230 *leye,* lay out.

That is unto our craft apertening,
Though I by ordre hem nat reherce can,
Bycause that I am a lewed man;
Yet wol I telle hem as they come to minde,   235
Though I ne can nat sette hem in hir kinde –
As bole armoniak, verdegrees, boras,
And sondry vessels maad of erthe and glas,
Our urinales and our descensories,
Violes, croslets, and sublymatories,   240
Cucurbites and alembykes eek,
And othere swiche, dere ynough a leek –
Nat nedeth it for to reherce hem alle;
Watres rubifying and boles galle,
Arsenik, sal armoniak and brimstoon;   245
And herbes coude I telle eek many oon –
As egremoine, valerian, and lunarie
And othere swiche, if that me liste tarie;
Our lampes brenning bothe night and day
To bringe aboute our craft, if that we may;   250
Our fourneys eek of calcinacioun,
And of watres albificacioun;
Unslekked lym, chalk, and gleyre of an ey,

---

²³² *That is . . . apertening*, that pertains to.
²³³ *by*, in.   *reherce*, rehearse, name (cf. 243 below).
²³⁴ *lewed*, uneducated (c).
²³⁵ *telle*, name.
²³⁶ *kinde*, order (according to their *kinds* or natures).
²³⁷ *bole armoniak*, Armenian clay (c).   *verdegrees*, verdigris (c).   *boras*, borax.
²³⁸ *sondry*, sundry, various.
²³⁹ *urinales*, phials (c).   *descensóries*, descensories (c).
²⁴⁰ *Violes*, vials.   *croslets*, crucibles.   *sublymatóries*, vessels used for sublimation (see 217n above and (c)).
²⁴¹ *Curcúrbites*, cucurbits (c).   *alembýkes*, alembics (c).
²⁴² *swiche*, such things.   *dere ynough*, etc., dear enough (at the price of) a leek – i.e. worth nothing.
²⁴³ *Nat nedeth it*, there's no need.
²⁴⁴ *Watres rubifying*, fluids' turning red (see 252 (c)).   *boles galle*, bull's gall, a bitter fluid secreted by the liver of oxen.
²⁴⁵ *sal armoniak*, sal ammoniac (cf. 237n above).   *brimstoon*, sulphur.
²⁴⁶ *many oon*, many a one.
²⁴⁷ *egremoine*, agrimony, a yellow wayside flower.   *valerian*, (prob. here) Great or Cat's Valerian.   *lunarie*, lunary, moonwort, a fern (c).
²⁴⁸ *if that me liste tarie*, if I wished to linger (over them).
²⁴⁹ *brenning*, burning.
²⁵⁰ *craft*, here = 'werk': the end we are seeking (cf. 66; 198, 232, with their respective senses of 'skill' and 'profession').
²⁵¹ *fourneys . . . of calcinacioun*, calcining-fire (cf. 218n and (c) above).
²⁵² *watres albificacioun*, fluids' whitening (c) (cf. 244 above).

Poudres diverse, asshes, dong, pisse and cley,
Cered pokets, sal peter, vitriole,   255
And divers fyres maad of wode and cole;
Sal tartre, alkaly, and sal preparat,
And combust materes and coagulat,
Cley maad with hors or mannes heer, and oile
Of tartre, alum-glas, berm, wort and argoile,   260
Resalgar, and our materes enbibing,
And eek of our materes encorporing,
And of our silver citrinacioun,
Our cementing and fermentacioun,
Our ingottes, testes, and many mo.   265
I wol yow telle as was me taught also
The foure spirites and the bodies sevene,
By ordre, as ofte I herde my lord hem nevene:
The firste spirit quiksilver called is,
The second orpiment, the thridde ywis   270
Sal armoniak, and the ferthe brimstoon.
The bodies sevene eek, lo! hem heer anoon:
Sol gold is, and *Luna* silver we threpe,
Mars yren, *Mercurie* quiksilver we clepe,
Saturnus leed, and *Jupiter* is tin,   275
And *Venus* coper, by my fader kin!
This cursed craft whoso wol exercyse,

[254] *dong*, dung.   *cley*, clay.
[255] *Cered pokets*, bags closed with wax (cf. 'poke', 'pocket'; Lat. *cira*, wax). *sal peter*, saltpetre (c).   *vitriole*, vitriol (c).
[256] *wode*, wood.   *cole*, coal.
[257] *Sal tartre*, salt of tartar (c).   *alkaly*, prob. soda-ash.   *sal preparat*, purified (common) salt.
[258] 'And substances both burnt and congealed.'
[259] *maad*, (here) treated, prepared.   *hors*, horse's.
[259-60] *tartre*, oil or cream of tartar (c).   *alum-glas*, alum crystal.   *berm*, barm (c).   *wort*, wort (c).   *argoile*, argol (c).
[261] *Resalgar*, realgar, disulphide of arsenic, red orpiment (cf. 206n).   *enbibing*, absorption of moisture (by the solids).
[262] *encorporing*, solidification.
[263] *citrinacioun*, citrination (c).
[264] *cementing*, cementation (c).   *fermentacioun*, fermentation (c).
[265] *ingottes*, 'ingots', moulds.   *testes*, earthenware vessels for assaying metals.
[267] *spirites, bodies*, vapours, metals (c).
[268] *nevene*, name.
[270] *thridde*, third.
[271] *ferthe*, fourth.
[272] *lo! hem heer anoon*, here they are, then!
[273] *Sol*, the sun.   *Luna*, the moon.   *threpe*, declare (to be) (c).
[274] *clepe*, call.
[275] *leed*, lead.
[276] *coper*, copper.   *by my fader kin*, by my ancestors (for the genitive case without *of*, cf. *GP*, 71n).

He shal no good han that him may suffyse –
For al the good he spendeth theraboute
He lese shal – therof have I no doute.   280
Whoso that listeth outen his folye,
Lat him come forth and lerne multiplye!
And every man that oght hath in his cofre,
Lat him appere and wexe a philosofre!
Ascaunce that craft is so light to lere?   285
Nay, nay, God woot – al be he monk or frere,
Preest or chanoun, or any other wight,
Though he sitte at his book bothe day and night
In lerning of this elvish nyce lore –
Al is in veyn, and parde, mochel more!   290
To lerne a lewed man this subtiltee –
Fy, spek nat therof, for it wol nat be!
Al conne he letterure, or conne he noon,
As in effect, he shal finde it al oon.
For bothe two, by my savacioun,   295
Concluden in multiplicacioun
Ylyke wel, whan they han al ydo:
This is to seyn – they faylen bothe two!
Yet forgat I to maken rehersaille
Of watres corosif and of limaille,   300

278 *good*, profit (cf. 58 (c), 279).
279 *good*, possessions, money.   *theraboute*, on it (alchemy).
280 *lese*, lose.   *doute*, doubt.
281 *listeth*, likes (to).   *outen*, display (verb from *out*).   *folye*, folly.
282 *lerne multiplye*, learn to be an alchemist.
283 *oght*, anything ('aught').   *cofre*, coffer (c).
284 *appere*, appear.   *wexe*, become (wax = grow into; cf. 315).   *philo-sofre*, philosopher (alchemist), alchemy being supposedly based on natural philosophy (science). (Cf. philosopher's stone, 309n below, 505.)
285 *Ascaunce*, 'so you think' (c).   *light to lere*, easy to learn (c).
286 *woot*, knows.   *al be he*, whether he be.   *frere*, friar.
287 *Preest*, priest (c).
289 *in lerning of*, in the study of.   *elvish*, strange.   *nyce*, foolish.   *lore*, subject, science.
290 'It's all a waste of time, and, by God, much worse besides!'
291 'As for teaching an ignorant man this subtle craft . . .' (c).
293 *Al*, whether (cf. 286n above).   *conne*, know (c).   *letterure*, book-learning.
294 *As in effect*, when it comes down to it (the *as* is redundant; cf. 29n).   *al oon*, all one, one and the same thing (c).
295 *bothe two*, both of them (cf. 298).   *savacioun*, salvation.
296 *Concluden*, etc., see 119n above.
297 *Ylyke wel*, (euphemistic for) equally badly.   *ydo*, finished.
298 'However, I forgot to mention . . .' (c).
300 *watres córosif*, corrosive fluids (i.e. acids).   *limaille*, metal filings (Lat. *lima*, file).

And of bodyes mollificacioun,
And also of hir induracioun;
Oiles, abluciouns, and metal fusyble –
To tellen al wolde passen any byble
That owher is; wherfor, as for the beste,   305
Of alle thise names now wol I me reste;
For, as I trowe, I have yow told ynowe
To reyse a feend, al loke he never so rowe.
A, nay, lat be! The philosophres stoon
(*Elixir* clept) we sechen faste echoon –   310
For hadde we him than were we siker ynow.
But, unto God of heven I make avow,
For al our craft, when we han al ydo,
And al our sleighte, he wol nat come us to.
He hath ymaad us spenden muchel good,   315
For sorwe of which almost we wexen wood –
But that good hope crepeth in our herte,
Supposinge ever, though we sore smerte,
To be releved by him afterward.
Swich supposing and hope is sharp and hard –   320
I warne yow wel, it is to seken ever.
That *futur temps* hath maad men to dissever,
In trust therof, from al that ever they hadde.
Yet of that art they can nat wexen sadde,

301 *bodyes mollificacioun*, softening (i.e. melting) of metals (cf. 272–6n above and (c)).
302 *hir induracioun*, their hardening.
303 *Oiles*, oils (possibly the vitriols).   *ablucions*, washings.   *fusyble*, that melts ('fusible').
304 *passen*, exceed (i.e. be too much to be written in).   *byble*, book, tome (alluding to the size of the Bible).
305 *owher*, anywhere.   *as for the beste*, as the best solution.
306 *me reste*, leave off, give a rest to.
307 *trowe*, believe.   *ynowe*, enough.
308 'To raise a devil, however angry (*rowe*, 'roughly') he may look' (c).
309–10 'The philosophers' stone, called the Elixir, (is what) we are, each one of us, seeking unremittingly' (c). And cf. 284, 505.
311 *him*, i.e. the Elixir (c).   *siker*, sure, secure.
312 *make avow*, swear.
313,314 *craft . . . sleighte*, skill . . . ingenuity (c).
316 *sorwe*, chagrin.   *wexen wood*, go mad.
317 *good hope*, hope of success (contrasted implicitly with *wan-hope*, despair, expectation of failure).
318 *Supposinge*, imagining, expecting (cf. 320).   *sore smerte*, smart, grievously.
319 *releved*, relieved, cured.   *him*, i.e. the Stone.
320 *sharp and hard*, 'agonizing'.
321 *to seken ever*, still to seek (i.e. never to be found).
322 *That futur temps*, that 'future tense' (i.e. expectation that someday they will find it).   *dissever . . ./from*, take leave of.
324 *sadde*, replete, surfeited (cf. sated, f. Lat. *satus*).

For unto hem it is a bitter-swete –   325
So semeth it – for, nadde they but a shete
Which that they mighte wrappe hem inne anight,
And a brat to walken inne by daylight,
They wolde hem selle and spenden on this craft;
They can nat stinte til no thing be laft.   330
And evermore, wher that ever they goon,
Men may hem knowe by smel of brimstoon;
For al the world they stinken as a goot!
Hir savour is so rammish and so hoot
That, though a man from hem a myle be,   335
The savour wol infecte him, trusteth me.
And thus by smell and by threedbare array,
If that men liste, this folk they knowe may;
And if a man wol aske hem prively
Why they been clothed so unthriftily,   340
They right anon wol rownen in his ere
And seyn, that if that they espyed were,
Men wolde hem slee by cause of hir science.
Lo, thus this folk bitrayen innocence!
Passe over this; I go my tale unto.   345
Er that the pot be on the fyr ydo,
Of metals with a certein quantite,
My lord hem trempeth, and no man but he –
Now he is goon I dar seyn boldely –

³²⁵ *bitter-swete*, i.e. sweet to the taste, bitter to digest (c).
³²⁶ *nadde they but*, had they no more than (*ne+hadde*).   *shete*, sheet.
³²⁷ *hem*, themselves.   *anight*, at night.
³²⁸ *brat*, cloak (and see Textual Note).
^{328,329} *inne* within, in.   *hem*, i.e. the sheet and cloak.
³³⁰ *stinte*, cease.   *laft*, left (cf. *lat*, 309, etc).
³³² *Men may hem knowe*, you can recognize them.
³³³ *goot*, goat.
^{334,336} *savour*, 'odour', 'aroma' (satirical euphemism for foul smell).   *rammish*, rank (f. *ram*).   *hoot*, powerful, intense
³³⁵ *from*, away from.
³³⁶ *infecte*, affect (with some implication that it will also *infect* him when it does) (c).   *trusteth*, trust.
³³⁸ *this folk*, these people (also 334).
³³⁹ *prively*, privately, confidentially.
³⁴⁰ *unthriftily*, badly (with implication that their dress reflects their lack of *thrift* or 'success').
³⁴¹ *rownen*, whisper.
³⁴² *espyed*, 'seen through'.
³⁴³ *slee*, kill.   *science*, knowledge (of alchemy).
³⁴⁴ *bitrayen innocence*, deceive innocent people.
³⁴⁵ *my tale*, see (c).
³⁴⁶ *ydo*, placed (cf. 186).
³⁴⁸ *hem*, i.e. the metals.   *trempeth*, blends ('tempers').
³⁴⁹ *dar seyn*, dare speak out.

For (as men seyn) he can doon craftily,   350
Algate I woot wel he hath swich a name –
And yet ful ofte he renneth in a blame.
And wite ye how? Ful ofte it happeth so,
The pot to-breketh, and farewel! al is go.
Thise metals been of so greet violence,   355
Our walles mowe nat make hem resistence
But if they weren wroght of lym and stoon,
They percen so, and thurgh the wal they goon;
And somme of hem sinken into the ground –
Thus han we lost by tymes many a pound;   360
And somme are scatered al the floor aboute;
Somme lepe into the roof; withouten doute,
Though that the feend noght in our sighte him shewe,
I trowe he with us be, that ilke shrewe!
In helle wher that he is lord and syre   365
Nis ther more wo, ne more rancour ne yre
Whan that our pot is broke as I have sayd:
Every man chit, and halt him yvel apayd.
Som seyde it was long on the fyr making,
Som seyde, "Nay, it was on the blowing."   370
(Than was I fered, for that was myn offyce.)
"Straw!" quod the thridde, "ye been lewed and nyce.
It was not tempred as it oghte be."
"Nay," quod the ferthe, "stint and herkne me:

---

350 *doon*, perform, carry out experiments.   *craftily*, skilfully.
351 'At any rate (*algate*) I'm certain he's reputed to' (*hath swich a name*).
352 *renneth in a blame*, makes mistakes, 'comes to grief' (rather than 'incurs blame', which is just possible).
353 *wite ye*, do you know.   *happeth so*, turns out that.
354 *to-brek'th*, breaks in pieces (the *to-* is intensive; cf. 82n).
356 *mowe nat*, could not.   *hem*, i.e. the metals.
357 *But if*, unless.   *lym*, limestone.
358 *percen*, pierce.
360 *by tymes*, on various occasions.
363 *him shewe*, actually appear ('show himself').
364 *ilke shrewe*, evil spirit (C).   *ilke*, same (cf. 'of that ilk').
366 *Nis*, (= *ne is*), there is not.   *yre*, wrath ('ire').
367 *broke*, broken.
368 *chit*, complains.   *halt him*, considers himself (C).   *yvel apayd*, hard done by (lit. ill-pleased) (cf. 496n).
369,370 *Som*, one (cf. the pl. form in 359, 361–2).   *seyde* (C).   *long on the fyr-making*, on account of the way the fire was made.
370 *on*, i.e. *long on* (as above).
371 *fered*, frightened.   *offyce*, job.
372 *Straw!*, rubbish!   *lewed and nyce*, stupid and ignorant.
373 *tempred*, controlled (with ref. to the temperature of the fire; cf. *tempreth*, 348n above and (C)).
374 *stint*, shut up.   *herkne*, listen to.

Bycause our fyr ne was nat maad of beech –   375
That is the cause, and other noon, so thee'ch!"
I can nat telle wheron it was long,
But wel I wot greet stryf is us among.
"What!" quod my lord, "ther is namore to done;
Of thise perils I wol be war eftsone   380
I am right siker that the pot was crased.
Be as be may, be ye no thing amased!
As usage is, lat swepe the floor as swythe;
Plukke up your hertes and beth gladde and blythe!"
The mullok on an hepe ysweped was,   385
And on the floor ycast a canevas,
And al this mullok in a sive ythrowe
And sifted and ypiked many a throwe.
"Pardee," quod oon, "somwhat of our metal
Yet is ther heer, though that we han nat al.   390
Al though this thing mishapped have as now,
Another tyme it may be wel ynow.
Us moste putte our good in aventure:
A marchant, parde, may nat ay endure
(Trusteth me wel) in his prosperitee.   395
Somtyme his good is drenched in the see,
And somtyme comth it sauf unto the londe."
"Pees," quod my lord, "the next tyme I wol fonde
To bringe our craft al in another plyte,

---

[376] *other noon*, no other.   *so thee'ch*, so help me (lit. so may I thrive, cf. 88).
[377] *whereon it was long, what* it was due to (cf. 369n above).
[378] *stryf*, quarrelling.
[379] *What!*, Ah, well!   *to done*, to do, to be done.
[380] *war . . . of*, careful about.   *eftsone*, next time.
[381] *crased*, cracked (cf. Fr. *craser*).
[382] *amased*, put out, upset.
[383] *As usage is*, as we usually do.   *lat swepe*, let's sweep.   *as swythe*, right away.
[384] *Plukke up*, etc., Cheer up! (c).
[385] *mullok*, rubbish.   *on an hepe*, in a pile.
[386] *a canevas*, a canvas (sheet).
[387] *sive*, sieve.   *ythrowe*, thrown.
[388] *ypiked*, picked over, sorted through.   *throwe*, time.
[389] *somwhat*, some.
[390] *Yet*, still.
[391] 'Although things have gone badly this time.'
[392] 'We must put our wealth at risk.'
[394] *marchant*, merchant.   *ay*, see 23n.   *endure*, remain.
[396] *drenched*, drowned.   *see*, sea.
[396,397] *Somtyme . . . somtyme*, one time, another time.
[397] *comth*, comes.   *sauf*, safely.
[398] *fonde*, attempt.
[399] 'To bring our efforts (*craft*) to quite another conclusion' (*plyte*; cf. 'plight').

And but I do, sirs, lat me han the wyte.   400
Ther was defaute in som what, wel I woot."
Another seyde, "The fyr was over-hoot" –
But be it hoot or cold, I dar seye this,
That we concluden evermore amis.
We fayle of that which that we wolden have,   405
And in our madnesse evermore we rave;
And when we been togidres everichoon,
Every man semeth a Salomon;
But al thing which that shyneth as the gold
Nis nat gold, as that I have herd it told,   410
Ne every appel that is fair at ÿe
Ne is nat good, what so men clappe or crye.
Right so, lo! fareth it amonges us:
He that semeth the wysest, by Jesus,
Is most fool whan it cometh to the preef,   415
And he that semeth trewest is a theef –
That shul ye knowe er that I fro yow wende
By that I of my tale have maad an ende.

The Tale

There is a chanoun of religioun
Amonges us, wolde infecte al a toun,   420
Though it as greet were as was Ninivee,
Rome, Alisaundre, Troye, and othere three.

400 *but*, unless.   *wyte*, blame.
401 *defaute*, a defect, a fault.
402 *over-hoot*, too hot.
404 'Our experiments come to nothing every single time.'
405 *fayle of*, fail to get.
407 *togidres everichoon*, all together ('ever-each-one').
408 *Salomon*, Solomon.
411 *appel*, apple (c).   *at ÿe*, to behold.
412 *clappe*, shout.
415 *preef*, proof, test.
416 *trewest*, most honest.   *theef*, thief.
417 *knowe*, realize.   *fro*, from.
418 *By that*, by the time that.
419 *of religioun*, belonging to a religious order.
420 *wolde*, i.e. *who* would.   *infecte*, infect, corrupt (cf. 336) (c).   *al a toun*,
a whole town.
421 *Ninivee*, Nineveh (c).
422 *Alisaundre*, Alexandria.   *othere three*, three more, too.

His sleightes and his infinite falsnesse
Ther coude no man wryten, as I gesse,
Thogh that he live mighte a thousand yeer.   425
In al this world, of falshede nis his peer,
For in his termes so he wolde him winde,
And speke his wordes in so sly a kinde,
Whan he commune shal with any wight,
That he wol make him doten anonright –   430
But it a feend be (as himselven is).
Ful many a man hath he bigyled er this,
And wol, if that he live may a whyle;
And yet men ryde and goon ful many a myle
Him for to seke, and have his aqueyntaunce,   435
Noght knowinge of his false governaunce.
And if yow list to yeve me audience,
I wol it tellen heer in your presence.
But worshipful chanouns religious,
Ne demeth nat that I sclaundre your hous,   440
Al though my tale of a chanoun be.
Of every ordre som shrewe is, parde,
And God forbede that al a compaignye
Sholde rewe a singuler mannes folye!
To sclaundre yow is no thing myn entente,   445
But to correcten that is mis I mente.

423 *sleightes*, cunning tricks.
424 *gesse*, guess.
425 *mighte*, should.
426 'In all this world he has no equal ('peer') for deceitfulness.'
427 *termes*, jargon.   *him*, i.e. the victim (c).   *winde*, ensnare.
428 *so sly a kinde*, so deviously subtle a fashion.
430 *make him doten anonright*, make a fool of him in a trice.
431 *But it*, unless he (i.e. the hypothetical victim).   *himselven*, he himself.
432 *bigyled*, tricked.
433 *wol*, i.e. will continue (or perhaps, 'and intends to continue') to do so.
434 *goon*, walk (contrasted with *ryde*).
435 *seke*, seek.
436 'Knowing nothing of his deceitful behaviour.'
437 'And if you are prepared to listen to me.'
438 *it*, i.e. a story of the 'falseness' of the Canon (the 'tale' anticipated from 418).
439 *worshipful*, honourable (cf. 'worshipful company').   *chanouns religious*, see
419n (c).
440 'Don't think I'm slandering your Order' (*hous* = religious house, metonymic
for Order).
442 'Every Order has its black sheep' (*som* is again sg.; cf. 369–70; on *shrewe*
cf. 364).   *ordre* (c).
443 *al a compaignye*, a whole group of people, a whole profession.
444 *rewe*, have to pay for ('rue').   *singuler*, individual, single.
445 *entente*, purpose.
446 *that is*, i.e. that which is.   *mis*, amiss.   *mente*, intended.

This tale was nat only told for yow,
But eek for othere mo; ye woot wel how
That among Cristes apostelles twelve
Ther nas no traytour but Judas himselve.   450
Than why sholde al the remenant have a blame,
That giltlees were? By yow I seye the same –
Save only this, if ye wol herkne me:
If any Judas in your covent be,
Remoeveth him bitymes, I yow rede,   455
If shame or los may causen any drede;
And beth no thing displesed, I yow preye,
But in this cas herkneth what I shal seye.

In London was a preest, an annueleer,
That therin dwelled hadde many a yeer,   460
Which was so plesaunt and so servisable
Unto the wyf, wher as he was at table,
That she wolde suffre him no thing for to paye
For bord ne clothing, wente he never so gaye;
And spending-silver hadde he right ynow.   465
Therof no fors; I wol procede as now,
And telle forth my tale of the chanoun
That broghte this preest to confusioun.
This false chanoun cam up on a day
Unto this preestes chambre, wher he lay,   470

---

447 *only*, solely.   *for yow*, on account of, concerning you.
448 *othere mo*, others, too.
448–9 *how/That*, how.
450 *nas no* (= *ne was*), was no (cf. 80 (c)).
451 *have a blame*, be condemned.
452 *giltlees*, guiltless.   *By*, concerning.
454 *covent*, convent (used in ME for houses of male religious as well as nuns).
455 *Remoeveth*, remove.   *bitymes*, promptly.   *rede*, advise.
456 'If (the prospect of) disgrace and opprobrium (is enough to) cause (you) any anxiety.'
457 *beth*, be. See 70 (c).
458 *in this cas*, as far as this instance is concerned.
459 *annueleer*, annueller (c).
461 *Which*, who (cf. '*which* art in Heaven').   *plesaunt*, charming.   *servisable*, willing to serve, helpful (c).
462 *Unto the wyf*, etc., to the woman who ran the house where he took his meals.
463 *suffre*, allow.
464 *bord*, board, food.   *wente he*, even if he should go about.   *gaye*, finely dressed (cf. *GP*, 74).
465 *spending-silver*, pocket-money.
466 *as now*, for the moment (c).
468 *confusioun*, ruin (cf. 530).
469 *on a day*, one day (cf. *GP*, 19).
470 *chambre*, room.   *lay*, was lodging.

Biseching him to lene him a certeyn
Of gold, and he wolde quyte it him ageyn.
"Lene me a mark," quod he, "but dayes three,
And at my day I wol it quyten thee;
And if so be that thou me finde fals,   475
Another day do hange me by the hals!"
This preest him took a mark, and that as swythe,
And this chanoun him thanked ofte sythe,
And took his leve and wente forth his weye,
And at the thridde day broghte his moneye,   480
And to the preest he took his gold agayn,
Wherof this preest was wonder glad and fayn.
"Certes," quod he, "no thing anoyeth me
To lene a man a noble, or two or three,
Or what thing were in my possessioun,   485
Whan he so trewe is of condicioun
That in no wyse he breke wol his day.
To swich a man I can never seye nay."
"What!" quod this chanoun, "sholde I be untrewe?
Nay, that were thing yfallen al of newe.   490
Trouthe is a thing that I wol ever kepe
Unto that day in which that I shal crepe
In to my grave, and elles God forbede!
Bileveth this as siker as is your Crede.
God thanke I (and in good tyme be it sayd!)   495
That ther was never man yet yvel apayd
For gold ne silver that he to me lente,

471 *lene*, lend.   *a certeyn*, i.e. a certain sum (cf. 223).
472 *quyte*, pay back (cf. 'requite').
473 *mark*, a 'money of account' (like the guinea today) worth about 67p. *but dayes three*, for only three days.
474 *my day*, the day I agree on.
476 *do hange me*, have me hanged.   *hals*, neck.
477 *took*, gave (c).   *as swythe*, right away.
478 *ofte sythe*, many times.
479 *leve*, leave.
481 *took*, see 477 (c).
482 *wherof*, at which.   *fayn*, pleased.
483 *no thing anoyeth me*, it's no trouble to me.
484 *a noble*, a gold coin worth 33½p (half a *mark*; see 473 above).
485 *what*, whatever.
486 *trewe*, honest.   *condicioun*, character (cf. *GP*, 38).
487 'Who will under no circumstances fail to keep his agreement.'
489 *untrewe*, dishonest, not keeping one's *trouthe* (see 491 below).
490 'No, that would be something quite unheard of!' (lit. 'a completely new occurrence').
491 *Trouthe*, my pledged word ('troth') (c).
494 *siker*, sure.   *Crede*, Creed.
496 *yvel apayd*, ill-pleased, dissatisfied (cf. 368n).
497 *For*, on account of.

Ne never falshede in myn herte I mente.
And, sir," quod he, "now of my privetee –
Sin ye so goodlich han been unto me,   500
And kythed to me so greet gentillesse –
Somwhat to quyte with your kindenesse
I wol yow shewe, and (if yow list to lere)
I wol yow teche pleynly the manere
How I can werken in philosophye.   505
Taketh good heed, ye shul wel seen at ÿe
That I wol doon a maistrie er I go."
"Ye," quod the preest, "ye, sir, and wol ye so?
Marie! therof I pray yow hertely."
"At your commandement, sir, trewely,"   510
Quod the chanoun, "and elles God forbede!"
Lo how this theef coude his servyse bede!
Ful sooth it is that swich profred servyse
Stinketh, as witnessen thise olde wyse,
And that ful sone I wol it verifye   515
In this chanoun, roote of al trecherye,
That evermore delyt hath and gladnesse,
Swich feendly thoughtes in his herte impresse
How Cristes peple he may to meschief bringe.
God kepe us from his fals dissimulinge!   520
Noght wiste this preest with whom that he delte,
Ne of his harm cominge he no thing felte.
O sely preest! O sely innocent!

499 *of my privetee*, out of my secret store (of knowledge).
500 *ye*, (c).   *goodlich*, obliging.
501 *kythed*, displayed, made known (cf. 'couth' in 'uncouth').   *gentillesse*,
magnanimity (c).
502 'To repay your kindness in some measure.'
504 *pleynly*, clearly, fully.
504–5 'What I know about alchemical operations' (cf. 284, 309).
506 *at ÿe*, with your own eyes.
507 *doon a maistrie*, demonstrate my skill (c).
509 *Marie!*, Mary (cf. 112 (c)).   *hertely*, earnestly.
512 *bede*, offer (c).
513 *profred servyse*, proffered service, solicitation.
514 *thise olde wyse*, wise men of old (c).
515 *it* is redundant.
516 *In*, in the case of.   *trecherye*, deceitfulness (the political meaning is a
specialized development; cf. *bitray*, 344, 539 and Fr. *tricher*, to cheat).
517 *delyt*, pleasure.
518 *feendly*, devilish.   *impresse*, imprint (themselves).
519 *How*, as to how.   *Cristes peple*, Christian people.   *meschief*, ruin.
520 *dissimulinge*, dissimulation (c).
521 *Noght wiste this preest*, this priest had no idea at all.   *delte*, was dealing.
522 *his harm cominge*, the evil in store for him.   *felte*, perceived.
523 'O simple priest! O silly, simple fool!' (c).

With coveityse anon thou shalt be blent!
O gracelees, ful blind is thy conceit,   525
No thing ne artow war of the deceit
Which that this fox yshapen hath to thee:
His wyly wrenches thou ne mayst nat flee!
Wherfor, to go to the conclusioun
That refereth to thy confusioun,   530
Unhappy man, anon I wol me hye
To tellen thyn unwit and thy folye,
And eek the falsnesse of that other wrecche,
As ferforth as that my conning may strecche.
This chanoun was my lord, ye wolden wene?   535
Sir Host, in feith, and by the hevenes quene –
It was another chanoun and nat he,
That can an hundredfold more subtiltee.
He hath bitrayed folkes many tyme –
Of his falshede it dulleth me to ryme!   540
Ever whan that I speke of his falshede,
For shame of him my chekes wexen rede –
Algates they biginnen for to glowe,
For reednesse have I noon, right wel I knowe,
In my visage, for fumes dyverse   545
Of metals which ye han herd me reherce
Consumed han and wasted my reednesse.
Now tak heed of this chanouns cursednesse:
"Sir," quod he to the preest, "lat your man gon
For quiksilver, that we it hadde anon,   550
And lat him bringen ounces two or three,
And when he comth, as faste shul ye see

---

524 *with coveityse*, through greed.   *blent*, blinded.
525 *gracelees*, wicked (lacking grace).   *conceit*, 'grasp of reality' (lit. conception;
cf. *Hamlet*, II, ii, 560).
526 *artow*, art thou.   *war*, wary, aware.
527 *yshapen*, contrived.
528 *wyly wrenches*, cunning tricks.
530 *refereth to*, relates to, is concerned with.
531 *me hye*, hasten ('hie me').
532 *unwit*, stupidity (un+*wit*, 'intelligence').
534 *As . . . that*, as far as.   *conning*, ability.   *strecche*, extend.
535 *wene*, suppose, guess.
536 *the hevenes quene*, Mary, the Queen of Heaven.
538 *can*, knows, is capable of.   *subtiltee*, subtle deceitfulness.
540 *it dulleth me*, it makes my head dizzy (lit. stupefies).
543 *Algates*, at any rate.
546 *Of metals*, (given off) by metals.   *reherce*, mention.
547 *wasted*, destroyed (see Textual Note on this line).
548 *cursednesse*, wickedness.
550 *that*, etc., 'so that we might have it immediately'.
552 *as faste*, right away.

A wonder thing which ye saugh never er this."
"Sir," quod the preest, "it shal be doon, ywis."
He bad his servant fecchen him this thing,   555
And he al redy was at his bidding,
And wente him forth and cam anon agayn
With this quiksilver, shortly for to sayn,
And took thise ounces three to the chanoun;
And he hem leyde fayre and wel adoun,   560
And bad the servant coles for to bringe,
That he anon mighte go to his werkinge.
The coles right anon weren yfet
And this chanoun took out a crosselet
Of his bosom, and shewed it the preest.   565
"This instrument," quod he, "which that thou seest,
Tak in thyn hand, and put thyself therinne
Of this quiksilver an ounce, and heer biginne
(In the name of Crist) to wexe a philosofre!
Ther been ful fewe whiche that I wolde profre   570
To shewen hem thus muche of my science.
For ye shul seen heer, by experience,
That this quiksilver wol I mortifye
Right in your sighte anon, withouten lye,
And make it as good silver and as fyn   575
As ther is any in your purs or myn,
Or elleswher, and make it malliable –
And elles holdeth me fals and unable
Amonges folk for ever to appere.
I have a poudre heer that coste me dere,   580
Shal make al good, for it is cause of al
My conning, which that I yow shewen shal.

555 *fecchen*, fetch.
556 *he*, i.e. the servant.
557 *wente him*, went (lit. turned himself, f. *wenden*, to turn).   *agayn*, back.
559 *took*, gave (cf. 477 (c)).
560 *leyde adoun*, laid down.   *fayre and wel*, 'carefully'.
564 *crosselet*, crucible ('crosslet').
565 *of*, from.   *the*, i.e. to the.
566 *thou* (c).
570 *whiche that I wolde profre*, whom I would be willing.
572 *by experience*, with your own eyes, experimentally (the phrase had both meanings; cf. Fr. *expérience*, experiment).
573 *mortifye*, 'mortify', a technical term (c); 'fix'.
574 *withouten lye*, 'believe me'.
575 *fyn*, fine.
577 *malliable*, malleable.
578 *elles*, otherwise, if not.   *holdeth*, think.   *unable*, unfit.
580 *dere*, dearly.
581–2 'which will bring us success, for it's the source of all my skill.'

Voydeth your man and lat him be theroute,
And shet the dore whyls we been aboute
Our privetee, that no man us espye   585
Whyls that we werke in this philosophye."
Al as he bad fulfilled was in dede:
This ilke servant anonright out yede,
And his maister shette the dore anon,
And to hir labour speedily they gon.   590
This preest at this cursed chanouns bidding
Upon the fyr anon sette this thing,
And blew the fyr and bisied him ful faste;
And this chanoun into the croslet caste
A poudre (noot I wher-of that it was   595
Ymaad, other of chalk, other of glas,
Or somwhat elles, was nat worth a flye)
To blinde with the preest, and bad him hye
The coles for to couchen al above
The croslet, "for in tokening I thee love,"   600
Quod this chanoun, "thyn owene hondes two
Shul werche al thing which that shal heer be do."
"Graunt mercy," quod the preest and was ful glad,
And couched coles as the chanoun bad;
And whyle he bisy was this feendly wrecche,   605
This fals chanoun (the foule feend him fecche!)
Out of his bosom took a bechen cole
In which ful subtilly was maad an hole,

---

[583] *Voydeth your man*, have your servant leave.   *theroute*, outside the room.
[584] *shet*, shut.   *whyls*, while (and 585, with *that*).
[585] *privetee*, private business.   *espye*, spy on.
[586] *werke*, see 69 (c).
[587] *bad*, bade, ordered.
[588] *anonright*, right away.   *yede*, went.
[592] *this thing*, i.e. the crucible.
[593] *him*, himself.
[595] *noot I* (= *ne woot I*), I don't know.
[596] *Ymaad*, made.   *other . . . other*, whether . . . or.
[597] *was*, i.e. that was.
[598] *to blinde with*, with which to pull the wool over the eyes of.   *hye*, hasten ('hie').
[599] *couchen*, lay down flat.   *al*, right.
[600] *in tokening*, to show that.   *thee*, see 572 (c).
[602] *werche*, carry out, perform.   *do*, done.
[603] *Graunt mercy*, many thanks ('*grand merci*').
[604] *bad*, instructed.
[605] *feendly wrecche*, devilish scoundrel.
[606] 'the devil carry him off!'
[607] *bechen*, beechwood.
[608] *subtilly*, cleverly.

And ther-in put was of silver lymaille
An ounce, and stopped was, withouten fayle,   610
The hole with wex, to kepe the lymaille in.
And understondeth that this false gin
Was nat maad ther, but it was maad bifore,
And othere thinges I shal telle more
Herafterward, which that he with him broghte: 615
Er he cam ther, him to bigyle he thoghte,
And so he dide, er that they wente atwinne –
Til he had terved him coude he not blinne.
It dulleth me whan that I of him speke!
On his falshede fayn wolde I me wreke   620
If I wiste how, but he is heer and ther –
He is so variaunt he abit nowher.
But taketh heed now, sirs, for Goddes love!
He took his cole, of which I spak above,
And in his hond he baar it prively,   625
And whyls the preest couchede busily
The coles, as I tolde yow er this,
This chanoun seyde, "Freend, ye doon amis.
This is nat couched as it oghte be;
But sone I shal amenden it," quod he.   630
"Now lat me medle therwith but a whyle,
For of yow have I pitee, by Seint Gyle!
Ye been right hoot, I see wel how ye swete;
Have heer a cloth and wype awey the wete."

609 *lymaille*, filings.
610 *withouten fayle*, have no doubt of it.
611 *wex*, wax.
612 *understondeth*, understand.   *false gin*, deceitful device.
613 i.e. it was prepared in advance.
614 *telle*, mention.
615 *Herafterward*, presently.
617 *wente atwinne*, separated (*atwinne*, in two).
618 'He couldn't stop (*blinne*) till he had bled him dry' (*terved*, lit, stripped; cf.
721 below).
619 *dulleth*, see 540n above.
620 *fayn*, gladly.   *me wreke*, revenge myself (c).
621 *wiste*, knew.
622 *variaunt*, changeable (with suggestion of deviousness).   *abit*, stays put
(= *abydeth*; see 48 (c)).
623 *taketh*, take.
624 *above*, a moment ago (c).
626 *couchede*, was arranging.
628 *ye doon amis*, you're doing it wrong (c).
630 *sone*, soon.   *amenden it*, put it right.
631 *medle therwith*, have a go at it.
632 'I feel sorry for you . . . .'   *Seint Gyle*, St Giles (c).

111

And whyles that the preest wyped his face,   635
This chanoun took his cole, with harde grace,
And leyde it above upon the middeward
Of the croslet, and blew wel afterward
Til that the coles gonne faste brenne,
"Now yeve us drinke," quod the chanoun thenne,   640
"As swythe al shal be wel, I undertake.
Sitte we doun and lat us mery make."
And whan that this chanounes bechen cole
Was brent, al the lymaille out of the hole
Into the croslet fil anon adoun –   645
And so it moste nedes, by resoun,
Sin it so even aboven it couched was.
But therof wiste the preest nothing, alas!
He demed alle the coles yliche good,
For of the sleighte he nothing understood.   650
And whan this alkamistre saugh his tyme,
"Rys up," quod he, "sir preest, and stondeth by me;
And for I woot wel ingot have ye noon –
Goth, walketh forth and bring us a chalk-stoon,
For I wol make oon of the same shap   655
That is an ingot, if I may han hap;
And bringeth eek with yow a bolle or a panne
Ful of water, and ye shul see well thanne
How that our bisinesse shal thryve and preve.
And yet, for ye shul han no misbileve   660
Ne wrong conceit of me in your absence,

636 *with harde grace,* either 'with ill-luck' (i.e. for the priest) or 'blast him!' (the phrase being used as an asseveration as at 112).
637 *middeward,* middle.
639 *gonne,* began.   *faste,* vigorously.
641 *As swythe,* in a jiffy (cf. 741).   *undertake,* warrant.
644 *brent,* burnt (up).
645 *fil,* fell.
646–7 'And so it couldn't help doing, of course, since it had been laid directly (*even*) above it.'
649 *demed,* thought.   *yliche good,* equally genuine.
650 *sleighte,* trick.   *understood,* perceived.
651 *alkamistre,* alchemist (c).   *tyme: by me,* on rhyme see (c).
652 *Rys,* rise.   *stondeth,* stand.
653 *ingot,* mould for casting metal.
654 *Goth, walketh,* go, walk.   *chalk-stoon,* piece of chalk.
655 *shap,* shape.
656 *That,* as.   *hap,* (good) luck.
657 *bolle,* bowl.
658 *thanne,* then.
659 *bisinesse,* operation.   *thryve and preve,* succeed.
660–1 'In order that you should put no misconstruction on what I do while you're away.'

I ne wol nat been out of your presence,
But go with yow and come with yow ageyn."
The chambre-dore, shortly for to seyn,
They opened and shette and wente hir weye,   665
And forth with hem they carieden the keye,
And come agayn withouten any delay.
What sholde I tarien al the longe day?
He took the chalk and shoop it in the wyse
Of an ingot, as I shal yow devyse.   670
I seye, he took out of his owene sleve
A teyne of silver (yvele mote he cheve!)
Which that ne was nat but an ounce of weighte.
And taketh heed now of his cursed sleighte!
He shoop his ingot, in lengthe and eek in brede,   675
Of this teyne, withouten any drede,
So slyly that the preest it nat espyde,
And in his sleve agayn he gan it hyde,
And fro the fyr he took up his matere
And in th'ingot putte it with mery chere,   680
And in the water-vessel he it caste
Whan that him luste, and bad the preest as faste,
"Look what ther is: put in thyn hand and grope.
Thow finde shalt ther silver, as I hope."
What (devel of helle!) sholde it elles be?   685
Shaving of silver silver is, pardee!
He putte his hond in and took up a teyne
Of silver fyn, and glad in every veyne
Was this preest whan he saugh that it was so.
"Goddes blessing and his modres also,   690

---

666 *carieden*, carried, took.
668 *What*, why.
669 *shoop*, shaped, moulded.   *wyse*, form.
670 *devyse*, describe.
671 *sleve*, sleeve.
672 *teyne*, plate.   *yvele*, etc., ill may he prosper!
673 *of*, in.
675 *brede*, breadth.
676 *of*, out of, with (c).   *withouten any drede*, have no fear!
677 *slyly*, dexterously (with 'sly' sense as well).
678 *gan it hyde*, hid it (cf. 3 (c)).
679 *matere*, materials.
680 *mery chere*, 'a smiling face' (cf. *GP*, 857 (c)).
682 *him luste*, he liked (impers. vb., pret.; the same word as *liste*).
683 *grope*, feel.
685 *What . . . elles*, what else.
688 *veyne*, vein.
690 *and his modres*, and his Mother's (the Virgin Mary).

And alle halwes have ye, sir chanoun,"
Seyde this preest, "and I hir malisoun,
But, and ye vouchesauf to techen me
This noble craft and this subtilitee,
I wol be youre in al that ever I may."   695
Quod the chanoun, "Yet wol I make assay
The second tyme, that ye may taken hede
And been expert of this, and in your nede
Another day assaye in myn absence
This disciplyne and this crafty science.   700
Lat take another ounce," quod he tho,
"Of quiksilver, withouten wordes mo,
And do therwith as ye han doon er this
With that other which that now silver is."
This preest him bisieth in al that he can   705
To doon as this chanoun, this cursed man,
Commanded him, and faste he blew the fyr
For to come to th'effect of his desyr.
And this chanoun right in the mene whyle
Al redy was the preest eft to bigyle;   710
And for a countenaunce in his hande he bar
An holwe stikke (tak keep and be war!)
In the ende of which an ounce and namore
Of silver lymaille put was, as bifore
Was in his cole, and stopped with wex weel   715
For to kepe in his lymaille every deel.
And whyl this preest was in his bisinesse
This chanoun with his stikke gan him dresse

691 *alle halwes*, (that of) all the saints (cf. 'All-Hallows,' and *GP*, 14).   *have ye*, may you have.
692 *and I hir malisoun*, and (may) I (have) their curse ('malison').
693 *But, and*, unless, if.   *vouchesauf*, have the goodness.
695 *youre*, yours.
696 *Yet*, further.   *make assay*, try it out (also 699).
697 *taken hede*, observe.
698 *been expert of*, become skilled in.   *in your nede*, as you need.
700 'This rigorous and skilful art' (c).
701 *Lat take*, take.   *tho*, then.
702 *withouten wordes mo*, without saying another word.
704 *other*, other (ounce)
705 *in al that he can*, as best he can.
708 *th'effect*, the fruits.
709 *mene whyle*, meanwhile.
710 *eft*, again.
711 *for a countenaunce*, for show (c).
712 *holwe*, hollow.   *keep*, heed.
716 *every deel*, every bit.
717 *in his bisinesse*, busying himself.
718–19 *gan him dresse/To* . . . approached.

To him anon and his poudre caste in
As he did er (the devel out of his skin   720
Him terve, I pray to God, for his falshede! –
For he was ever fals in thoght and dede)
And with this stikke, above the croslet
That was ordeyned with that false get,
He stired the coles til relente gan   725
The wex agayn the fyr, as every man
(But it a fool be) woot wel it mot nede –
And al that in the stikke was out yede
And in the croslet hastily it fel.
Now, gode sirs, what wol ye bet than wel?   730
Whan that this preest thus was bigyled ageyn,
Supposing noght but trouthe, soth to seyn,
He was so glad that I can nat expresse
In no manere his mirthe and his gladnesse;
And to the chanoun he profred eftsone   735
Body and good. "Ye," quod the chanoun sone,
"Though povre I be, crafty thou shalt me finde.
I warne thee, yet is ther more bihinde.
Is ther any coper herinne?" seyde he
"Ye," quod the preest, "sir, I trowe wel ther be."   740
"Elles go by us som, and that as swythe.
Now, gode sir, go forth thy wey and hy the."
He wente his wey and with the coper cam,
And this chanoun it in his handes nam,
And of that coper weyed out but an ounce.   745

---

721 *him terve*, flay him (cf. 618).
724 *That* refers to the stick.   *ordeyned*, prepared.   *get*, device (pronounce 'jet').
725 *relente*, melt.
726 *agayn*, before.
727 *But*, except.   *woot*, etc., 'is perfectly aware that it must'.
728 *out yede*, came out.
729 *hastily*, quickly.
730 'What more could you ask?'
732 *Supposing*, imagining.   *trouthe*, honesty, plain dealing (i.e. on the Canon's part).
734 *mirthe*, joy.
735 *eftsone*, forthwith. (On rhyme see (c).)
736 *Body and good*, himself and all he possessed.
737 *povre*, poor.   *crafty* (c).
738 *warne*, tell.   *bihinde*, 'to come'.   *thee* (c).
739 *herinne*, i.e. in the house.
740 *I . . . be*, I'm sure there is.
741 *Elles*, if not.   *by*, buy.   *as swythe*, see 383n (cf. 756 below).
742 *hy the*, hurry up ('hie thee').
744 *nam*, took (c).

Al to simple is my tonge to pronounce
(As ministre of my wit) the doublenesse
Of this chanoun, roote of al cursednesse!
He semed freendly – to hem that knewe him noght –
But he was feendly, bothe in herte and thoght.   750
It werieth me to tell of his falsnesse,
And nathelees yet wol I it expresse
To th'entente that men may be war therby,
And for noon other cause, trewely.
He putte his ounce of coper in the croslet   755
And on the fyr as swythe he hath it set
And caste in poudre, and made the preest to blowe
And in his werking for to stoupe lowe
As he dide er – and al nas but a jape:
Right as him liste, the preest he made his ape.   760
And afterward in the ingot he it caste
And in the panne putte it at the laste
Of water, and in he putte his owene hond;
And in his sleve (as ye biforenhond
Herde me telle) he hadde a silver teyne.   765
He slyly took it out, this cursed heyne,
(Unwiting this preest of his false craft)
And in the pannes botme he hath it laft,
And in the water rombled to and fro,
And wonder prively took up also   770
The coper teyne (noght knowing this preest)
And hidde it, and him hente by the breest
And to him spak and thus seyde in his game,

746 *Al to*, far too. *simple*, ineloquent. *pronounce*, utter.
747 *ministre*, (the) instrument. *wit*, mind. *doublenesse*, duplicity.
748 *roote*, etc., source of all damnable wickedness (c).
750 *feendly*, devilish (c). *thoght*, mind.
751 *werieth*, wearies.
752 *expresse*, declare.
753 *To th'entente that*, in order that (c).
758 *stoupe*, stoop (c).
759 *jape*, deceitful trick.
760 'Exactly as he wished, he made a monkey of the priest' (c).
762 *at the laste*, finally.
764 *biforenhond*, previously (c).
766 *heyne*, wretch.
767 *Unwiting*, knowing nothing (cf. 771 below). *craft*, trick (cf. 737 (c) above).
768 *laft*, left (cf. *lat, thanne*, above).
769 *rombled*, 'rumbled' (c).
770 *wonder prively*, 'with a remarkably unobtrusive movement'.
771 *noght knowing*, (cf. 767n above).
772 *hente*, gripped. *breest*, i.e. the front of his gown.
773 *in his game* (c).

"Stoupeth adoun, by God, ye be to blame!
Helpeth me now as I dide yow whyler.   775
Putte in your hand and loketh what is ther."
This preest took up this silver teyne anon,
And thanne seyde the chanoun, "Lat us gon
With thise three teynes which that we han wroght,
To som goldsmith, and wite if they been oght.   780
For, by my feith, I nolde for myn hood
But if that they were silver fyn and good;
And that as swythe preved shal it be."
Unto the goldsmith with thise teynes three
They wente, and putte thise teynes in assay   785
To fyr and hamer – mighte no man sey nay,
But that they weren as hem oghte be.
This sotted preest, who was gladder than he?
Was never brid gladder agayn the day,
Ne nightingale in the sesoun of May –   790
Nas never noon that luste bet to singe,
Ne lady lustier in carolinge
Or for to speke of love and wommanhede,
Ne knight in armes to doon an hardy dede
To stonde in grace of his lady dere   795
Than had this preest this sory craft to lere;
And to the chanoun thus he spak and seyde,
"For love of God, that for us alle deyde,
And as I may deserve it unto yow –
What shal this receit coste? Telleth now!"   800

---

774 *Stoupeth*, bend (C).
775 *whyler*, a moment ago.
776 *loketh*, see.
780 *wite*, find out.   *oght*, (worth) anything (C).
781–2 'I wouldn't for the life of me have them turn out to be anything but good,
fine silver.'   *for myn hood*, a common asseveration.
783 *preved*, put to the proof (*that* is the subject; *it* is redundant).
785–6 *putte . . . in assay/To*, had assayed by (C).
786–7 'no one could deny that they were as genuine as they ought to be' (i.e.
because of their appearance).
788 *sotted*, deluded (OF *sot*, a fool).
789 *brid*, bird.   *agayn*, at the coming of.
791 *Nas never noon*, there was never any (nightingale).   *luste bet*, derived more
pleasure, delighted more.
792–3 'more full of joy as she danced (*in carolinge*) or spoke of love and the
affairs of the heart (*wommanhede*)' (C).
794 *to doon*, in doing.
795 *in grace of*, in favour with (C).
796 *Than had*, than was.   *this sory craft*, this pernicious art (C).
799 *deserve it unto yow*, pay you back, make it worth your while (C).
800 *réceit*, formula (cf. 'recipe').   *telleth*, tell (me).

"By Our Lady," quod this chanoun, "it is dere,
I warne yow wel, for, save I and a frere,
In Engelond ther can no man it make."
"No fors," quod he, "now sir, for Goddes sake –
What shal I paye, telleth me, I preye?"   805
"Ywis," quod he, "it is ful dere, I seye.
Sir, at o word – if that thee list it have,
Ye shul paye fourty pound, so God me save!
And nere the freendship that ye dide er this
To me, ye sholde paye more, ywis."   810
This preest the somme of fourty pound anon
Of nobles fette, and took hem everichon
To this chanoun for this ilke receit.
Al his werking nas but fraude and deceit!
"Sir preest," he seyde, "I kepe han no loos   815
Of my craft, for I wolde it kept were cloos,
And as ye love me, kepeth it secree;
For and men knewe al my subtilitee –
By God, they wolden han so greet envye
To me, bycause of my philosophye,   820
I sholde be deed – ther were non other weye."
"God it forbede!" quod the preest, "what sey ye?
Yet hadde I lever spenden al the good
Which that I have (and elles wexe I wood!)
Than that ye sholden falle in swich mescheef."   825
"For your good wil, sir, have ye right good preef,"
Quod the chanoun, "and farwel, *grant mercy*!"

---

801 *By our*, pronounce '*By'r*' as in Shakespeare (c).
802 'I assure you – for except for myself and a friar. . . .'
803 *can*, knows how to.
804 *No fors*, never mind.
805 *I preye*, I beg you.
806 *ful dere*, very costly.
807 *at o*, in a.   *thee list*, you wish (to).
808 *Ye shul*, you will have to.
809 *nere*, (= *ne were*), were (it) not (for).   *freendship*, act of friendship.
811 *somme*, sum.
812 *of*, in (c).
815–16 'I set no store by having (*kepe han no*) fame (*loos*, f. Lat. *laus*) as a result of my art'.   *cloos*, hidden ('close').
818 *and*, if.   *men*, people.
820 *To*, towards.   *philosophye*, alchemical knowledge.
821 'I'd end up dead – there'd be no way of avoiding it.'
822 *it*, i.e. that the Canon should be murdered.
823 *lever*, rather ('liefer').
824 *and elles wexe I wood*, may I go mad (if I wouldn't)! (c).
825 *mescheef*, ill-fortune.
826 *have ye*, etc., may you prosper.

He wente his way and never the preest him sy
After that day, and whan that this preest sholde
Maken assay, at swich tyme as he wolde,   830
Of this receit – farwel! it wolde nat be.
Lo, thus bijaped and bigyled was he!
Thus maketh he his introduccioun,
To bringe folk to hir destruccioun.

   Considereth, sirs, how that in ech estaat,   835
Bitwixe men and gold ther is debaat
So ferforth that unnethes is ther noon.
This multiplying blent so many oon
That, in good feith, I trowe that it be
The cause grettest of swich scarsetee.   840
Philosophres speken so mistily
In this craft that men can nat come therby
For any wit that men han now-a-dayes.
They mowe wel chiteren as doon thise jayes,
And in her termes sette hir lust and peyne,   845
But to hir purpos shul they never atteyne.
A man may lightly lerne, if he have aught,
To multiplye, and bringe his good to naught.
Lo! swich a lucre is in this lusty game,
A mannes mirthe it wol torne unto grame   850
And empten also grete and hevy purses,
And maken folk for to purchasen curses

---

⁸²⁸ *sy*, saw (c).
⁸²⁹ *sholde*, should (happen to).
⁸³⁰ *Maken assay*, try the experiment.
⁸³² *bijaped . . . bigyled*, tricked . . . deceived.
⁸³³ *he*, i.e. the Canon. *introduccioun*, 'overtures'.
⁸³⁵ *Considereth*, consider. *estaat*, division of society ('estate').
⁸³⁶ *debaat*, contention, quarrelling.
⁸³⁷ 'on such a wide scale (*so ferforth*, lit. so far forth) that scarcely (*unnethes*) is there any left' (c).
⁸³⁸ *multiplying*, see 116n. *blent*, blinds, deceives (*blendeth*).
⁸⁴⁰ *scarsetee*, scarcity (of gold).
⁸⁴¹ *Philosophres*, alchemical writers. *mistily*, obscurely (c).
⁸⁴² *come thereby*, attain it (the Stone).
⁸⁴³ *For*, in spite of. *wit*, intelligence, knowledge.
⁸⁴⁴⁻⁵ 'Let them go on chattering like jays and finding both their pleasure and their trouble in the fancy jargon they use.'
⁸⁴⁶ *purpos*, end. *atteyne*, attain.
⁸⁴⁷ *lightly*, easily. *aught*, any wealth.
⁸⁴⁸ *his good*, what he has.
⁸⁴⁹ *lucre*, monetary reward. *lusty*, pleasant.
⁸⁵⁰ *grame*, sorrow.
⁸⁵¹ *empten*, empty. *grete*, large.
⁸⁵² *purchasen*, get.

Of hem that han hir good therto ylent.
O fy, for shame! they that han been brent –
Allas! can they nat flee the fyres hete? 855
Ye that it use, I rede ye it lete,
Lest ye lese al – for "bet then never is late."
Never to thryve were to long a date!
Though ye prolle ay, ye shul it never finde.
Ye been as bolde as is Bayard the blinde, 860
That blundreth forth and peril casteth noon;
He is as bold to renne agayn a stoon
As for to goon besydes in the weye;
So faren ye that multiplye, I seye.
If that your eyen can nat seen aright 865
Loke that your minde lakke nought his sight.
For though ye loke never so brode, and stare,
Ye shul nat winne a myte on that chaffare,
But wasten al that ye may rape and renne.
Withdrawe the fyr, lest it to faste brenne – 870
Medleth namore with that art, I mene,
For if ye doon, your thrift is goon ful clene!
And right as swythe I wol yow tellen here
What philosophres seyn in this matere:
Lo, thus seith Arnold of the Newe Toun, 875
As his *Rosarie* maketh mencioun,
He seith right thus, withouten any lye,
"Ther may no man Mercurie mortifye
But it be with his brother knowleching,

---

853 *Of*, from.   *therto*, for that purpose.
854 *brent*, burnt.
856 *use*, practise.   *lete*, give up.
857 'Better late than never!'
858 *a date*, a time to wait (cf. 'Never is a long time').
859 *prolle*, search widely (cf. 'prowl').   *ay*, for ever.   *it*, the Stone.
860 *Bayard, the blinde*, 'blind Bayard', a blind horse (c).
861 *blundreth*, stumbles (cf. 117n).   *peril casteth noon*, imagines (there to be) no danger.
862 'He is equally confident (*bold*) that he is going straight when he bumps against a stone as when he strays off the path.'
865 *If that*, even if.   *eyen*, eyes.
866 *lakke*, lack.
867 *loke never so brode*, open your eyes never so wide.
868 *myte*, mite, farthing.   *on that chaffare*, at that business.
869 *rape and renne*, get hold of by hook or by crook (c).
871 *Medleth*, meddle.
872 *thrift*, see 186n.
874 *in*, concerning.
878 *mortifye*, see 573 (c).
879 *But*, unless.   *his brother knowleching*, along with his brother (lit. with the knowledge of) (c).

How be that he, which that first seyde this thing,   880
Of philosophres fader was, Hermes –
He seith how that the dragoun, doutelees,
Ne deyeth nat but if that he be slayn
With his brother – and that is for to sayn,
By 'the dragoun' *Mercurie*, and noon other   885
He understood, and brimstoon by 'his brother',
That out of *sol* and *luna* were ydrawe."
And therfor seyde he, "Tak heed to my sawe:
Let no man bisy him this art for to seche
But-if that he th'entencioun and speche   890
Of philosophres understonde can,
And if he do, he is a lewed man.
For this science and this conning," quod he,
"Is of the secree of secrees, parde."
Also there was a disciple of Plato   895
That on a tyme seyde his maister to
(As his book *Senior* wol bere witnesse),
And this was his demande, in soothfastnesse;
"Tel me the name of the privy stoon."
And Plato answerde unto him anoon,   900
"Tak the stoon that *Titanos* men name."
"Which is that?" quod he. "*Magnasia* is the same,"
Seyde Plato. "Ye, sir, and is it thus?
This is *ignotum per ignotius*!
What is 'Magnasia', good sir, I yow preye?"   905
"It is a water that is maad, I seye,

880 *How be that,* although ('howbeit').
881 'was the father of alchemists, Hermes' (c).
882 *dragoun,* dragon (c).   *doutelees,* undoubtedly.
883 *Ne deyeth nat,* does not die.   *but if that,* unless.   *slayn,* killed.
887 *sol,* the sun (gold).   *luna,* the moon (silver). See 882 (c).   *ydrawe,*
extracted.
888 *my sawe,* my words.
889 *seche,* seek, pursue.
890 *entencioun,* intention.
892 *if he do,* i.e. 'if he *does* pursue it (without understanding their language)'.
lewed man, ignorant man (i.e. fool).
893 *conning,* knowledge.
894 'Is concerned with (*of*) the secret of secrets' (c).
896 *on a tyme,* on one occasion.
897 *bere,* bear.
898 *demande,* request.   *soothfastnesse,* truth.
899 *privy,* secret.
901 *men name,* people call.
904 *ignotum per ignotius,* (the explanation of) an unknown thing by (recourse to)
something still more unknown.
906 *water,* fluid.

Of elementes foure," quod Plato.
"Tel me the roote, good sir," quod he tho,
"Of that water, if that it be your wille."
"Nay, nay," quod Plato, "certein, that I nille!   910
The philosophres sworn were, everichoon,
That they sholden discovere it unto noon,
Ne in no book it wryte in no manere.
For unto Crist it is so leef and dere
That he wol nat that it discovered be,   915
But wher it lyketh to his deitee
Man for t'enspyre, and eek for to defende
Whom that him lyketh; lo, this is the ende!"
Thanne conclude I thus: sin that God of hevene
Ne wil nat that the philosophres nevene   920
How that a man shal come unto this stoon –
I rede as for the beste, lete it goon!
For whoso maketh God his adversarie,
As for to werken any thing in contrarie
Of his wil – certes, never shal he thryve,   925
Thogh that he multiplye terme of his lyve.
And ther a poynt: for ended is my tale.
God sende every trewe man bote of his bale! *Amen*   928

Here is ended the Chanouns Yemannes Tale

908 *roote*, source, basis.
910 *nille*, (= *ne wille*), will not.
912 *discovere*, reveal (cf. 915).
914 *leef*, precious ('lief').
915 *wol nat*, is unwilling.
916–18 'Except under (special) circumstances – where it pleases his Godhead to reveal it to one man by inspiration and withhold it from another – and that's the end of the matter.'
919 *sin that*, since.
920 *nevene*, declare (lit. name).
922 *rede*, advice.
923 *whoso*, whoever.
924 *As for to*, in such a way as to.   *in contrarie/Of*, contrary to.
926 *terme of his lyve*, the rest of his life, till his life's end.
927 *poynt*, period, full-stop (with pun on 'point' meaning 'argument').
928 *trewe*, honest.   *bote of his bale*, remedy for his ills.

Commentary

The General Prologue

1–4. The basic metaphor here is a sexual one: April is seen as 'impregnating' March in order to bring forth from the barren winter earth the vegetation of spring. (Contrast the opening lines of T. S. Eliot's *The Waste Land*, which allude to Chaucer's poem.) 'Shoures' (l. 1) had the meaning both of 'rain-showers' and of 'showers' of falling missiles or weapons. This military metaphor is present here in a subdued way. As a result, 'pierced' (l. 2) comes to assume associations of violence and pain (as well as the obvious sexual implications underlying the literal sense). But, paradoxically, the showers are also 'sweet' – because the 'wound' experienced by the last winter month is a 'wound' of love, bringing at once death (of the old) and a new life. (For this meaning of 'shoures' cf. Chaucer's *Troilus and Criseyde*, Book I, l. 470 and Book III, l. 1064.) This kind of complexity of meaning (which incorporates both ambiguity and paradox) is not *typical* of Chaucer's poetry but is nonetheless quite common in his later work. (For a discussion of this whole stylistic question see William Empson's brilliant book *Seven Types of Ambiguity*, Chapter II.)

6. Note the whispering spirant sounds in this line ('hath . . . holt . . . heeth').

7. The sun, like the months of March and April, is unobtrusively personified: Chaucer sees it as a young athlete running a race (its course through the heavens).

7–8. The 'Ram' is *Aries*, the first of the twelve signs of the zodiac. In Chaucer's day, as is clear from his *Treatise on the Astrolabe*, the sun was thought to enter the sign of Aries on 12 March and leave it on 11 April, to enter the sign of the Bull, Taurus. This means that the sun would run a 'half-course', (i.e. half of the whole course, the period from 12 March to 11 April) in the sign of the Ram during the month of April, and then go on to run a 'half-course' in the next sign, that of the Bull. Where was the sun now? To answer this we need to turn to the Prologue of the *Man of Law's Tale* (ll. 5–6) where 18 April is given as what is probably the second day of the pilgrimage. So in l. 8 of the *General Prologue* Chaucer must be referring to 16 April, at which date the sun would have moved several degrees in the second zodiacal sign, Taurus. Thus the phrase 'his halfe-cours' must refer to the *second* of the two half-courses into which the sun's progress in Aries may be divided. And this half-course is now completed ('*hath* run'), so that the sun has completed approximately five degrees in Taurus (16 minus 11). The day on which the pilgrimage begins (see l. 822) is 17 April.

This manner of indicating time, place and season is typical of Chaucer (though not of medieval poets generally). He was a keen student of astronomy, which in this period was a mixture of real astronomy and what we would now call 'astrology'. (For further explanation of the zodiac, etc., see the chapter on 'The Heavens' in C. S. Lewis's brief and lucid book *The Discarded Image*, which describes the medievals' picture of the universe.)

9. 'Fowls' is a common ME synonym for 'birds' ('briddes') – as in the title of Chaucer's poem *The Parliament of Fowles*. Its meaning narrowed to '(barn) fowl' around the sixteenth century. *Maken*; plural verbs in ME end in *-n* (like the infinitive), though this is sometimes omitted for metrical and other reasons (it had already disappeared in more northerly dialects than Chaucer's). It is not clear from the text whether Chaucer was an old-fashioned speaker who actually retained the *-n* in his speech (as opposed to inserting it for metrical convenience or because he was writing 'poetry'. At any rate, it appears in his prose works too). Other examples of verbs ending in *-n* are *slepen* (9), *longen* (11). The point will not be noticed from here on.

10. Either Chaucer thought there were birds which slept with an eye open or (more likely) this is a poetic way of saying 'that do not sleep at night at all' (cf. l. 98 below).

1–12. Beginning with a description of different kinds of 'awakening', these lines reach a climax in the action of setting out on pilgrimage, thus bringing the world of human beings into the orbit of Nature's revival after winter, when weather was bad and roads dangerous.

11. In medieval literature 'Nature' was sometimes personified as a beautiful goddess who governs the vegetable and animal world. The idea has a complex history but there is no better introduction to it than Chaucer's poem *The Parliament of Fowles*, in which Nature 'presides' over a gathering of birds which she has convoked on St Valentine's day to choose their mates. Chaucer saw the renewed activity of birds as the symbol par excellence of the coming of spring. A famous passage in the prologue to *The Legend of Good Women*, written a year or two before the *General Prologue* (hereafter called *GP*) (1386–7) also describes this vision in verse of ecstatic buoyancy (F-version, 125–47). In ll. 4–6 of the *GP* Chaucer seems to be echoing ll. 171–3 of this poem:

> And Zephirus and Flora gentilly
> Yaf to the floures, softe and tenderly,
> Hire swote breeth, and made hem for to sprede . . .

13–18. *palmers*, originally pilgrims to the Holy Land, who brought back palms as tokens. Here, a pilgrim who travels to *any* distant place. The main *ferne halwes* were those named in 463–6. *Thomas Becket* (1118?–70) became Archbishop of Canterbury in 1162 and was killed by knights of Henry II in Canterbury Cathedral on 29 December 1170. He was canonized in 1174 and his shrine, built on the site of his murder, became one of the most magnificent in Europe and a great centre of pilgrimage. It was destroyed in 1538 by Henry VIII. (For a satirical sixteenth-century view of the Canterbury pilgrimage, see Erasmus's Colloquy on 'The Religious Pilgrimage', translated by Roger L'Estrange.) In contrast to the *devout corage* with which Chaucer claims he set out (22), medieval pilgrims often went in a holiday mood, rather than one of penance or devotional piety: their aim was to see the world in pleasant company. This was especially true of pilgrimages overseas, of which the Wife of Bath was so fond (463–7). In days when travellers faced hazards from shipwreck and robbers it was prudent to travel in company, and to security was added the pleasure of meeting people and making friends. Not a few like the Wife of Bath made their 'visitaciouns' to 'thise pilgrimages' in order 'to se, and eek for to be seye/Of lusty folk'. (Wife's Prol., D 552–7). Pilgrims often brought back replicas of relics as souvenirs, though Chaucer's contemporary Langland suggests that their main acquisition was a heap of lying tales –

> Pilgrims and palmers·plighted them together,
> To seek St James·and saints of Rome;
> Went forth in their way·with many wise tales,
> And had leave to lie·all their lives after.
> *(Piers Plowman, B, Prol. 46–9)*

Chaucer seems to take a more indulgent view of his characters' mixed or unserious motives for making a pilgrimage, and it is not until the end of the *Tales* as a whole that he makes the Parson recall to the company that a pilgrimage to a shrine is an image of the 'pilgrimage' (*peregrinatio*, wandering) of man's life on earth, and has for its goal the 'Jerusalem celestial' of Heaven.

17. *seke*: *seeke* – identical rhyme. For a different kind of homophonic rhyme, cf. ll. 187–8, where the second rhyme word ('-served') is etymologically related to 'served' (l. 187) in a way that *seke*: *seeke* are not related. (Cf. also ll. 523–4, 671–2 and comment.)

20. The Tabard Inn still stood in the sixteenth century. This is the first of the many references to actual places known to his audience by which Chaucer achieves a general effect of realism. In spite of the pronoun 'I', we should not necessarily suppose that Chaucer had himself made the pilgrimage to Canterbury, although this seems probable enough. The distinction between Chaucer *the man, the author* and *the dramatic character* is discussed interestingly by E. T.

Donaldson in his essay 'Chaucer the Pilgrim' in Schoeck and Taylor (eds), *Chaucer Criticism*, Vol. I.

24. This line is puzzling, since there are clearly *thirty* pilgrims (excluding Chaucer). William Blake, in his essay on the Canterbury Pilgrims (1809), suggested ingeniously that the 'Webbe' and the 'Dyer' in l. 362 were one and the same man, and that Chaucer originally wrote 'a Webbe Dyer' ('a Cloth Dyer'). But he may simply have counted the number wrongly, possibly recalling the *three* priests of his initial plan as *two* when he actually wrote l. 24. (See comment on l. 164.)

37–42. These lines suggest that Chaucer may have intended to describe the pilgrims in an order which really *did* accord systematically with their 'degree' (see Introduction). Yet at ll. 743–6 he apologizes for not having done so. Either he changed his mind after completing the first five portraits (which observe priority of social rank) or deliberately began 'acordaunt to resoun' in order to indicate a clear-cut intention to his reader, and then, no less deliberately, proceeded to follow a less rigid, more casual and natural-seeming order, so as to avoid the risk of monotony.

37. The modern word 'think' comes ultimately from the Old English *thencan*, but the '-thinks' in 'methinks' derives from the word *thyncean*, 'to seem'. In Chaucer's time the two were distinct but had begun to merge, owing to the closeness of the two ideas they expressed: what 'seems so' to me is hard to distinguish from 'what I think'.

The Knight

43, etc. The word 'worthy' appears five times in this portrait. Contrast its meaning here with the one it acquires in 217 or 243.

45–6. The best way to appreciate the *chivalrye* of the Knight is to read a chivalric romance like Malory's *Morte D'Arthur* or the Knight's own *Tale*. In the latter the dying hero Arcite praises his friend and former rival Palamon (in words closely akin to 45–6) for possessing

> . . . trouthe, honour, knighthede,
> Wisdom, humblesse, estat, and heigh kinrede,
> Fredom, and al that longeth to that art . . .   [belongs
>
> (A 2789–91)

Estat (= wealth) and *heigh kinrede* were not essential to a knight but *wisdom* and *humblesse* were (cf. *GP*, 68, 69). In Chaucer's *Franklin's Tale* the importance of *trouthe* is illustrated in the character of Arveragus (see also *Burrow* on *Sir Gawain and the Green Knight*), and the whole poem illustrates varieties of *fredom*. The 'art' of chivalry was basically that of the mounted warrior-knight – the word came from Fr. *cheval* – but Chaucer is stressing in the *chivalrye*

loved by the Knight (45) an ideal concept, a faint remnant of which
survives in the modern 'chivalrous action, gesture'. If we punctuate

> . . . he loved chivalrye:
> Trouthe and honour, etc.

(or, 'chivalrye –', as in the text) the various abstract qualities then
become not *further* objects of the Knight's 'love' but rather *component
elements* of an all-embracing ideal. (The fact that we must in any
case pause in reading at the end of 45 means that both this interpreta-
tion and the usual one ['chivalrye,/Trouthe, etc.'] are possible and
can even be held simultaneously in the mind.)

The *chivalric* was, of course, only one side of 'knighthood'. There
was also a social side and a corresponding social ideal, for knights
had a key place in the structure of society as the lowest but most
numerous section of the nobility, below the lesser barons. Langland
stresses the duty of this class to protect the church and common
people 'from wasters and from wicked men that this world destroy'.
The social ideal of knighthood requires that knights should treat
their tenants with fairness and compassion, should refrain from
ordering their inferiors to do evil, and should avoid evil company
themselves. Their exalted position in society is merely temporary
and death levels all men – 'For in the charnel-house at church who
can tell a churl/Or a knight from a knave there?' Like Chaucer's,
Langland's ideal knight must cultivate a 'true tongue' and pursue
'wisdom and wit'. (*Piers Plowman*, B. VI, 29, 50–1.) That Chaucer's
knight *is* a landowner is attested by the very existence of his yeoman
(a forester); but Chaucer has isolated one aspect of the many-sided
reality of the fourteenth-century knight (part sportsman, part land-
lord, part justice, part mercenary-soldier) in order to make him the
personification of the ideal of chivalry.

47. The Knight's true 'lord' was either the King (of England), or
God; in the latter case, it is the Crusades that Chaucer has in mind.
But *lordes* may also mean 'any lord he happened to be fighting for at
the time' (as a mercenary), or it may be plural – 'his lords' war (s)'.
The fact that *werre* is singular does suggest that Chaucer meant *one*
'war', not a series of wars; but the rest of the sentence, from 'therto'
to 'hethenesse' points to a plural meaning, because all the knight's
campaigns are included. Perhaps it is best to say 'his lord's war' and
leave it as indefinite as the original.

51–66. The Knight's campaigns seem to cover a period of some
forty years (from *c.* 1345 to 1385) and this would make him a man
in his late fifties. He had fought against the Moors in Spain (*Algezir*,
1344) and North Africa (the date of *Belmarye* is uncertain); against
the Saracens in Egypt (*Alisaundre*, 1365) and Asia Minor (*Attalia* and
Lyeys, 1361, 1367); for the Turkish Sultan ('the lord of Palatye');
with the Knights of the Teutonic Order against the Lithuanians,

who accepted Christianity in 1385, and against the Russian Tartars. The Lithuanian campaign may have been intended as the one from which he is returning (the date of the *GP* being *c.* 1387), but Chaucer has not given the campaigns in chronological order, rather as an illustration that 'no Christian man had ridden further than he'.

66. The 'other heathen' mentioned here is being distinguished from the one he fought against at Tremezen; but since the lord of Palatye was himself a heathen, Chaucer could mean that the knight fought (as a mercenary) for one heathen ruler against another.

70. The double negatives here – as so often – are emphatic rather than logical: they do not 'cancel out' to give a positive meaning.

74–8. The knight's soiled clothes, which he has not stopped to change, contrast strikingly with the smart array of several other pilgrims (including his son the Squire). They also hint at his awareness of the penitential purpose of a pilgrimage – *he* is not setting out 'to se, and eek for to be seye'.

The Squire

79 ff. The Squire's portrait combines an impression of elegance and of strength – he is fighter and lover, where his father is only the fighter. Another contrast with the Knight's portrait is the strong emphasis on visual details where the latter concentrated on the moral qualities and achievements of the subject. The Squire is not 'superficial' in a bad sense, but he clearly *is* concerned with outward appearance (looks, manners) in a way the Knight is not. His *curteisye* lacks the deep moral proportions of the Knight's 'gentleness'. Appropriately, therefore, his (unfinished) Tale turns out to be a treatment more of the superficies of the chivalric life than the Knight's, which penetrates beneath the trappings to the moral essence of knighthood.

Various details in the portrait recall the descriptions of *Mirth* and the *God of Love* in Chaucer's *Romaunt of the Rose*, a translation of the French *Roman de la Rose*: with ll. 83–4 compare

> With lymes wrought at poynt devys,
> Delyver, smert, and of gret myght.
> (Mirth, Romaunt, 830–1)

and also 89–90:

> His garnement was everydell
> Yportreied and ywrought with floures,
> By dyvers medlyng of coloures, etc.
> (God of Love, Romaunt, 896–8)

But the *GP* lines are no mere repetition – and the whole portrait has a compression and wit that the translation (written some twenty years before) lacks. Thus in 89 the phrase 'Embrouded was *he*' fuses the ideas of clothing and man in one image of springtime freshness and growth, so that the 'floures whyte and rede' (90) can refer equally to the flower pattern on the young man's clothes and to his complexion. Both thoughts are as it were held in suspension in the one effortlessly simple expression. Mirth in the *Romaunt* is given a complexion 'rody and whit in every place' (820) and the God of Love a flowery robe, which is lengthily described (888–906). The Squire's portrait condenses details from both into a new (and more poetically effective) whole. (This power of condensation is a key feature of Chaucer's mature verse.) Lines 81, 97–8 also convey a witty, detached attitude which is more interesting (as well as more complex) than the somewhat naïve catalogue-style of the *Romaunt* description. (The latter can be categorized as 'medieval' in a delimiting sense; the art of the former is timeless; cf. also Intro. p. 10–11.)

80. The Southern English form *lovyere* is more emphatic than Chaucer's normal East Midland 'lovere' (the metre requires the word to be stressed and followed by a short pause). A *bachelor* was a probationer-knight – one who was proving himself in arms. (Compare the title 'bachelor' in the Universities – the grade between 'scholar' and 'master'; and that of 'journeyman' in the craft-gilds – between 'apprentice' and 'master-craftsman'.)

86. *Flaundres*: Chaucer probably had in mind the notorious 'crusade' against Pope Clement VII's supporters (1383), led by Henry Despenser, Bishop of Norwich. Note too that Chaucer himself took part in campaigns of the Hundred Years' War in Artois and Picardy (1369). On the 'crusade' and on the historical background generally see M. McKisack's valuable study *The Fourteenth Century* (esp. pp. 429–33).

92. May was sometimes represented as a youth (resembling the Squire) in the illuminated Books of Hours. But the phrase here seems a spontaneous response to the vigour and 'freshness' suggested by Squire and month alike. Chaucer seems to have had a special liking for the word 'fresh' (rather like Keats's for 'rich'). It fittingly characterizes a major part both of his poetry and of his attitude to life generally.

99–100. Compare these lines with the descriptions of the two (rather less idealized) squires Damian and Aurelius in the *Merchant's* and *Franklin's Tales* respectively.

The Yeoman

101 ff. The Yeoman, though a servant, may have been an independent farmer holding land from the Knight (by 'yeoman-service'), judging by the evidence of his 'gay' dagger and silver 'Cristofre'. He could have easily combined this with acting as a forester on the Knight's estates. He is, with the Plowman, the only pilgrim to receive a full description but no tale. Chaucer may have intended

to rewrite the tale of *Gamelyn* (an anonymous romance telling the same story as Shakespeare's *As you Like It*) which is found in several MSS of the *Canterbury Tales* along with Chaucer's genuine works.

The image of the Yeoman clad in green conveys an impression of full summer after the springtime image of the Squire which precedes. This is reinforced by the detail of his *broun visage* (109) – either a naturally dark complexion or, more likely, tanned by the summer sun in his mainly outdoor existence (cf. the Shipman, 394). The details of the description are both 'naturalistic' and serve a decorative, semi-symbolic function; they provide both colour-contrasts and a 'seasonal' contrast with the Squire's portrait (red-and-white/spring: brown-and-green/summer) in a way that is both 'painterly' and 'poetic' and gives literal force to the term 'portrait' as a description of Chaucer's art.

107. 'His arrows did not fall short in their flight as a result of having the feathers too close to the shaft of the arrow (giving it inadequate support in its flight through the air)'. In this reading *with* = virtually 'on account of' and the reference in 'dresse' (106) is to the Yeoman's *making* his arrows, rather than to his placing them in the quiver in such a way that the feathers do not get crushed and give the arrows an appearance of 'drooping'.

The Prioress

118 ff. In the portrait of the Prioress, one of the most delicately subtle in the poem (see Introduction, p. 22), the main irony lies in the fact that one who should be a representative of the spiritual life is described as an epitome of refined worldliness, a creature better cut out for court life than the constraints of convent-discipline.

120. St Eligius (seventh century), a goldsmith, became Bishop of Noyon. He was noted for his personal beauty and his courtesy, and is thus an appropriate figure for the Prioress to swear by. *If* she swore, that is – for Chaucer may be alluding to the story of Eligius's refusal to take an oath, as a way of saying that 'she did not swear at all' (cf. l. 10 and Commentary above), *by* being read as 'according to, in the manner of (St Loy)'. But the allusion might be missed, and a more natural meaning is that 'she *did* swear, but used only genteel-sounding oaths' – i.e. not the ferocious oaths 'so grete and so damp-nable' common in the period, like those used by the Miller (*Prologue* to his *Tale*, A 3125) or the Host (Intro. to *The Pardoner's Tale*, C 288) and denounced by the Pardoner in the opening of his *Tale* (C 472). Nuns, like all religious, were forbidden to swear.

121. *Madame* was the title of all nuns (priests were called 'sir'). *Eglentyne*, a name more suitable for a heroine of the courtly romances (they had names like 'Alundyne' and 'Blancheflour') than a nun; but there is a 'Madame Argentyn' on record (on the relation between the portrait and contemporary actuality see the entertaining

chapter on 'Madame Eglentyne' in Eileen Power's *Medieval People*).

122. The 'divine service' consisted of the set prayers of the eight canonical Hours of the Breviary, which monks and nuns were obliged by their rule to sing or recite.

123. Nasal singing (which is still practised) was less tiring than the usual method, and was useful during the long hours of the *servyce divyne*.

125. The Prioress could speak French of the kind she had learned at the Benedictine convent of St Leonard, near Stratford-Bow, Middlesex. This would be, probably, 'school-French' and not the more correct and polished Parisian French of the type spoken by the English Court (and, possibly, Chaucer himself, who had travelled in France). The line would thus be deflating the Prioress's pretensions to 'chere of court'. If there is a further cryptic meaning – e.g. that 'Stratford French' was peculiarly bad – it is lost on Chaucer's modern readers.

127–35. These details about table-manners are taken almost verbatim from a passage in the thirteenth-century French poem, the *Roman de la Rose*.

136. *raughte*. Copland argues that *raughte* comes not from OE *ræhte* (pret. of *ræcan*, 'reach') but from the pret. of *hræctan*, 'belch', the frequentative form of *hræcan*, 'spit', 'hawk'. *after* then becomes a preposition expressing time. The argument is unconvincing. Chaucer has gone out of his way in 127–35 to emphasize the Prioress's conscious stress on elegant table-manners, with which 'belching', 'decorous' (*semely*) or not, would surely be totally inconsistent – to the Prioress, at any rate!

151. Nuns were not permitted to wear pleated wimples, which were a form of 'ornament'.

152. 'Grey' eyes seem to have been much admired in the Middle Ages, but it is not certain exactly what colour 'grey' signified. Chaucer may have had in mind the type of stained glass called *grisaille*, a translucent grey-green ('greye as *glas*'), of which there are good examples at York Minster.

154–6. Broad foreheads were thought beautiful at this time – but nuns were supposed to keep theirs covered to just above the eyebrows. *undergrowe* need suggest no more than that she was big-built – i.e. her forehead was not excessively large, because she was quite a big woman anyway. Criseyde in Chaucer's *Troilus and Criseyde* is a model of beauty and yet Chaucer says of her 'She nas nat with the leste of hir stature' (i.e. not the smallest of women) – a similar 'litotic' description. (See further, Introduction, p. 11.) There is no hint whatever that the Prioress's size makes her 'comic . . . and a bit pathetic', as one scholar has suggested.

158–9. The five *gaudes* stood for the five 'Our Fathers' dividing the decades of 'Hail Marys' in red (*coral*, 158). The rosary, intended as an aid to meditative prayer, here seems by its form more of a decorative ornament than anything else.

120, 146, 154, 160 all describe various small breaches of the rules governing the lives of nuns (note that they *are* small, but it is the attitude they reflect that is important): they were forbidden to swear, keep pets, expose their foreheads or wear ornaments. The Prioress's indulgences spring from personal vanity; her worldliness is obvious but not blatant. But it may be that her foibles would look more serious since as a Prioress she was supposed to set an example to the nuns under her authority in the convent.

162. The brooch's capital **A** surmounted by a crown, standing for AMOR (the 'crowning' virtue, love) is ambiguous (cf. also *charitable*, 143). The Virgilian motto had long been referred to heavenly love (charity, CARITAS), but the setting of this little detail raises doubts in our minds – and is meant to. The Prioress's *Tale* however, does not increase them: slightly sentimental (cf. 11, 144, 148 of the portrait), it is nonetheless unimpeachably in character for a nun.

164. The '*Second Nun*', as she is usally referred to, tells the story of the life of St Cecilia, which precedes the arrival of the Canon and his Yeoman (see *Prol.* to *Canon's Yeoman's Tale* in this vol.). Chaucer seems to have reduced his 'preestes three' to one, giving him one of the finest of the tales, the story of Chantecleer and Pertelote (the *Nun's Priest's Tale*). See also l. 24 and Commentary, above.

The Monk

165 ff. The Monk's worldliness is rather more forthright than that of the Prioress, and it leads Chaucer to commend (ironically) his blatant rejection of the ascetic ideals of monasticism:

> And I seyde, his opinioun was good.
>
> (183)

This line can be read in one of two ways, both of which yield an ironic meaning: either Chaucer is presenting himself as a naïve person impressed by the Monk's manner and way of life ('Chaucer the Pilgrim') in order to indicate that to a *man of sense* the Monk's outrageous attitude is clearly to be condemned; or else, we can take the 'I' of this line as standing more or less for the poet Chaucer himself, who is making the directly ironic statement: 'I *said* his opinion was a *good* one (but of course *meant* that it was a very *bad* one'). The third possibility, that Chaucer really *was* naïve (or cynical) and genuinely impressed by the Monk's 'opinion' seems hardly worth considering. Later developments in the *Canterbury Tales* lend support to the first reading (which is now widely accepted), but the second one seems equally valid in the context of the *GP*. (See also 20 (c) and *Robertson*, p. 255.)

168. *deyntee*; the noun (from which the adj. derives) comes ulti-

mately from Lat. *dignitas* (worthiness, dignity) and meant 'choice', 'worth'. The adj. later narrowed its meaning from 'choice' to 'fastidious' ('choosy'), and from 'precious' to 'delicately pretty or pleasing'.

172. *lord* was a title usually confined to bishops and abbots among the clergy (cf. also 121, above) whereas this Monk seems to have been no more than a prior or sub-prior at the most, although 'to been an abbot *able*'. Chaucer may be suggesting that though not an abbot yet he *behaved* like one.

173–6. Either 'held his course (Lat. *spatium*, 'space') in accordance with the way the modern world was going' (i.e. was not ascetic, but worldly like your contemporary monk) or else '(left the past behind) and *in the meanwhile* ['*the space*' used absolutely] followed the new fashion'. The lines seem to echo a couplet from a Latin work by Chaucer's friend John Gower, the *Vox Clamantis*: 'Nowadays the rule of St Bernard or St Maur counts for little – nay more, positively displeases these modern monks'.

177. The 'text' was St Jerome's comment on Esau: 'you will scarcely find in the scriptures one holy man who was a hunter; holy fishermen, yes'. The 'hunting-monk' was no rarity in the fourteenth century. Chaucer may particularly have had in mind the notorious William de Cloune, abbot of the Augustinian canons at Leicester, who had died some ten years before the *GP* was written. He was an expert hare-hunter and master of greyhounds.

180. A Latin proverb said that 'Just as a fish without water lacks life, so does a monk away from a monastery'. Langland paraphrases it:

> Right as fishes in flood·when water fails them,
> Die for drouth·when they dry are lying,
> Right so religion·rots and starves [dies]
> That out of convent and cloister·covets to dwell.
> (*Piers Plowman*, C, VI. 149–52)

and he also describes a monk who is

> A priker on a palfrey·from manor to manor,
> An heap of hounds at his arse·as he a lord were.
> (B, X, 308–9)

185. *cloistre*, meant literally: fourteenth-century monks read their books at 'carrells' or study-spaces formed from the arches of the cloister (as at Gloucester Cathedral, for example).

187. 'How shall the *world* be served?' Heavily ironic: monks by profession renounced 'the world' for a life of dedicated service to God.

190, 191–2, 194, 196. Monks were forbidden to hunt, keep greyhounds, wear expensive fur on their habits or sport ornaments (cf. the Prioress, above). They supposedly aspired to a more ascetic standard of life than the ordinary ('secular') clergy who lived 'in the world' (Chaucer's Parson is a powerfully contrasting example).

191. 'Hunting the hare' sometimes symbolized in medieval art the 'Hunt of Venus' (i.e. an allegorical representation of an amatory pursuit or chase, the prey being the hare, which had a sexual significance). See, for example, the illustrations in *Robertson*, pls. 27, 28, *61*; also pp. 113, *253–6*. Whether we should find innuendoes in *manly* (167) and the *love-knotte* of 197 is not certain, but it is suggested by the possible sexual pun on *venerye* (166) and *priking* (191). (cf. also the Host's later remarks in the Monk's *Prologue*, 1944–64, and the satire on the lascivious monk – also an 'outrider' – in the *Shipman's Tale*.)

The Friar

208 ff. Various details in the Friar's portrait echo Hypocrisy's description of himself in the *Romaunt of the Rose*. With 245–50 compare

> For how that I me povre feyne,
> Yit alle pore folk I disdeyne . . .
> For whan I see beggers quaking
> Naked on mixnes, al stinking,   [middens
> For hungre crye and eke for care,
> I entremete not of her fare.
> > [have nothing to do with
> > (6489–90, 6495–8)

Chaucer did not specify which of the 'ordres foure' his Friar belonged to, presumably because he felt his satire was equally applicable to all of them. Apart from his general worldliness, this friar is characterized by greed for money, amorousness and a liking for pomp and display. Line 261 says that he is '*like* a Master'; two further points suggest that he *was* a graduate of one of the universities. One is his *Tale*, a brilliantly clever and subtle attack on Summoners. The other is lines 2184–8 of the Summoner's *Tale*, a reply to this attack, which become doubly effective if the real Friar is a 'Master' like his fictional counterpart.

209. A 'limiter' was a Friar appointed to beg within a certain *limited* area and also (with the bishop's permission) to preach, bury, and hear confessions. *solempne* was a word of many meanings; here the word points to the Friar's sense of his own importance, as illustrated by lines like 243–5, 261, etc.

210. These were the Franciscans, Dominicans, Augustinians and Carmelites, all founded at various times in the thirteenth century.

218–20. Certain grave sins could not be forgiven by an ordinary parish priest but were 'reserved' for the bishop. Some friars had the privilege of absolving these sins, without the leave of the parish priest. *As seyde himself* suggests that perhaps the Friar's claim was not genuine.

227-8. I make 'dorste make avaunt' parenthetical; but taking 'He wiste that . . .' as a noun-clause object of 'dorste make avaunt' (main verb) gives the meaning 'he could boldly declare *that* he knew him to be (truly) repentant'. This latter reading stresses that the Friar was able to state publicly his knowledge of the (rich) sinner's 'true' repentance.

238, 264. The white neck and the lisping were associated with licentiousness. But this is not to suggest that the Friar was *effeminate*, as l. 239 shows.

246-7. Note the suggestion here that 'honest' (i.e. respectable) people avoid contact with the poor – a gross perversion of the original ideal of the mendicant orders – poverty!

250. This line echoes line 99, with the ironic suggestion that the amorous Friar resembles the Squire.

253. It is curious to note that in his *Tale* the Friar himself satirizes the *Summoner* for his greed in attempting (howbeit unsuccessfully) to extort a saucepan from an old widow.

256. The phrase was proverbial and usually means that what a man *earns* is more than his income from his own property. The problem here is that the Friar supposedly had *no* property, and his 'income' should have been no more than what he obtained by begging. Perhaps Chaucer meant to suggest by 'purchas' in this context kinds of income to which the Friar was not entitled, or else that the Friar used to keep back part of what he received (the 'purchas' in question), which actually amounted to more than he turned in to his superiors in the Order (his 'rente').

257. This line almost certainly hides a sharply satirical attack on the Friar's sexual vices under the supposedly mild comparison of him to a playful puppy. The *Chaucer Concordance* shows that the word *rage* usually has a sexual connotation in Chaucer's poetry. Taken together with 238, 264, and 212-13, the line more than bears such a reading. 212-13 contains an innuendo that the young women whose marriages the Friar arranged at his own expense were girls whom he himself had seduced (cf. also 211, 234, 241).

258. Love-days were days on which legal disputes could be settled out of court. The local clergy (or the friars) sometimes took part as arbitrators. Perhaps Chaucer intends this line as satire rather than as praise of the Friar's 'help'. Love-days would be yet another means of increasing his 'purchas' (see above). He may also have been amused at the overtones of the name 'love-days' when associated with the amorous Friar. (The clergy at this period were, as it happens, forbidden to take part in love-days unless on behalf of the poor – an unlikely occupation for this Friar.)

263. An allusion to his stoutness (cf. 216, 248).

Satire of the friars, often exceedingly bitter, abounds in poetry of the later Middle Ages. How just it was is difficult to assess, but hardly any writers of the period have anything *good* to say about them. The friars had clearly declined from the high ascetic standards of the founders of their Orders, but we need to allow for exaggeration in the poetry of both Chaucer and Langland. (Cf. the virulent satire of the hypocritical gluttonous Doctor of Divinity – a friar – in *Piers Plowman*, B, Passus XIII, 25 ff.)

The Merchant
270 ff. In the portrait of the Merchant Chaucer is satirizing less the mercantile spirit than a variety of hypocrisy (cf. the preceding portrait of the Friar). Merchants were widely disliked in the fourteenth century (see Langland's tart remarks, B, II, 212–14; VII, 18–37) as a relatively new class of people, difficult to accommodate in the old threefold division of society (see below, Commentary on 529 ff), who made quick fortunes, often by devious means. Chaucer's own father was a wine-merchant and he probably did not dislike them as a *class* (as Langland seems to have done), but he expresses, although with understatement, an unusual contempt. Perhaps he disliked the merchant because he was not a simple trader but also a moneylender, the ancestor of the modern financier. Lending money at interest, whether or not the rates were exorbitant, was regarded as a sin (usury) and Christians were forbidden to engage in it (see Ch. I of Tawney's classic study). For a further picture of *chevisaunce* cf. the merchant in the *Shipman's Tale*.

276–7. Orwell, near Harwich, lay opposite the Dutch port of Middleburg. The wool-staple was located at the latter town between 1384 and 1388 (the period when Chaucer probably started on the *GP*). This indicates that the Merchant had a special interest in wool (the biggest and most profitable trade in late medieval England). But the portrait remains unparticularized, probably because Chaucer was more concerned with his pilgrim's character and attitudes (particularly to money-making) than with his precise enterprises. The only commodity he *sells* is 'sheeldes' (278; i.e. French *écus*) – an illegal practice. In this he corresponds to the modern speculator.

284. The London merchant Gilbert Maghfield, whose career and interests closely resembled the Merchant's, has been seen as the model for Chaucer's portrait. (Chaucer himself borrowed money from him in 1392.) But if a real man *did* lie behind this character, then this was all the more reason for refusing to name him if an effective satire was aimed at. (In Pope's words: 'a nameless character can never be found out, but by its *truth* and *likeness*'.)

The Clerk of Oxford

285 ff. The Clerk of Oxford, one of Chaucer's idealized creations, is nevertheless subject to a few touches of the blandest satire (287–9 and possibly 297–8). Chaucer, admirer of learning as he was, seems to have been a man of the world. But the piety, dedication, disinterestedness and seriousness of the Clerk would have exercised a certain attraction on one brought up in luxurious courts and not in the austere atmosphere of medieval Oxford. The Clerk contrasts strongly with characters like Langland's gluttonous Doctor of Divinity, who ate 'many sundry meats, mortrewes and puddings . . . wild brawn and eggs y-fried with grease' (B, XIII, 62–3) or the lecherous young students of the *Miller's* and *Reeve's Tales* and the clerk of Orleans in the *Franklin's Tale*, whose hobby was magic! His dedication to logic contrasts sharply with that of the

> yonge clerkes, that been likerous   [eager
> To reden artes that been curious

and who

> Seken in every halke and every herne
> Particuler sciences for to lerne.   [nook and cranny

(Franklin's Tale, F 1119–22)

286. Robinson takes this as meaning he had 'long since proceeded to logic' but 'was still pursuing his studies, perhaps . . . for the Master's degree'. But the natural sense is 'he had long been a student of logic' (and still was one). In his *Prologue* the Clerk claims to have

> Lerned at Padowe of a worthy clerk   [i.e. Petrarch

the tale of Griselda that he tells, and this suggests he may once have been one of the *scolares vagantes* described so fascinatingly by Helen Waddell as wandering over Europe from university to university to learn what they had to teach.

289. The Clerk's 'hollowness' is due to both protracted study and ascetic living.

291–2. Probably he had not been looking for a benefice. Clerks were usually (though not necessarily) men who had received one of the 'minor orders' of the Church which preceded full or 'holy orders', terminating in the priesthood. 291–2 suggest both that the Clerk *was* in minor orders and also uninterested in the type of secular employment medieval graduates (including those in holy orders) frequently sought, e.g. with nobles or the king. The Clerk wished to remain a scholar because he sought learning as an end in itself.

293–6. Contrast the way of life of the Oxford clerk Nicholas in *The Miller's Tale*, who had at *his* bed's head

a gay sautrye,
On which he made a-nightes melodye.

(A 3213–14)

Nicholas, moreover, had a private income ('rente') as well as support from his 'freendes' (the usual Middle English term for family and relatives (A 3219–20).

The Man of Law

309 ff. The portrait of the Man of Law is rather similar to that of the Merchant, but less hostile. Chaucer both admires his learning and efficiency (which are quite genuine, and issue in a more solid success than the Merchant's activities) and regards with mild scepticism his appearance of being wise (313) and of having more business than he can handle (322). With acute psychological insight, Chaucer realized that to impress the world (and attract clients) a lawyer needs to appear in great demand – and there are times when this state of affairs has to be simulated. Langland (*Piers Plowman*, B, VII, 39–61) and other satirists attacked lawyers for their greed, dishonesty and indifference to justice, but Chaucer's criticism is less fundamental and at the same time more subtle and delicate. Lines 316–17 do not necessarily imply dishonesty, but there is no doubt that the Lawyer is being *ironically* praised for putting his 'science' and 'heigh renoun' at the service of his own profit. Coming hard upon the portrait of the unworldly Clerk (who refused *offyce* and put *his* 'science' to such a different use) the description gains in ironic emphasis.

309. Sergeants-at-law (*servientes ad legem*) were senior barristers from whose ranks the judges of the King's court were chosen. The Man of Law is obviously more distinguished than the types of petty avarice usually attacked by medieval satirists. (But cf. *Prologue to Piers Plowman*, 212–14.) Chaucer's is not a *radical* satire which probes the very basis of moral and social life, but is nearer to that of Jane Austen than that of Swift. Langland writes that if evil is punished and good rewarded in society lawyers will become superfluous (B-text, V, 146). He attacks lawyers for seeking profit rather than seeking to advance justice irrespective of their clients' ability to pay large fees (B, VII, 57 ff). Chaucer, by contrast, accepts the *status quo* as usual and is more interested, as a satirist, in the *foibles* of human nature (e.g. the Sergeant's efforts to seem busier than he was) than absolute principles of right and wrong. His art is realistic in its holding up the mirror to nature (in Hamlet's words) 'to show virtue her own feature, scorn her own image, and the very age and body of the time his form and pressure'.

323. *termes* may possibly refer to the legal year-books compiled under the headings of the law-terms (Hodgson).

326. The word *pinche* is perhaps a punning allusion to Thomas Pynchbeck of Lincolnshire, a well-known sergeant-at-law whose career closely resembles that of Chaucer's pilgrim.

The Franklin
331 ff. The Franklin's portrait shows Chaucer's satire at its most genial. (His *Tale* is an exploration of the idea of *gentillesse*, a theme which Chaucer wrote about with obvious personal conviction in the short poem of that name). One suspects that Chaucer was himself something of an 'epicure', too (see his tale of *Sir Thopas*, Prol. B, 1890–1 and the *Envoy* to his friend Scogan [*Robinson*, p. 538], both of which allude to his corpulence). He obviously admires the Franklin's exuberant hospitality (to get some idea of its scale, cf. Thrupp, pp. 150–1) and the criticism in 353 ff is of the mildest sort.

332. The daisy was Chaucer's favourite flower (see his rapturous description of it in the Prologue to *The Legend of Good Women*) and the choice of this simile indicates his sympathy and admiration for the Franklin.

333. That is, his character was benevolent, warm-hearted and good-humoured (see Commentary below on 420–1 and cf. 458, 587, 624 and Commentary).

336. The medieval view that Epicureanism identified pleasures of sense (such as eating and drinking) with the highest good ('perfect felicity') was a distorted oversimplification, but it has determined the modern meaning of the word 'epicure'.

355–6. Chaucer himself had also held these offices (see Biographical Note).

361 ff. The passage on the *Gildsmen* is a piquant commentary on the 'rising middle classes' of Chaucer's day and on the social pretensions of the richer craftsmen's wives. The gildsmen are not given any tales, and they are obviously, in their anonymity, the most expendable of the pilgrims (their servant the Cook is far more of an individual).

377. The desire to take precedence at religious services was a foible shared by that other notable representative of the new bourgeoisie, the Wife of Bath (see 450).

379 ff. The gildsmen's *Cook* had probably been hired for the occasion (we learn later in the *Tales* that he had a cook-shop in London and it was perhaps here that Chaucer acquired the first-hand acquaintance with his cooking implied by 387). His *Tale*, a bawdy fabliau (see Introduction, p. 6, n.), was left unfinished.

The Shipman
388 ff. The Shipman's portrait is a superb instance of Chaucer's satirical method. A seemingly objective description of the man's craft (396–7) and cold-blooded callousness (398–400), it makes its

point far more effectively than direct moral comment. (See also Introduction, pp. 25, 26.) Chaucer can appreciate the man's expert seamanship while quietly (and devastatingly) exposing his villainy. The Shipman has been thought to be modelled on a Peter Risshenden of Dartmouth, captain of a ship called *Maudelayne*.

390. The Shipman is unused to riding a horse.

397. Bordeaux was, then as now, a great centre of the French wine trade.

410. 'Maudelayne' = 'Magdalen' (cf. the modern pronunciation of 'Magdalen(e) College'). From the name comes the adj. 'maudlin' (tearfully sentimental), after Mary Magdalen, traditionally identified with the woman who wept over the feet of Jesus (Luke, vii, 38).

The Doctor of Phisyk

411 ff. The Doctor of Phisyk is treated a little like the Man of Law. Chaucer acknowledges his learning (429 ff) and his efficiency (419) but at the same time exposes his adroitness in making profit from the sick – whether through association with apothecaries (427) or through capitalizing on the results of the plague (442). The satirical touches, almost casual in their lightness, are all the deadlier. Contrast the direct invective and exhortation of Langland (B, VI, 275–6): 'Many leeches [doctors] are murderers. . . . They do men die through their drinks [potions] ere destiny will it'. The 'leeches' were usually barbers. The other types of medieval physician were the operating *surgeons*, men of practical experience often noted for their scientific skill and professional integrity; and, more respected but probably less reliable, the university-trained *physicians*, whose knowledge was based on books and theory. Chaucer's Doctor, whose title is not generic but denotes his university degree, belongs to this last group. (See *Power* [ii].)

414. *Astrology* formed the 'ground' of much medieval medical theory and practice because of the belief that man (the 'microcosm' or little world) was influenced in innumerable ways by the greater universe (or 'macrocosm'). Astrology was the art of interpreting the influences of the stars and planets on man in order to use them for one's own ends. *Astrological medicine*, like alchemy (see *Canon's Yeoman's Tale*, Introduction, in this volume), was inherited from the Greeks and accepted on authority, but not all physicians believed in it. (See below on 429 ff).

416. The planetary *hours* were twenty-four divisions of the day (of varying lengths according to the time of year), measured from dawn to dusk and from dusk to dawn. In astrological medicine the Doctor had to know which hours were propitious for his patient, and this was determined by reference to the latter's horoscope. 'Natural magic' here means roughly the same as astrology (it is this which is practised by the Clerk of Orleans in *The Franklin's Tale*;

see esp. F 1125 and 1261–96). The Church disapproved of this type of magic, along with alchemy, etc., while reserving its severest condemnation for *black* magic (witchcraft). Note 438 and (c).

417–18. The *ascendent* was the degree of the zodiacal circle[1] ascending above the eastern horizon at any moment. The time propitious for making *images* would be determined by the ascendant at the exact moment of the patient's birth. (The 'images' were not like those used in the sympathetic magic of savage tribes but were rather instruments for focusing upon the patient the power of the beneficent planet whose influence was felt during the chosen 'hours'.)

420–1. *The Theory of Humours* is one of the fundamental medieval conceptions which has vanished totally from modern thinking but which must be properly grasped if a great deal of literature, from Chaucer to Shakespeare and Jonson, is to be understood. The theory derives from *Galen* (see 429 (c) below) via the medical writings of the school of Salerno. The following typical summary comes from a twelfth-century English medical compendium:

> [The] *four humours* are dominant each in their own place: *blood* in the right side (the liver), also in the heart; *red bile* in the gall-bladder; *black bile* on the left side, where the spleen lies; *phlegm* in the head and bladder.
>
> Blood is hot, moist, and sweet; red bile bitter and active; black bile acid and cold; phlegm cold, salt and moist.
>
> Each has its special *season* – spring for the blood, summer for red bile, autumn for black bile, winter for phlegm.
>
> The humours give rise to certain types of *character* according to the degree of dominance in a man's body: blood makes men benevolent, simple, moderate, sluggish and stout; red bile makes men fearless, just and lean; black bile, irascible, covetous, melancholy, envious and often lame; phlegm produces a composite type – watchful, introspective, often prone to go grey early.
>
> The body contains *four qualities* – cold, hot, moist and dry.

The humours were further linked with the *four elements* of which all matter was thought to be composed – blood with *air*, red bile (also known as choler) with *fire*, black bile (also called melancholy) with *earth*, and phlegm with *water*. The author explains that a man's 'temperament' depends on the *mixture* or *balance* (*temperamentum*) of the humours in his body and takes its name from the dominant humour (e.g. a melancholy temperament comes from an *excess* of black bile). *Sicknesses* were thought to be caused by an imbalance of the humours and various remedies used to right the balance included

---

[1] The (imaginary) belt, divided into twelve parts or signs, extending 8 or 9 degrees on each side of the ecliptic (the great circle which is the apparent orbit of the sun).

diets, purges and blood-letting (often by means of leeches – whence the term 'leech' for doctor.'[2] A man's *complexion* or *temperament* could be deduced from his *appearance* (e.g. a ruddy face betokened a sanguine temperament, from the predominance of blood). From the connexion of medieval medical theory with the art of physiognomy (divining character from the features) the word 'complexion' has come to assume its modern meaning. (Other old terms that survive in common usage, but with a meaning that is psychological rather than physiological, are sanguine, phlegmatic, choleric.) Some of the *GP* portraits relate physiology to character (see the Franklin, Reeve and Summoner especially, and compare Pertelote's 'physiological' intepretation of Chanteclere's dream in *The Nun's Priest's Tale*, B 2923–69). Chaucer's knowledge of the humours was probably derived from popular compendia of the type quoted from rather than directly from a systematic study of Galen, and his references presuppose a range of knowledge which was probably as common among the more aristocratic and educated of his readers as terms from psychoanalysis (like 'unconscious' or 'complex') are to their modern equivalents.

422. An (?ironic) echo of 72: 'verray, parfit, gentil knight'.

425. The apothecaries of fourteenth-century London belonged to the Spicers' Gild and were mainly Italians.

429 ff. This list of famous physicians is as much a tribute to Chaucer's learning as to the Doctor's. But note the possible ironic hint – that the Physician's skill was *entirely theoretical* (see 412–13 and footnote). The authorities named are

a. Greek. Aesculapius was the legendary founder of the science of medicine. Dioscorides and Rufus of Ephesus belong to the second century A.D. Hippocrates (*Ypocras*), fifth century B.C., conceived the notion of *dieting* (cf. 435) and the *theory of humours*, which was transmitted to posterity by Galen (*Galyen*), who practised at Rome in the second century A.D.

b. Moslem. Haly Abbas and Rhazes (*Razis*) lived in the tenth century A.D., Serapion in the eleventh or twelfth. *Avicen* is Avicenna or Ibn Sina, tenth to eleventh century A.D., and *Averrois* is Averrhoes, twelfth century A.D. Both were also famous philosophers.

c. Christian. St John Damascene (*Damascien*) was a celebrated eighth-century theologian to whom various medical works were wrongly attributed. Constantine the African, eleventh century, studied at Salerno and translated the medical works of the Arabians (see above). The three writers named in 434 were all British – Gilbert the Englishman (*Gilbertyn*), Bernard of Gordon and John of Gaddesden (*Gatesden*). The last, an older contemporary of Chaucer, has been thought to be the 'model' for the Physician; but he actually rejected astronomy as a part of 'physic' and a better candidate is

[2] *Singer,* pp. 22–53 (condensed and translated).

another contemporary, John of Burgundy, who wrote that 'the science of astronomy is in physic wonder needful . . . for why astronomy and physic rectify each other in effect' (mentioned in *Cholmeley*). But there were doubtless many doctors 'grounded in astronomy' (see *Curry*). There is much amusing information on doctors in the chapter called 'The Medieval Physician' in Cholmeley's book.

438. Physicians had a reputation for religious scepticism even in the twelfth century. (Cf John of Salisbury's *Policraticus*, ch. 29.)

442. Chaucer may have had in mind the outbreaks of the Black Death in 1369 or as recently as 1379 (in the North of England). On the plague and its effects, see *McKisack*, 331–6.

The Wife of Bath

445 ff. The best 'commentary' by far on the portrait of the Wife of Bath is her own *Prologue*, an amazing soliloquy of nearly 850 lines, in which she spills out the whole story of her life and five marriages. Witty, gossipy, obscene and pathetic in turns, this is one of Chaucer's greatest poetic achievements, and a high point in medieval literature. Chaucer may have envisaged this enormous expansion of the Wife's character when he wrote l. 462 of the *GP* – 'But thereof nedeth nat to speke *as nouthe*'. When the Wife is 'on stage' she dominates the whole company through her sheer vitality, like Falstaff in *Henry IV*. The *Prologue* to her tale tells us more about her vanity, her love of fine clothes, her taste for pilgrimages (a good way of meeting future husbands) and her passion to dominate men. We learn that she got her deaf ear (446) when her fifth husband hit her soundly for tearing a leaf out of a book he was reading. We also learn that she regards her wide-spaced teeth as 'the print of Saint Venus' seal' – i.e. as a sign of her hyperactive sexuality.

445. The phrase 'goodwife' corresponds to 'goodman' and means 'woman possessing goods' (contrast the phrase 'good man' in 477). The Wife came from the parish of St Michael *iuxta Bathon* ('beside Bath').

448. It would be high praise to say that the Wife's skill surpassed that of the weavers of Ypres and Ghent, the centres of the Flemish weaving industry; but Chaucer may be writing ironically, since Bath cloth was not of the best.

458. The Wife's red face indicates her *sanguine temperament* (see Commentary on 420–1, and cf. 333, 587, 624) but, because she was born under Mars, who gave her 'sturdy hardynesse' (*Prologue* to her *Tale*, 612), she is not only pleasure-loving but also aggressive (cf. also the implications of her hat and spurs, 471, 473).

460. Marriages were conducted at the *chirche dore* until the sixteenth century. After the spousal ceremony, nuptial mass was celebrated at the altar. The *housbondes fyve* serve to link the Wife with the Woman of Samaria in John, iv, 18. The medieval church

discouraged (without actually prohibiting) people from marrying more than twice.

467. cf. Introduction p. 17.

The Parson

477 ff. The Parson is idealized, but not beyond belief. Poor, and brother to a Plowman, he is obviously of humble origin, like many medieval parish priests (the Church was not a preserve of the middle classes in Chaucer's day). But *unlike* many of the latter, he was learned, holy, industrious, charitable and also brave (521–3). In lines 507–11 Chaucer may be echoing Langland's stinging lines (B. *Prol.* 85–6) on parsons who 'have a licence and leave at London to dwell,/And sing there for simony – for silver is sweet'. (Cf. also Introduction pp. 20–2.)

478–9. His poverty was only in material things. Cf. Matthew, vi, 19–20; also Proverbs, xiii, 7: 'There is that maketh himself rich, yet hath nothing: there is that maketh himself poor, yet hath great riches'. The Parson derived his income from *tithes* (cf. 486).

486. The 'cursing' in question was not solemn excommunication (with 'bell, book and candle') but simply deprivation of the sacraments.

497. Cf. Matthew, v, 19, the passage alluded to in 498 ('tho wordes').

496, 504, etc. The shepherd–sheep imagery derives from John, x, 1–16.

499–500. The 'figure' is elucidated in 501–2; cf. also Introduction, pp. 29–30.

504. *shiten shepherde.* The alliteration lends emphasis to the word, which was 'strong' but not vulgar in Chaucer's day.

510. A *chantry* was an endowment whereby a priest said masses for the souls of deceased people and received money for doing so.

514. Perhaps an allusion to the 'chaplains mercenary' who made their living entirely by saying masses (Robinson). And cf. John, x, 12.

517. *daungerous* comes from OF *dangere*, derived f. late Lat. *dominiarium*, the power of a lord (over his retainers). The line means that the Parson did not stand upon his dignity or throw his weight about; cf. 663, and on *dygne*, 141 above.

524. Perhaps the strongest contrast with Chaucer's Parson is the priest in *Piers Plowman*, VII, 106 ff, who is certainly both 'daungerous' and 'dygne' – as it was all too easy for clergy with uneducated parishioners to become.

526. The rendering 'over-scrupulous' for *spyced* does not suggest complacency (*Hodgson*, p. 123) but fits in well with 515–20 (cf. also Introduction p. 20).

The Plowman

529 ff. The Plowman represents the class of *laboratores* (workers), as the clerical pilgrims (theoretically) represent the *oratores* (those who pray) and the knight the *bellatores* (those who fight to protect the realm). In the portraits of the Plowman, the Parson and the Knight, Chaucer may be deliberately offering idealized specimens of each 'estate'. (For a good exposition of the idea see Piers Plowman's speech to the Knight, B, VI, 24 ff; and cf. (c) on *GP* 45–6). Langland's perfect Christian labourer probably influenced Chaucer's Ploughman (compare 536–8 with *Piers*, B, VI, 220 ff). Against the background of contemporary social discontent amongst agricultural workers (demands for higher wages, opposition to feudal obligations, etc.) the portrait would have seemed all the more of an ideal or model.

533–5 Cf. Matthew, xxii, 37–9.

The Miller

545 ff. The Miller's detailed physical description contrasts strongly with the preceding (unvisualized) portrait. (Cf. also the description of the Miller in the *Reeve's Tale* (A 3925 ff), a satirical attack on the pilgrim-Miller.) The animal imagery of the portrait (*sow*, *fox*) anticipates interestingly the Miller's own description of the girl Alison in his tale (A 3221), which compares her to a weasel, a kid, a calf and a colt. Both passages underline the character's pronounced animality. The medieval physiognomists would have recognized in the Miller's features unmistakable signs of a violent, lustful and scurrilous nature (all these characteristics are exemplified in his *Tale*).

559. With the 'forneys' image cf. the description of the Monk's head 'That stemed as a forneys of a leed' (202).

560. *Goliardeys* comes from the followers of the fictitious 'Bishop Golias', the Wandering Scholars or *Goliardi* (see *Waddell, passim*), many of whom wrote bawdy Latin verses. The word is prob. from Lat. *gula*, 'gluttony', but was also associated with the boastful giant Goliath (I Sam., xvii, 43–4).

562. i.e. he took three times the legal 'toll', usually one twentieth, of the corn ground at his mill. (The 'toll' was exacted over and above the ordinary money payment for grinding the corn.)

563. 'And yet he was honest, as millers go (i.e. not honest at all).' It was a proverbial expression that 'An honest miller has a thumb of gold'. Coming after the account of his practices in line 562 the phrase *must* be ironical here. The expression may also allude to the Miller's *skill*, since he tested the fineness of the flour by rubbing it between thumb and finger (gold here signifies the excellence of his 'feel').

The Manciple

567 ff. The Manciple exemplifies 'canny' commonsense, which is often more effective in practical matters than the wisdom of the formally educated. His tale of the Crow is very much in character: its moral is the prudent maxim 'Beware – and take heed what you say'. Chaucer does not specify whether the Manciple belonged to the Middle or the Inner Temple (so-called because they occupied the site formerly belonging to the order of Knights Templar, dissolved in 1312). There is a tradition that Chaucer was a student at the Inner Temple (see Biog. Note).

570. The tally-stick was a means of recording debts. It was cut with notches and divided in two, one part being kept by the debtor and one by the creditor. The interlocking of the two pieces confirmed the exact sum to be paid. (Cf. 'indenture'.)

574. *Lewed* meant both 'uneducated' (neutral sense) and 'ignorant' (adversely critical sense). Chaucer's question in this line makes it clear that education and practical wisdom are far from identical (cf. also *CYT*, 234 (c) in this vol.). A dialogue between the Host and the Manciple in the Prologue to the latter's tale suggests that the 'lewd' lawyers' steward knew enough to be able to 'cook the books' (his 'rekeninges') – and that the Cook, moreover, knew about this. But the *GP* portrait holds no hint of actual dishonesty.

586. *hir aller* is genitive plural (cf. *oure aller*, 823). The idea is perhaps that of tilting someone's hat at such an angle as to make him look ridiculous (Pollard). Uses of the phrase in A 3143 and A 3911 (*howve* ['hood'] for *cappe*) support the meaning 'discomfit, put out (a person) by displaying greater ingenuity'.

The Reeve

587 ff. The functions of the Reeve, who was the representative of the Lord of the Manor were 'to direct the cultivation of the estate, to call for the labour services and see that they were properly carried out, to levy taxes, and to keep good order among the tenants' (*Bloch*, II, 337). Chaucer's Reeve is, like the Manciple, a servant whose shrewdness exceeds his master's, but he is obviously 'crooked' where the latter is 'sharp'. Physical details abound in the portrait and illustrate Chaucer's contempt for the Reeve (the skinny legs (591–2) and rusty blade (618) are examples). The Reeve's irascibility emerges in the *Prologue* to his *Tale*, an ill-humoured reaction to the Miller's story of the cuckolding of an old carpenter (A 3864 ff). In this speech he complains about his impotence, and a new factor is explicitly introduced which is only implicitly present in the *GP* – the Reeve's old age. (The juxtaposition of varieties of the same type (Manciple, Reeve) is also found elsewhere in the *GP* (cf. Clerk, Man of Law and Introduction, p. 18).)

587. The Reeve's 'choler' (another name for *bile*; see (c) on 420–1) makes him irascible (605) and physically thin (591–2).

589–90. The close-cropped hair was a sign that he was a serf. This makes the hold he has acquired over his master all the more striking.

602. He always collected the rents due to his lord in good time.

603. He was probably 'head-bailiff' of the whole manor, with other bailiffs under him. Originally the bailiff (or serjeant) was a higher manorial official than the reeve, but the latter's status improved during the fourteenth century. (See *McKisack*, 317–19, on Reeves.)

An alternative interpretation of 'That he ne knew his . . .' would make *he* refer to the bailiff, herdsman, etc., and *his* to the Reeve: 'there wasn't a soul who didn't know about the Reeve's dishonesty (except his master, of course)'. The *grammar* certainly supports this reading (*Hodgson*, p. 130) but the fear of 605 would make more sense if it was the *Reeve* who knew about *everyone else's* secret dishonesty (cf. 663–5 (c)).

605. *the deeth* may be abstract (like Fr. *la mort*, 'death') or may allude to the pestilence or Black Death (cf. 442 (c)).

616. The name *Scot* may be a pun: *scot* meant 'tax' and the allusion may be to the customs or dues paid to the reeve of a manor. The Reeve would be 'riding high' on his money.

620. *Baldeswelle* belonged to the estates of the earl of Pembroke. No satisfactory explanation for the choice of the name has been given (cf. *Hodgson*, p. 131).

The Summoner

623 ff. The Summoner is even more grotesque a creation than the Miller, but the satire is not cruel, as it could have been (against 624–33, set 647–8, which are not necessarily ironic). 641–5 imply smiling condescension, not the contempt hidden in the cooler accounts of the Merchant or Reeve. Chaucer seems more tolerant of the *ignorant* vice of the Summoner than the subtler hypocrisy of the Friar. As a *churl* he is given one of the crudest of all the tales. In it he exposes the greed and hypocrisy of a friar, the pilgrim-Friar having provoked him with a tale exposing the extortionist practices of a summoner. The tales together throw a lurid light on ecclesiastical 'low-life' in the period.

The summoner or apparitor was a church-official, usually a layman, whose job was to summon people guilty of various offences dealt with by the bishop or the archdeacon, the commonest of which were fornication and adultery. The institution provided ample room for blackmail (663–5) and extortion (see the *Friar's Tale*); but 649–51 indicate that receiving bribes was a main source of this Summoner's revenue. The comic exaggeration of Chaucer's

147

portrait is pure caricature. There is much direct comment on the subject's character (626, 645, 647–8, 659), not all of it hostile. Chaucer almost feels sympathy for his creation, like Langland for his miserable Glutton (B, V, 304 ff). A comparison of the two poets' treatment of drunkenness is particularly interesting.

624. 'Cherubin' is singular here, though 'cherubim' is a Hebrew plural. (Cf. *Othello*, IV, ii, 64). *Ecclesiasticus*, xlix, 10, applies the name 'cherubim' to the 'living creatures' seen by the prophet Ezekiel, whose 'appearance was like burning coals of fire' (*Ezek.* i, 13). The term is grotesquely incongruous as applied to the unholy and disease-ridden Summoner.

625. See 420–1 (c). The Summoner is suffering from *alopicia*, a type of leprosy thought to be caused by infection of the blood due to excess of wine and 'hot foods' (onions, etc.) and to intercourse with women infected with it (*Curry*, pp. 43–7). The remedies suggested in 629–31 are those recommended by the medieval physicians. The narrowing of the eyes is probably due to swelling, another effect of *alopicia*.

626. Sparrows were traditionally called 'lecherous' and the bird is 'Venus' son' in *The Parliament of Fowls*.

627. The black brows were taken by the physiognomists as a sign of a lecherous nature (cf. Alison in the *Miller's Tale*, whose brows were 'blake as any sloo').

638–45. The scraps of Latin would have been picked up by the Summoner in his dealings in the ecclesiastical courts.

643. 'Jays' or jackdaws were taught to cry *Wat* as parrots nowadays to say 'Poll'.

655. On archdeacons, see the *Friar's Tale* (opening lines). The villainous character there satirized pounces on people guilty of offences ranging from witchcraft and usury to failure to pay tithes:

But certes, lecchours dide he grettest wo (D 1310).

661. The meaning is that (solemn) excommunication (cf. 486) 'kills' the soul by depriving it of the sanctifying grace obtained through the sacraments, the excommunicate already being presumably in a state of 'mortal sin'. Chaucer seems to be denying indignantly in 659 that 'excommunication kills' *in the same sense as* (*'right as'*) absolution 'saves', rather than that neither of them is efficacious.

662. The *Significavit* was properly a writ for the imprisonment of an excommunicate if he failed to pay his fine within forty days, whereupon he was handed over by the bishop to the Chancellor.

663. On *daunger* see 517 (c) above.

663–5. The Summoner's 'hold' over the youth of the diocese was doubtless due to his knowledge of their sexual activities.

668. The buckler made of a cake is a final grotesque touch bring-

ing out the absurd frivolity with which this unlikely character has embarked on the pilgrimage.

The Pardoner

669 ff. The Pardoner is, along with the Wife of Bath and the Canon's Yeoman (see text in this vol.), one of the characters who receives a long and revealing prologue to his *Tale*. In 130 lines of astonishing frankness, he unfolds the methods by which he extracts money from the unwary and gullible.

The pardoner's function was to convey papal indulgences ('pardons') to individual men and women. When a person had confessed his sins to a priest and received absolution, though now freed from the guilt of sin, he was still subject to 'temporal punishment' – i.e. he had to make satisfaction here and now (as opposed to in Purgatory) by performing penance. This could be severe, involving public humiliation, and it became common to remit all or part of the punishment through an *indulgence* granted by the Pope or his representatives the bishops. The Church taught that there existed a 'treasury of merit' acquired by Christ through his life and death and through the merits of the Saints, which far outweighed the debt of punishment incurred by humanity. The Church as a unified spiritual entity enabled its sinful members to 'draw upon' the 'treasury' to make satisfaction for sin. Though this could be achieved partly through temporal punishment, sinners still had to suffer for a period in Purgatory after death to complete their expiation for sin. But by indulgences part or all of this period could be remitted. 'Plenary indulgences' (remitting *all* punishment) could be granted only by the Pope himself exercising the 'Petrine privilege' conferred on St Peter (and on the Popes as his successors) by Christ in the words 'Whatever you loose upon earth it shall be loosed also in heaven' (Matthew, xvi, 19). Indulgences were earned by special acts like almsgiving and *pilgrimage*. In theory, merely to go through the motions of these acts was not enough: the recipient also had to have the right spirit and intention, without which indulgences could (and did) degenerate into a kind of 'spiritual commodity' to be bought.[3] The fact that the plenary kind had to come from Rome made them a rather expensive commodity! The pardoners also took their 'cut', and unscrupulous ones were free to use their authority to exploit the simple faithful (including the less-educated clergy) by making them pay to venerate their supposed relics. This Pardoner seems to have been *genuine* (671) – though there were certainly impostors – but he misses no chance to make money from his profession. Being in minor orders (708 (c)), he can preach

[3] This account is based on Aquinas, *ST*, suppl. Qq. 25-6: cf. *Langland* B, VII, 173 ff.

in churches, and he uses this means to talk his congregation into a sense of their sinfulness in which they will come forward to venerate his trinkets. The Pardoner is a kind of parody of the elegant Squire in his negligent dandyism – but the whole description produces a nasty impression (see 673, 684). *Curry* (pp. 54–70) identifies him from the description as what the medievals called a *eunuchus ex nativitate* (a man wholly or partially impotent – by nature as opposed to castration; see 691).

670. Members of this convent were notorious for their unauthorized sale of pardons (*Hodgson*, 137).

673. The line probably contains an obscene pun (*burdoun* also meant 'staff' or 'shaft').

685, etc. The relics and mementoes sported by the Pardoner could have been picked up by any wandering pilgrim. Langland's description of a pilgrim (B, V, 526–31) may have been known to Chaucer: 'A bowl and a bag he bore by his side, a hundred *ampullae* (holy-water vials) sat on his hat – tokens from Mount Sinai and shells from Galicia, crosses on his cloak and keys from Rome, and in front a *vernicle* (cf. *GP*, 685) to show people which shrines he had been to'. The name *veronike* was applied to copies of the handkerchief which St Veronica (according to tradition) used to wipe the face of Christ on the way to Calvary, and which was thought to have received a miraculous imprint of his face.

692. Ware in Hertfordshire, the word perhaps suggested by the need for a rhyme to *mare*.

702. The *povre persouns* clearly did not resemble the pilgrim-Parson, who would have seen through the Pardoner at a glance.

708. The Pardoner was at least in *minor orders* (i.e. not ordained priest or deacon, but nonetheless a *clericus*).

709. The 'lesson' and 'story' (Lat. *lectio, historia*), may both be parts of the Canonical Office (the daily round of worship in monastic orders) or, more likely, the Epistle and Gospel sections of the Mass (cf. 710). The *historia* was often a rhymed office honouring local saints (*Young*, I, 191–2).

715–24. These lines sum up in the clear and rational manner of Chaucerian narrative all that has gone before, and prepare us for the beginning of the 'tale' of the pilgrimage (747–end). (*shortly, in a clause*, is of course a joke – since the description has occupied over 700 lines up till now!) But in between Chaucer has an important digression which stands (with some lines in the *Miller's Prologue*) as a kind of manifesto of realism. Chaucer appeals to authority (739–41) to vindicate his literary method – the faithful reporting of all he sees and hears (this, of course, is only a fraction of what the poetry actually offers us). The quotation from Plato (742) comes via Boethius's *Consolation of Philosophy*, which Chaucer translated a few years before the *GP*: '(. . . the sentence [statement] of Plato) that nedes the wordes moot be cosines to the thinges of whiche they speken' (Bk. III, prose 12).

746. An example of the famous (or notorious) 'modesty-*topos*' (convention) – the intentionally insincere statement of the author's stupidity or incompetence. The use of the cliché must have drawn a smile to the lips of Chaucer's original audience as it was intended to.

747 ff. The rest of the *GP* is dominated by *the Host*, who becomes a key-figure in the whole pilgrimage-story. His name is Harry Bailey (*Cook's Prol.*, A 4358). Bustling, aggressive and high-spirited, he typifies the new London middle classes – a 'burgess' worthy to be a 'marshal' in the hall of a great lord. He is certainly a more attractive example of the English *bourgeois* than the five gildsmen, and Chaucer clearly admires the man to whom he gives the inspiration that the pilgrims should tell tales to pass the time on the way to Canterbury. The arrangement agreed upon in 810–15 remains unfulfilled, however, since Chaucer never completed the *Tales* according to his original design.

754. *Cheapside* was the home of the richer London citizens, and the reference seems to be a compliment to the Southwark innkeeper.

858. *as ye may here* reminds us that medieval audiences usually *heard* poetry read out aloud (see also Textual Note), though the *Miller's Prologue* (A 3176–7):

> And therfore, whoso list it nat *yheere*,
> Turne over the leef and chese another tale

suggests that 'hear' was not always literal, and that Chaucer also expected his works to be *read*.

The Canon's Yeoman's Prologue and Tale

1. The Second Nun (see *GP* 163–4 (c) in this vol.) has just finished telling her tale, the Life of St Cecilia.

3. Boughton was some five miles' distance from Ospringe on the old pilgrims' road to Canterbury.

gan (short for 'began') is often used as a mere metrical filler in ME poetry (cf. modern *did*) and when followed by the infin. can be rendered as an ordinary past tense.

7. *wonder* (sb.) is often used adjectivally (and adverbially) –
'wonderful(ly)' (cf. 76).

10. The terminal *-n* of *gon* signifies the infin. in ME verbs as well
as the plural (cf. *wondren*, 16; *dwellen*, 103).

12. The white foam that flecked his black clothing made him look
like a magpie, which has black and white plumage. The simile also
suggests the proverbially thievish habits of the bird.

13. Perhaps the bag was *folded* over because nearly empty.

16. *I.* The speaker is Chaucer himself, who tells the story of the
Canterbury pilgrimage in the first person. See *GP* Introduction p.
14.

20. *Canons* were either *secular* (living 'in the world' – e.g. in
collegiate churches or cathedrals) or *regular* (living in a religious
order according to a Rule). This one seems to be a Canon Regular
who has abandoned the religious house he was attached to for a
wandering life.

27. The simile is apt, since the man turns out to be an alchemist.
He sweats like the distilling apparatus used by alchemists in the
search for the Elixir.

28. Both plants have medicinal qualities: plantain leaves are
astringent; pellitory was reputedly good against 'choleric inflam-
mation'. Their precise use in alchemy is not clear.

29. Cf. *GP*, 1; for similar uses of 'that' see *what that, til that* (17),
how that (18), *bycause that* (32), *which that* (38).

36. The inn in question is probably that at Ospringe (see line 3
and *Commentary* above). On the pilgrims' arrival at Southwark and
their arrangement for telling tales on the way to Canterbury, see
GP, 20–7, 747 to end, in this vol.

37. The modern sense of *warn* is a specialized development; in
ME the word often meant 'to inform' generally, not only of danger.

41. For a description of the *Host*, see *GP*, 746 ff.

48. The *-eth* ending denotes both the 3rd pers. sg. pres. and also
(as here) the imperative pl. (the context prevents confusion). In
ME the pl. is often a polite form, as in French. Alternations between
the sg. and pl. forms of a vb. often indicate significant changes of
meaning in the work of writers as late as Malory (fifteenth century)
and even (to some extent) Shakespeare. See below, 500, 566–71,
628, etc.

49. 'And yé him knéwe ‖ as wel as do Í.'

51. *wyse* survives as the termination in *likewise, crosswise*, etc. and
has been revived in spoken American in the sense 'with respect to'
(e.g. 'entertainment-wise').

52. The final *-n* of the past participle is often omitted (cf. 367,
etc. below).

55. *homely* is here advbl., with the basic meaning of 'simply',

'plainly' (cf. our use of the adj. 'homely' to describe looks; also *GP*, 328 (c). *rit* is the contracted form of *rydeth*, 3rd. pers. sg. pres. indic. of *ryden*. Cf. also 129, etc.

58. *good* in the sg., meaning 'goods, property, possessions, money' occurs several times in the *CYT* (cf. also *GP*, 445 (c)).

63. A *clerk* ('clericus') was one who knew Latin, and in ME the word generally means 'an educated man' (cf. also *GP*, 480). *Lered* (or *lerned*) men were contrasted with *lewed* (unlearned or ignorant men) and often enough in practice 'clerks' were members of the clergy (cf. also *GP*, 285–301 (c)), while the unlearned were laymen.

69. The Yeoman is a mere assistant in an alchemical laboratory, not an alchemist himself. *werking* is the usual ME word for 'operations, activities, experiments'. In its verbal forms, *werchen*, *worchen* and as the noun *werk*, it occurs frequently in the *CYT*. 'The Work' was alchemical cant for the experiment in which the Elixir is precipitated.

70. *been* is the normal Chaucerian form of the pres. pl. indic.; *be* in the sg. is the subjunctive, *beth* is always the pl. imperative (the 3rd pers. sg. pres. ind. being *is*). The form *aren*, which was to prevail in later English, sometimes occurs in Chaucer as an alternative to *been*, but not in this tale. (Cf. also 10 (c).)

78. The construction with *men* (sometimes abbreviated to *me*) is common in ME for the passive (cf. Ger. *man*, Fr. *on*; and see *GP*, 149; cf. 332, 338).

78–83. In Chaucer's day even more than in ours 'clothes made the man'. See *GP*, Introduction p. 17–18.

80. Doubling of the negative for emphasis is common in Chaucer. Cf. also *GP*, 70n.

81. *Oaths* and *asseverations* (esp. the latter) are very frequent in ME, especially in a consciously colloquial writer like Chaucer (see as early a work as his *Boke of the Duchesse* (1370)). They serve as line-fillers and often supply rhymes, in *CYT* to such an extent as to suggest carelessness or lack of revision (about 9 per cent of the rhymes use asseverations, and the frequency of phrases like *ywis*, *God forbede*, *trewely*, *I seye*, *I trowe* in the conspicuous rhyme-position produces a cumulative effect of slackness). The 'dramatic' argument that the verse appears tired and flat because it mirrors the speaker's inner state is unconvincing (cf. the *Wife of Bath's Prologue*, where asseverations form only about 4 per cent of the rhymes, and where Chaucer achieves an effect of garrulous spontaneity without impoverishing his verse). The number of asseverations *within* the line in the *CYT* is also high and the writing accordingly lacks the tautness of Chaucer's best verse (cf. the *Pardoner's* or *Merchant's Tales*).

95–6. Cf. Dryden's lines (*Absalom and Achitophel*, 163–4):

> Great wits are sure to madness near allied,
> And thin partitions do their bounds divide.

153

104. The Yeoman is being deliberately vague about the *toun* out of caution, but the *suburbes* perhaps hint at the capital (it is in London, too, that the False Canon of the *Tale* – whom there is good reason for identifying with the Yeoman's Canon (see 535–42, below) – carries out his gulling of the Priest).

106. *this* and *thise* have a generalizing sense in Chaucerian English rather like Shakespearian *your* ('Than are dreamt of in your philosophy').

112. Swearing by the saints is very common in ME literature: cf. also 509, 536; *GP*, 120 (c); and 798 (c).

116. *Duncan*[1] (p. 635) points out that 'multiplication' is used in Arnald's *Rosary* (see 875 (c)) with the specific meaning of 'the operations by which the transmuting elixir was tremendously increased in strength and efficacy' and argues that Chaucer 'imaginatively enlarged its meaning' (i.e. to signify 'transmutation' generally). But the latter meaning is already found in Gower, writing about 1390 (*CA*, IV, 2573–4):

> It [the stone] makth *multiplicacioun*
> Of gold, and the fixacioun   [solidification
> It causeth

and (*CA*, IV, 2459–61):

> . . . Alconomie
> Wherof the selver *multeplie*
> Thei made and ek the gold also.

Skeat (V, 420) sees a pun in 'multiply': the alchemists supposed that they could '*multiply* gold by turning as much base metal as a piece of it would buy into gold itself'. The word here (as frequently in the *CYT*) is rich with ironic potentialities. The more the Yeoman and his associates attempt to 'multiply' the little gold they start out with, the more they actually end up by *reducing* it (cf. the Yeoman's gloomy realization of this fact at 836–7 (c)).

135. *Dionysius Cato* (*c.* fourth century A.D.) wrote the *Disticha de Moribus*, moral apophthegms in couplets which were very popular in the Middle Ages. The source of the quotation is Book I, Dist. 17.

157. *Ernest* and *game* (like *lust* and *lore*, *doctryne* and *solas*) are often contrasted in ME idiom.

169. The *y*- prefix (OE *ge*-) denotes the past participle (cf. mod. Ger. *ge*-). While not grammatically necessary in Chaucer's day, it was metrically very useful.

172. *array* virtually repeats *clothing* in the same line (cf. also 'that clothed was in clothes blake', 4). This tendency to repeat the same idea is characteristic of the *CYT*.

175. *leden* has many associations – 'dull, heavy' (appropriate to the Yeoman's psychological state); 'of the base metal lead' (again

appropriate to one whose life is spent in a *fruitless* quest for *gold*.)
The two meanings are of course closely linked in the case of the
Yeoman, whose unsuccess has made him dejected. There is also a
hint that the Yeoman has, as it were, been himself 'transmuted' (in
reverse) from his original 'gold' (*reednesse*, 544) to his present
'discoloured' hue by the Alchemy to which he has been so long
addicted.

177. 'To blear someone's eyes' also meant 'to deceive' or 'to hood-
wink' them, and the implication is appropriate here (and generally)
in a tale one of the main themes of which is moral and mental
blindness. The metaphor grows from the literal fact that the Yeoman's
eyes *have* suffered from his labours.

190. *jupartye* (from which our 'jeopardy' comes) derives from Fr.
jeu parti (a game in which the chances are exactly even). If the word
still retained this precise connotation in Chaucer's day then it is
clearly a euphemism here: alchemy, as the Yeoman reveals, offered
far less than a 50–50 chance of success.

194. Semi-proverbial. The exact source is unknown. Cf. Marlowe's
Dr Faustus, 474: 'Solamen miseris socios habuisse doloris'.

215. The temperature of the fire in alchemical experiments was
very important. Tending the fire was the Yeoman's special task, as
we learn from 922–4 (cf. earlier 113). See also 373 (c).

217. *sublimation*: the process whereby solids under the influence of
heat turn to vapour or gas without first passing through the liquid
state, and return directly to the solid state on cooling.

218. *amalgamation*: the close mingling of elements through solution
in mercury.

calcination: the reduction of a metal or mineral to fine powder
(Lat. *calx*) usu. by heating.

Lines 217–25 echo Gower, *CA*, IV, 2513–24. The processes are
well described in *Holmyard*, ch. 4, 'Alchemical Apparatus'.

225. *spirites ascencioun*, the turning to a gaseous state of the sub-
stances known as *spirits* (see 267–71 (c) below).

226. These are the solids that remain after the gases have been
given off.

234. The modern sense of the word *lewd* is a deterioration or cata-
chresis of the original meaning, 'lacking the education of a *clerk*'
(see (c) on 63 above).

237. *armoniak* is a corruption of *armeniak* ('Armenian'). Perhaps
Chaucer confused the word with 'ammoniac', which he gives as
armoniak at 245 below (and cf. the form *sal armoniak*, in Gower, *CA*,
IV, 2480). *bole* is f. Lat. *bolus*, a clod. *Bole armeniak* was a reddish clay
with astringent properties. *verdigris* ('green-of-Greece'), the greenish
acetate of copper. *borax*, a white crystalline salt.

239. *Urinals*, used by physicians, may also have been used by the
alchemists to contain urine (see 254). *descensories* were used in

'downward distillation' (i.e. by descent of the vapour through a glass tube surrounded by cold water).

241. The *cucurbit* was a gourd-shaped retort (Lat. *cucurbita*, gourd) forming the lower part of an *alembic*, the whole apparatus for distilling (*alembic* was also used specifically of the cap or upper part of the apparatus).

247. All these herbs were used in medicine. Cf. also 28n (c).

253. 'Unslaked lime' is quicklime (calcium oxide) before it has been hydrated ('slaked' with water).

255. *Saltpetre* (potassium nitrate), the basis of gunpowder. It is not surprising that the pot blew up so often! *vitriol*, the general name for the various metallic sulphates.

257, 260. *Salt of tartar*, crude potassium carbonate. *Oil of tartar*, white crystals formed from *argol*, a product of fermentation which is deposited on the sides of wine casks as a hard crust. *barm*, the yeast formed by the fermentation of beer. *wort*, the malt infusion used in making beer.

263. *silver citrination*, colouring silver so that it looks like gold by fusing into the metal, under great heat, prepared and refined compounds of sulphur and mercury. *citron* is a very pale lemon colour (*Duncan*[ii] p. 249).

264. *fermentation*, the production of chemical change in metals by a 'ferment' resembling that produced by leaven in dough.

265. *cementation*, the combining of solids at high temperatures so as to change the properties of one of them without liquefaction.

267–71. The (four) 'spirits' of alchemy (substances which volatilize completely on heating) were mercury, the arsenic sulphides realgar and orpiment (Chaucer names only the latter, 270), sal ammoniac and sulphur.

272–6. The seven 'bodies' were the metals gold, silver, copper, iron, tin, lead and mercury (the latter also a 'spirit'; the alchemical authority Geber makes the seventh 'Chinese iron' [*Holmyard*, p. 91], an unidentified substance; Gower (*CA*, IV, 2474–8) also calls mercury a 'body'). The planetary correspondences were based on analogies with the (apparent) movements of the planets (Saturn slow, Mercury swift), their colours (golden sun, silver moon), their etymology (copper, *Cyprian* Venus) or their associations (iron/Mars, God of War). Only Jupiter's connexion with tin seems arbitrary. The planetary names are commonly found in alchemical writings as a cryptic shorthand.

273. *threpe* usually means 'argue, dispute'; in the sense of 'assert' it seems dragged in here for the sake of the rhyme.

283–4. For the rhyme *cofre : philosophre* see also *GP*, 297–8.

284. *Philosopher* and *philosophy* in the *CYT* nearly always mean 'alchemist', 'alchemy'. The term was a cant euphemism, 'alchemy' having suspect overtones. However, alchemy was widely believed

to be based on the principles of 'natural philosophy', the old name for 'science'. Cf. also Philosopher's Stone, etc.

285. *Ascaunce* comes from the adv. *as* +OF *quanses* ('as if') and means usually 'as though (to say)', but here rather 'perhaps' or 'so?' *craft so light to lere*, cf. the opening line of Chaucer's *Parliament of Fowls*, 'The lyf so short, the craft so long to lerne,' where the 'craft' in question is *love*.

287. The references to clerics as assumed exponents of alchemy is explained by the fact that historically alchemical learning flourished amongst the religious Orders (see *Duncan*[i], p. 635) – examples are the Dominicans (Albertus Magnus) and the Franciscans (Roger Bacon) – in spite of repeated prohibitions.

291. Note the different meanings of *lerning* (289, 'studying'), *lere* (285, 'learn'), *lerne* (291, 'teach').

293. *connen* means 'be acquainted with' (*witen* = 'know for a fact'; Cf. Fr. *connaître* and *savoir*).

293–4. The learned man and the ignorant alike will find their pursuit of alchemy futile.

298. The haphazard way in which the Yeoman pours out his picked-up scraps of knowledge reveals how completely he too is lost in the mazes of alchemy.

303. The *metal fusible* referred to an alloy of bismuth, lead and tin that melts at the heat of boiling water.

308. The Yeoman means that his outlandish terminology sounds like the conjuring abracadabra of magicians. Alchemy was often linked with magic as a forbidden practice; cf. *Piers Plowman*, A-text, XI, 160–1, with its reference to

> Experiments of alchemy of Albert's making, [Albertus Magnus'
> Necromancy and pyromancy, the puck [devil] to raise –
> If you think to do well, deal therwith never!

309–10. *The Stone*, the object of the alchemists' quest, was thought to be a substance capable of transmuting the base metals lead, iron, tin, copper and mercury into the precious metals silver and gold. The term *Elixir* (Arabic *al-iksr*, f. Gk. *xéron*, 'dry residue') was used as an alternative name for the Stone, and for a tincture (made from the Stone) possessing the power of restoring youth and prolonging life indefinitely.

311. The 'him' (cf. also 313, 314, 'he') suggests that the Stone has become in the Yeoman's mind an elusive, Pimpernel-like person desperately pursued by the alchemists (cf. *sechen faste*, 310).

313. The word 'craft' and its synonyms meaning '(scientific) skill' echo throughout the tale with an increasingly ironic hollowness.

318–19. Literal and figurative meanings are mingled here. The pain of the disappointed alchemists is internal (mental) but they see it as an almost bodily pain which the Elixir (see 309–10 above) will remedy – once they have found it. (Cf. also the last line of the *Tale*.)

325. *bitter-swete* carries on the metaphor from feeding implicit in *sadde* (324n).

335. See also Introduction p. 36.

345. In fact the Canon's Yeoman is so engrossed in recounting the story of his life that he goes on for another seventy-five lines before beginning his 'tale' proper (as he would have it) at 420.

363–4. The 'violence' of the exploding metals suggests to the Canon's Yeoman's disordered imagination that the 'very devil' is amongst them (cf. also 308). The recurring references to the fiend, the devil, hell, etc., help to prepare us for the moral conclusion or 'poynt' voiced at 915–26 – that alchemy is a rebellion against the will of God.

368. A contracted form of the verb (= *holdeth*); cf. *rit*, 55 *and* (c).

369–70. *seyde*: the tense changes from pres. to past as if the Yeoman were now no longer describing his day-to-day routine but recalling a particular occasion (which is, nonetheless, typical of what used to happen).

373. Alchemical experiments frequently came unstuck because there was no adequate means of controlling the heat of the flame, a factor the importance of which all the authorities emphasized (cf. also 215 (c)).

379. *done*, the inflected form of the infin., is the ME equivalent of our passive infin. ('to be done').

384. The repetitions (*glad, blythe*) here seem to suggest the insincerity of the Canon (but cf. (c) on 172 above).

409–12. Chaucer's source for these proverbial expressions is the *Parabolae* of the twelfth-century Latin writer Alanus de Insulis. 'Do not think that everything that glitters is gold, or every fair apple a sound one.' The gold-image in particular is ironically appropriate in the context.

420. *Infecte* has a moral sense here, but also recalls the physical meaning of the word at 335. The avarice in his victims' natures to which the Canon appeals is of course the true infection and the Priest in the story that follows is not an 'innocent' (cf. 344), only gullible and blinded by greed.

421. Nineveh was the ancient capital of Syria, a city famed for its size.

427. *him* could just possibly be reflexive, the image being one of the Canon 'winding' *himself* round and round in words until his true purpose is concealed. But Chaucer probably intended an image of ensnaring, or trapping in a winding maze.

442. *ordre* may be more general than 'religious Order' and may mean 'division of society', 'estate'. The singular *som shrewe* would then acquire a general meaning: 'there are wicked characters in every walk of life'.

443. The pious asseveration is taken up by the Canon at 493 and 511 and serves as part of his Tartuffe-like insinuation of himself into the Priest's confidence.

447. For *was* we would expect *is*, since the tale has not yet been told.

439–58. This address to 'honest canons' has sometimes been taken as implying that the *Tale* was originally intended for an actual audience of canons before Chaucer used it in the *Canterbury Tales*. But the passage is surely no more than a rhetorical apostrophe, with the author speaking through the mouth of the Yeoman to declare that the tale isn't meant to be an attack on Canons Regular taken collectively. This is not to deny that in making the villain of the tale a canon Chaucer may not have had a particular man in mind, as has been suggested for the Monk in the *GP* (see 177 (c) in this vol.). A likely candidate is Canon William Shuchirch of Windsor, a notorious alchemist.

459. An *annueller* was a priest who said 'annuals' or Masses of commemoration (celebrated every day for a year after the donor's death or once a year on the anniversary of his death) instead of being in charge of a parish (cf. also *chantry*, *GP*, 510). This Priest makes enough money from his annuals and from his landlady's generosity to afford his own servant (555 below).

461. The context indicates that *servisable* is scarcely complimentary as it usually is (see 464–5) and cf. *GP*, 99).

466. The phrase 'as now' (*as nowthe*, *GP*, 482) provides a useful rhyme as well as a transition from description to narrative.

477. *take* often has the meaning *give* in ME (cf. also 744 (c) below).

488. A line pregnant with unconscious irony. The Priest indeed turns out to be unable to say 'nay' to the Canon, though the latter does not turn out to be 'swich a man' (i.e. 'trewe of condicioun') as the Priest imagined.

491–4. The excessive solemnity of the oath (a typical confidence-trickster's 'ploy') would alert any but the avarice-blinded to the Canon's speciousness.

491. On *trouthe* see *GP*, 46 (c) and cf. *The Franklin's Tale*, 1479: 'Trouthe is the hyeste thing that man may kepe'.

500. The polite form of the pronoun, *ye*, here replaces the casually intimate *thee* used by the Canon at 474. The subtle shift to a respectful tone, an instrument of flattery, again reflects the Canon's mastery of 'craft'.

501. *Gentillesse* is a high term of praise; see *GP*, 331 ff. (c).

507. Again ironic: the skill displayed is that of a trickster, not that of a genuine 'master' of alchemy. The expression 'to make a Magistery' was alchemical jargon for 'transmuting a base metal to a higher one' (*Duncan*[ii], p. 243).

512. Note the rich rhyme (*forbede: bede*), which was permissible in ME poetry (see (c) on *GP*, 17–18).

514. The source is prob. St Jerome: *Merx ultronea putet* ('Unasked-for merchandise stinks').

520. A line indicating first-hand knowledge of the Canon's devices and support for the view that the latter is identical with the Yeoman's ex-master (see also 535 below).

523. *sely* (from which 'silly' and 'seely' both derive) is ult. f. OE *sælig*, 'blessed'. Here it means 'foolish', and *innocent* in this line is thus nearer to 'gullible fool' than to our 'innocent'.

524. Covetousness or greed (*Avaritia*) was one of the Seven Deadly Sins. The *CYT* is an implicit attack on avarice and the folly to which it gives rise (cf. also *The Parson's Tale*, I, 738 ff). It was regarded by the medievals as 'the grettest synne that may be, after the synne of Lucifer' (*sc.* Pride) (*Pars. T.* 787).

527. The *fox* was a traditional symbol of cunning and deceit (cf. Chaucer's *Nun's Priest's Tale*, also Luke, xiii, 32).

535–42. This passage is one of the main reasons for identifying the Canon of the *Tale* with the Canon of the *Introduction*. How could the Yeoman know so much and feel so strongly about the former if he were a completely separate person? There is no need for an elaborate theory involving the displacement of the Yeoman's hostile emotions from his ex-master onto the False Canon. It is simpler to take *shame* in 542 as 'embarrassment' (or indeed 'shame') rather than as a generalized indignation against villainous conduct. The Yeoman's invisible (but real) blush is due to his former association with a man he knew to be a 'fox' (cf. also 606, 620 (c), 720–2, 751, etc.).

563. *anon* recurs here for the fourth time in thirteen lines. The Priest's impatience springs from his avarice (cf. 574, 588, 589, 592, also *speedily*, 590, and *ful faste*, 593).

566–71. The Canon now uses the more intimate *thou* as one revealing a cherished secret to a close and trusted friend. The change of tone indicated by the reversion to *ye* between 572 and 600, when the Canon invites the Priest to tend the coals, is perhaps due to the fact that he is here 'making a speech' – solemnly declaring his powers, rather like the traditional mountebank (which is what, in reality, he is) (cf. also 500, 628). The oath at 569 is ironically out of place in the mouth of a character who has been persistently linked with 'the fiend' (431, etc.) and echoes the ref. to Judas at 459 ff as well as the Yeoman's statement at 519 about the Canon's diabolical mission in life. But the irony is heightened (if we recall 519) by the Priest's being scarcely a good representative of 'Cristes peple'. While this doesn't excuse the Canon's cynicism, it removes any sympathy we might feel for the victim. (Chaucer enjoyed the spectacle of fools [as well as villains] being undone by cleverer villains. The motif is characteristic of Chaucer's *fabliaux* as of the *fabliau*-genre as a whole [cf. the tales of the Miller, Reeve, Shipman and Friar, also *GP*, Introduction p. 6n.].)

573. *mortifye* (lit. 'put to death') graphically describes the chemical alteration of *quick*silver ('*argentum vivum*') to plain silver sought by the alchemists (cf. further 878 and the brief allegory that follows). The word also meant generally 'bring about any change in the substance', but not here.

574. The impudent 'withouten lye' shows the extent of the Canon's cynicism and the ref. to his own purse (576) – soon to be filled with the Priest's forty pounds – underlines his open contempt for his victim. But the latter is so blind that the hasty cover-up of *elleswher* (577) is scarcely necessary.

580. The powder is supposedly the Philosophers' Stone (see 309–10 (C) above) and – if genuine – could have 'cost' the Canon both effort and money. In many accounts of transmutations the Stone is described as a powder in form (e.g. the highly circumstantial one of Helvetius, in *Holmyard*, 259–67).

620. Yet another hint that the two Canons are one person: the wish for revenge here is more than a general hope. (Note also the strength of feeling in the heavy alliteration of 606, and cf. 535–42 (C), 751 (C).)

624. Note Chaucer's small lapse from dramatic decorum in *above*, which is more appropriate to someone writing rather than telling a story.

628. The Canon again reverts to *ye*. The sentiment expressed is friendly concern (feigned) and the polite pronoun adds to the effect (cf. 500–66 above).

632. The seventh-century Greek saint Giles (Aegidius) was very popular in the Middle Ages, judging by the frequency with which people swore by him.

634. The metaphorical blinding of the Priest becomes literal at this point as he is inveigled into wiping his face and so missing what the Canon is about.

637. A metrically irregular line with a dactylic movement in the first two feet (cf. 928).

651. The word 'alchemist' (f. Arab. *al* [the article]+*kimia* < Gk. *khemeia*, 'transmutation') appears only once in the *Tale*. Its sudden use at this point (where a more opprobrious expression might be expected from the incensed speaker) has the effect of making all alchemists and alchemy identical with frauds and trickery.

651–2. *tyme: by me*. This type of rhyme is common in ME and does not necessarily have a comic effect as in Byron and most modern poets. (This particular rhyme occurs seven times in Gower.) The *-me* of *tyme* is pronounced [mə] and that of *me* [me] but the rhyme was acceptable nonetheless (cf. 741).

675 ff. The Canon's trick is not described with perfect clarity, for all the Yeoman's eagerness to expose and warn against the 'sleighte'. At 675 we need to read '*an* ingot' (mould) for 'his ingot' – i.e. a mould fashioned out of an easily bent tin plate. There is already some silver in the crucible, released when the hollow beech-coal was burnt up, and the idea now is to give the impression that the ounce of quicksilver put in the crucible has been turned into an ounce of silver 'good and fine' by the process of 'mortification', effected through the power of the Stone (the powder). The *ingot* of 680 is the chalk one, which the Canon fills with the *matere* from the crucible and transfers to the water to cool off. The shaped *teyne* which the Canon hides in his sleeve is to be used in the third experiment (764–6); its mention at this stage is just a little confusing.

682. *him luste* = *him liste*, 'it pleased him' (hence 'he liked'). The impersonal construction is a common ME idiom.

700. The Canon's sarcasm adds insult to injury. We have seen the 'art' to be relatively simple – only the 'craft' (bad sense) of the Canon requires 'skill'. In calling the 'assay' a 'discipline' the Canon is mocking the Priest for his lack of wit.

711. The stick is supposedly for stirring but in fact the instrument of the trick. (It is 'for show' only in that it serves to conceal its real purpose under its ostensible one.) As the wax stopper melts, the *lymaille* is released.

735–6. On identical rhyme see (c) on *GP*, 17 in this vol.

737. *crafty*, both 'skilful' and 'cunning'; a consciously ironic pun (cf. 767).

738. *thee* maintains the intimate tone.

741–2. *swythe: hy the*. Cf. 651–2 (c) for the rhyme. Note the monosyllabic briskness of the lines, which seem to express the Canon's mounting impatience and desire to get his money and make his escape. The sg. imper. (*go, hy*) reinforces this impression, which is not gainsaid by the hollowly rhetorical *gode sir*, and seems curt rather than amicably informal.

744. *niman* was the common OE word for 'take' (cf. Ger. *nehmen*) but was supplanted by ON *taka* in the pres. though surviving in the pret. (its use here is obviously determined in part by the need for a rhyme and if Chaucer had used *took* it could have meant 'gave'; cf. 477 (c) above).

748. The Yeoman's hyperbole is characteristic. The 'root of all wickedness' was the devil, as the following lines make explicit (749–50, and cf. 519, 566–71 above). ME *roote* was more graphic than our 'source', the etymological meaning of which ('spring') is lost. Cf. also *The Man of Law's Tale*, 358, 361: 'O sowdanesse, *roote of iniquitee*! . . ./Lyk to the serpent depe in helle ybounde.'

749–50. *feendly* is deliberately contrasted with *freendly* and the fact that the two words are phonetically identical except for one consonant helps to express Chaucer's *theme* through the very nature of the words used. The Canon's *craft* ('skill') is really 'craft' (cunning) and he appears honest only to the blindly gullible, just as the written word *feend* can be easily mistaken for *freend* if one doesn't look too closely. *Modern paraphrase* destroys the near-homophone, but even if we do not substitute 'devil' for 'fiend' the change produced by the *modern pronunciation* of this word and 'friend' equally destroys the subtlety of the verbal contrast. This is a striking instance of the value of knowing how to pronounce Chaucer's words.

751. Compare 540 (c), 619 (c). These frequent self-intrusions by the Yeoman help to keep his personal animus against the Canon in our minds and so assert what he himself has denied – the identity of the two Canons.

753. The metre is again irregular, *to* being slurred.

754. A sermon-like touch: the case is offered as exemplary. But it is hard to believe the Yeoman's denial of personal motives in denouncing the Canon (cf. 751 above).

756. The use of the perfect tense instead of the simple past has the effect of making the action seem immediate, a device familiar to modern readers from the Ballads (also 768).

758. The word has a faint overtone of opprobrium. The avaricious Priest literally 'stoops' to further his quest for lucre and in doing so is duped.

760. Skeat says the image is taken from the medieval showmen (apewards) who led apes on a string (hence the meaning is 'to lead someone at will') but perhaps the idea is rather the well-known faculty for mimicry of monkeys (*ape* prob. denoted a chimpanzee, not a gorilla). Here the Canon has made the foolish Priest follow his instructions faithfully but with no more *understanding* of what he is doing than a monkey (cf. also 758 (c) above).

761–2. *it*, i.e. first the mixture in the crucible, then the mould containing the mixture.

763. The Canon uses his own hand this time because he has to transfer the silver plate unseen from his sleeve into the mould. By this time he can afford so blatant a deception because he has his unsuspecting victim completely in his confidence.

764. i.e. at 678. On the rhyme see 735–6 (c) above.

766. The meaning of *slyly* is here influenced by the neighbouring *heyne*.

769. The word here has the relatively unusual meaning of 'producing a rumbling noise by agitating something' – i.e. here the silver plate on the bottom of the pan.

773. The routine of gulling people is a 'game' or joke for the Canon. The phrase normally implies that the playfulness is perceptible as such.

774–5. The resumed formality of the pl. imper. restores a tone of gravity appropriate to the end of an experiment in which (had it been genuine) the Canon would have revealed the secrets of alchemy to the Priest.

779–80. The Canon's knowledge of the psychology of human weakness almost merits the term 'fiendly'. While – like the real fiend in *The Friar's Tale* – he allows his victim virtually to undo himself, he is also a past master of flattery ('which that *we* han wroght') and self-disparagement ('oght').

785–6. The silver was melted (to see if it was *pure*) and hammered (to see if it was *malleable* like real silver or brittle like an alloy). The first method was prob. the one called *cupellation* (see *Taylor*, p. 50).

789–96. This passage of similes is stylistically the most curious in the poem and has often been noticed because of the incongruity with which it evokes contrasting realms of value and conduct to those of the 'besotted' Priest. The natural, instinctive delight of the bird and the young woman and the dedicated knight's chivalric nobility are genuine and praiseworthy emotions (caused by light, youth, love) and there is something unnatural and perverted about the Priest's exaltation (which, we remember finally, should have been induced in *his* case by religion, not money, anyway). The medieval *carole* (793) was a round-dance accompanied by music (and often words, from which the first 'carols' developed). *wommanhede* (794) here refers to 'the things that interest (or concern) women' rather than 'femininity'. With 794–5, lines evoking the ethos of 'Courtly Love', cf. *GP*, 88 (c) in this vol.

795. A metrically awkward line whether we read *stonde* as *stonden* (which forces the stress onto the naturally unemphatic *in*) or pronounce final *-e* in *grace* (which produces hiatus).

796. A line of pungent irony. Not only is the craft *sory* to the Priest, but he doesn't in any real sense 'learn' it (or anything).

798. The 'pious' allusion to the death of Christ certainly expresses the *strength* of the Priest's lust for gold – a discrepancy further illustrating his 'blindness' (cf. also 804, 789–96 (c) above and 801 (c) below).

799. A very rare and unusual meaning of the expression (recorded in the *OED* under *deserve*, sense 6, citing Malory, II, ix: 'I have ill deserved it unto him for his kindness'.

801. The Canon ripostes to the Priest's oaths (cf. *for Goddes sake* later as well as 798) with his own (808 as well as 801) – though not without a hint of mockery. *His* blasphemy however is conscious and cynical. Like the true mountebank, he is now playing 'hard to get'. Chaucer captures beautifully the Canon's 'act' of making a great concession – from the understatement of *dere* at 801 to the *ful dere* ('*very* expensive') of 806 to the sudden anticlimax of *fourty pound* at 808 as the Canon (who doesn't wish to overplay his hand but who

also wishes to appear to be acting out of gratitude for the Priest's disinterested generosity) puts his victim out of his misery.

812. The Priest pays over a total of 120 gold coins, a quantity over which the narrator lingers with incredulity ('took hem *everichoon*', 'gave every last one of them!')

815–21. The danger from other men's envy incurred by alchemists was given by the Yeoman (by implication) as a reason for his master's 'bawdy' clothing at 90.

821–2. *weye: sey ye*, see 651–2.

824. The asseveration is dramatically ironic, foreshadowing the frustrated rage the Priest will feel when he gets round to trying out the 'receit' for himself.

828. The normal Chaucerian preterite of *seen* is *saugh* (saw) but the alternative *sy* is here used for the sake of the rhyme.

835. On the Three Estates of society (clergy, nobility, labourers) see *GP*, 529 ff (c).

836–7. The Yeoman visualizes the dabbling in alchemy of people from all the estates as a kind of 'quarrel' between men and gold the result of which is to diminish the actual quantity of available gold (i.e. through its use in unsuccessful efforts at transmutation which destroy the old gold without producing any new). This is a poetic exaggeration, of course, since the gold 'disappears' more through changing hands than through being wasted in laboratories.

841–3. In spite of intelligence or learning (*wit*) men cannot achieve the Stone because they start from a shaky basis – i.e. the confused and inconsistent terminology and instructions of the alchemical writers, which they further misinterpret themselves, as well as the false physical theory underlying alchemy (see Introduction, section on the 'slyding science'). The Yeoman's strictures on 'mistiness' are amply borne out by the account of the 'mortification' of mercury from Arnald of Villanova given below (878–94).

854–5. The allusion to the proverb ('Burnt bairns fear fire') suggests by implication that alchemists are *more* foolish than children. 855 is peculiarly piquant coming from the Yeoman, whose 'office' was to blow the fire.

860. Proverbial: 'As bold as blind Bayard' (*Bayard* was a common name for a horse – orig. 'bay-coloured'). 860–1, with their heavy alliteration, both recreate the ungainly movement of the blind horse and express the speaker's contempt for the (mental) blindness of the oft-bitten but still unshy breed of alchemists.

869. Lit. 'seize' (*rape*, f. Fr. *raper* or OE *hrēapian*, 'handle') and (?) 'run' (*renne* f. OE *hrinan*, 'touch').

870. The metaphor here is from kindling: 'Don't even dabble in alchemy, or before you know it you'll have run through your whole fortune.'

875. *Arnaldus of Villanova* ('the Newe Toun'), *c.* 1235–1311, was

a physician and alchemist. The work Chaucer calls the *Rosarie* (Lat. *rosarium*, 'rose-garden') was 'The Treasure of Treasures, *Rosary* of Philosophers and Greatest Secret of all Secrets' (cf. 876, 894 below), a treatise in two parts on the theory and practice of alchemy. (On Arnald, see *Holmyard*, 122–6). 878–87 are translated from a passage in Ch. iv of Arnald's treatise *On the Philosophers' Stone* (printed in *SA*). Chaucer's rendering is somewhat confusing because of the connective *How be that* at 880 which implies that what follows is a contradiction of 878–9 and yet is attributed to the same person. The Latin source shows that the speaker of 878–9 is a disciple who is asking the Master why alchemists say that 'Mercury dies not unless slain with his brother' (*cum fratre*, Chaucer's 'with his brother knowleching') and in fact the reply merely confirms and expands this statement. The confusion may ultimately derive from the fact that Chaucer (no less than ourselves) was not clear what this gibberish really meant. The 'brother' of Mercury was of course sulphur (*brimstoon*).

881. *Hermes Trismegistus* (the 'thrice-great') was the name of the reputed author of many alchemical writings, notably the *Smaragdine* [Emerald] *Tablet*, one of the earliest. He was identical with *Thoth*, the Egyptian god of mathematics and science (see *Holmyard*, 97–100). From *Hermes* comes the name 'Hermetic Art' (alchemy) and the expression 'hermetically sealed'.

882. The 'dragon' was another name for mercury.

884. The 'sulphur' (see end of 875 (C)) was not ordinary sulphur as we know it but a hypothetical substance thought to be contained in gold and silver, from whence it could be extracted. The process here described is the making of the Elixir, which requires mercury to 'die' or 'be killed' ('mortified'), i.e. *solidify* (the Lat. has *congelatur*) in the presence of the 'sulphur' mentioned above. The basic notion underlying this experiment was the 'Sulphur–Mercury Theory', according to which these elements (in their ideal form) were the 'proximate constituents' of all metals, from which they had to be isolated to be of use in the 'projection' (precipitation) of the Elixir or Stone. Roughly speaking, the alchemists sought to achieve an equilibrium between the ideal substances they called 'sulphur' and 'mercury' so as to bring about the solidification of the mercury to form silver and gold. The isolation of the 'sulphur' and 'mercury' supposedly present in *all* metals formed the preliminary stages of the 'great Work' (i.e. those prior to projection). Any metals could be used, but the best were, of course, silver and gold (*luna* and *sol*) – a factor accounting for the expensiveness of alchemy. Chaucer changed (or misunderstood) his source. The plural verb at 887 gives the meaning '(Mercury and sulphur), which were extracted from gold and silver (respectively)', whereas Arnald states merely that by 'his brother' is meant 'gold and silver' (by implication, the 'sulphurs' present in these metals).

894. The knowledge of the nature of the Elixir or Stone was called the most secret of all secrets because it was thought to give the possessor the power to control the production of all the metals. Since alchemy was a means of 'speeding up' the chemical processes by which nature formed metals it placed in a man's hands a power analogous to that of creation and so made him a kind of god. This reason (as well as the more obvious financial one) conduced to secrecy and was the basic reason for the alchemists' resort to 'mystical' writing that made use of allegory and symbolism (there was also a variety of speculative or 'esoteric' alchemy which was not in fact concerned with practical operations at all but with inner spiritual states although using the language and imagery of experimental or 'exoteric' alchemy). The name *Secret of Secrets* was that of many books, including Arnald's (see 875 (c) above).

895–918. The second alchemical work Chaucer quotes from is the *Tabula Chemica* of a writer called 'Senior', now thought to be the Arabian physician *Muhammad ibn Umail* (see *SA*, 686). Chaucer takes 'Senior' as the title of the book – a fact which suggests he had only glanced at it. The *his* of 897 obviously refers to the disciple, not Plato. The story is spurious.

874–end. The last lines of the tale have been thought to be out of character for the 'lewed' Yeoman because of their grave tone and learned references (to Arnald, Senior, etc.). In a sense they are, but only if we interpret 'character' narrowly, taking psychological consistency as all-important. For Chaucer, 'character' is a function of his total poetic statement, which here requires the invocation of *authorities* to support the moral so amply illustrated from the Yeoman's account of his own *experience*. (The conception of character is, so to speak, the product of the medieval notion of the nature of a literary work.) Chaucer could hardly deliver the last lines *in propria persona* – he had to give them to the narrator of the tale (i.e. speak through the Yeoman as a mouthpiece). Like the long speech on *gentillesse* in *The Wife of Bath's Tale*, these lines are not strictly an *expression* of character and taken as such they must appear incongruous. Taken as the poet's explicit summing-up of the moral (or morals) implicit in the poem, they are acceptable enough (even if they add little to what has gone before) and indeed help to underline the Yeoman's earlier point that 'lered' and 'lewed' 'Concluden . . ./Ylike wel . . .'

This is to seyn, they faillen bothe two.

Sources and Abbreviations

Arnold, Matthew Arnold, 'The Study of Poetry', in *Essays in Criticism*, 2nd series, ed. S. R. Littlewood. Macmillan, 1958.

Bayley, John Bayley, *The Characters of Love*. Chatto and Windus, 1960.

Bloch, Marc Bloch, *Feudal Society*, trans. L. A. Mańyon. 2 vols. Routledge and Kegan Paul, 1965.

Brewer, D. S. Brewer, 'The Fabliaux', in Beryl Rowland (ed.), *Companion to Chaucer Studies*. Oxford University Press, 1968.

Burrow, J. A. Burrow, *A Reading of Sir Gawain and the Green Knight*. Routledge and Kegan Paul, 1965.

Cholmeley, H. P. Cholmeley, *John of Gaddesden*. Clarendon Press, Oxford, 1912.

Copland, R. A. Copland, note on line 136 of the *GP* in *Notes and Queries*, vol. 17, no. 2 (Feb. 1970), 45–6.

Curry, W. C. Curry, *Chaucer and the Medieval Sciences*. New York, Barnes and Noble, rev. edn, 1960.

Dryden, John Dryden, 'Preface to the Fables', in *English Critical Essays* (XVI, XVII and XVIII centuries), ed. Edmund D. Jones. World's Classics, Oxford University Press, 1959.

Donaldson, E. T. Donaldson, 'Chaucer the Pilgrim', *PMLA* LXIX (1954), 928–36, repr. in R. J. Schoeck and J. Taylor (eds), *Chaucer Criticism*, I, 1–14. Notre Dame, Indiana, University of Notre Dame Press, 1960.

Duncan,ⁱ Edgar H. Duncan, 'The Literature of Alchemy and Chaucer's *CYT*: Framework, Theme and Characters', *Speculum* XLIII (1968), 633–56.

Duncan,ⁱⁱ Edgar H. Duncan, 'The Yeoman's Canon's "Silver Citrinacioun",' *Modern Philology*, XXXVII (1940), 241–62.

Gower, *The English Works of John Gower*, ed. G. C. Macaulay. Early English Text Society, Oxford, 1900; repr. 1957.

Hodgson, Phyllis Hodgson (ed.), Chaucer's *General Prologue*. Athlone Press, 1969.

Holmyard, E. J. Holmyard, *Alchemy*. Pelican, 1968.

Hulbert, J. R. Hulbert, 'The Canterbury Tales and their Narrators', *Studies in Philology*, XLV (1948), 565–77.

Kittredge, G. L. Kittredge, 'Chaucer's Discussion of Marriage', repr. in Schoeck and Taylor (eds.), *Chaucer Criticism*, I, 130–60.

Langland, *Piers Plowman* (B-text), ed. W. W. Skeat, 2 vols. Clarendon Press, Oxford, 1888.

Lumiansky, R. M. Lumiansky, *Of Sondry Folk*. University of Texas, Austin, 1955.

McKisack, May McKisack, *The Fourteenth Century* (1307–99), Oxford History of England, Vol. V. Clarendon Press, Oxford, 1959.

Muscatine, Charles Muscatine, *Chaucer and the French Tradition.* University of California Press, Berkeley, 1957.

Owen, Charles A. Owen, 'The Design of the Canterbury Tales', in Beryl Rowland (ed.), *Companion to Chaucer Studies.* Oxford University Press, 1968.

Payne, R. O. Payne, *The Key of Remembrance*: *a study in Chaucer's Poetics*, publ. for the University of Cincinnati by Yale University Press, New Haven, 1963.

Pollard, Alfred W. Pollard, Chaucer's *Canterbury Tales*: *Prologue.* Macmillan, repr. 1921.

Pope, Alexander Pope, 'Advertisement' to his 'Epistle to Dr Arbuthnot', in *The Poems of Alexander Pope*, ed. John Butt. Methuen, 1963.

Power,ⁱ D'Arcy Power, *English Medicine and Surgery in the Fourteenth Century*, repr. from *The Lancet*, 1914.

Power,ⁱⁱ Eileen Power, *Medieval People*. Methuen, 1924.

Pratt, R. A. Pratt, 'The Order of the Canterbury Tales', *PMLA* LXVI (1951), 1141–67.

Robertson, D. W. Robertson, *A Preface to Chaucer*. Princeton University Press, Princeton, New Jersey, 1962.

Robinson, F. N. Robinson (ed.), *The Works of Geoffrey Chaucer*. Oxford University Press, 2nd edn., 1957.

Singer, Charles Singer (ed.), MS 17, St John's College, Oxford, in *A Review of the Medical Literature of the Dark Ages, with a new Text of about 1100*. Repr. from the *Proceedings of the Royal Society for Medicine*, vol. IV, pp. 107–60, 1917.

Skeat, W. W. Skeat (ed.), *The Works of Geoffrey Chaucer*, 6 vols. Clarendon Press, Oxford, 2nd edn., 1900.

Tawney, R. H. Tawney, *Religion and the Rise of Capitalism*. Pelican, 1961.

Taylor, Gerald Taylor, *Silver*. Pelican, 1965.

Thrupp, Sylvia L. Thrupp, *The Merchant Class of Medieval London*, repr. Ann Arbor pbk., 1962.

Waddell, Helen Waddell, *The Wandering Scholars*. Pelican, 1954.

Young, Karl Young, *The Drama of the Medieval Church*, 2 vols. Clarendon Press, Oxford, 1933.

CA, the *Confessio Amantis* of John Gower (see *Gower*, above).

CYT, the *Canon's Yeoman's Tale*   *GP*, the *General Prologue*

ME, Middle English   *OE*, Old English   *ON*, Old Norse

SA, *Sources and Analogues of Chaucer's Canterbury Tales*, ed. W. F. Bryan and G. Dempster. Humanities Press, New York, 1958.

ST, St Thomas Aquinas's *Summa Theologica* (3rd edn.). La Editorial Catolica, Madrid, 1961.

Appendix I

How to Read Chaucer's Verse

To read Chaucer's verse properly we need to combine a basic knowledge of the original sound-values of his words with the ordinary sensitivity we would bring to the reading of any poetry. A great deal can never be recovered, of course – for instance, the *tone* of the poetry as read aloud or recited – but on the whole the meaning is a reliable guide to the latter.

The sounds

No manuscript of Chaucer's work survives in his own hand, and, since spelling was not yet fixed in the fourteenth century, Chaucer's poetry shows inconsistencies of spelling. But the Ellesmere MS of the *Canterbury Tales* (on which this text is based) has a fairly regular spelling which indicates the pronunciation quite clearly. This has been further regularized and simplified (e.g. long *i* is spelt *y* in this edition).

Consonants

These are always pronounced – including the *w* in *wryte*, *k* in *knowe*, etc. The letter *r* is rolled or trilled in any position – e.g. *flour* as well as *croppes*. *ng* is pronounced like *ng* in our finger; *gh* is like *ch* in German *ach* except after *i* and *e*, when it is more like *ch* in German *ich* (thus *night* has one sound, *droghte* another).

Vowels

		EXAMPLE
Short a	as in German *Mann*	*whan, that*
Long a	as in father	*bathed, name*
Long open e ('slack' e)	as in there	*heeth, were*
Long close e ('tense' e)	as in French *é*, or, less closely, fame	*swete, meeke*
Short e	as in set	*engendred*
Unaccented or neutral e	as in *ado*, mill*er*	*swete, falle*
Long i (y)*	as in mach*ine*	*ryde, wys*
Short i	as in switch	*swich, blisful*
Long close o ('tense' o)	roughly as in tone, but closer to French *rôle*	*sote*
Long open o ('slack' o)	as in broad	*goon*

*Always spelt *y* in this edition.

Short o	as in long	*croppes*
Long u	as in true	*devout, shoures*
Short u	as in put	*ful, ronne*
'French' u	as in Fr. *tu*, Ger. *Dürer*	vertú, natúre

Diphthongs

These are sounds composed of two vowels spoken more or less rapidly together. Some are still heard in English:

| au | as in brown | *bawdrik, ytaught* |
| oi | as in joy | *coy, Loy* |

About the others scholars still disagree, but the following simplified guide is not too far from the truth:

The sound represented variously by the spellings *ai, ay, ei, ey* (e.g. *day, veyne*) may be pronounced as either a combination of the short *a* in our *man* plus the short *i* of our *thin*, lengthened somewhat (as in *mayde, lay*); or else as a sound like '*ai*' in our *aisle*. But there are other possibilities.

In diphthongs containing *w* it is simplest to sound the first vowel separately and then articulate the *w* gently: *tre – we, kno – we.*

Au in the group *aun* (mainly in words from the French, like *straunge, daungere*) may be pronounced either as in our *haunt*, or as in *brown*.

Note that the spelling *o* sometimes indicates other than 'o' sounds: *ronne* (*o* = short *u*), *droghte* (*o* = long *u*). Contrast *also* (long open *o*), *doon* (long close *o*), *oft* (short *o*).

A rough guide to the difference between open and close vowel-sounds is the *modern spelling* of the equivalent ME word (where it still exists). Thus modern *ea* usually indicates an original open *e* sound (e.g. head, *heed*), *ee* or *ie* an original close *e* sound (e.g. green, *grene*; lief(er), *levere*); *oa* indicates an original open *o* sound (e.g. broad, *brood*), *oo* an original close *o* sound (e.g. root, *ro(o)te*).

Chaucer's Verse provides no difficulty of 'scansion' if we remember that it is basically the same as the verse of Shakespeare or Pope – somewhat less strict than the latter and less free than the former. *Two rhythms* are played off against each other in this as in most English verse – a musical rhythm and a speech rhythm, or, in other words, the rhythm of the metrical pattern and the rhythm dictated by the voice interpreting dramatically the meaning of the poetry. In practice, the musical rhythm is suppressed nearly always and exists only by implication at the back of the reader's (or listener's) mind while the dramatic rhythm operates actively. Thus in the opening lines of the Prologue, we stress '*Whán that*' '*Áprill*' '*shoures*' and '*sóte*' because these are the *important* words, pausing briefly after 'Aprill'. It is unlikely that Chaucer read the line

$$\text{Whán that Áprill wíth his shóures sóte}$$

but of course we cannot know. The general impression conveyed by Chaucer's late verse is one of great flexibility, a lyric sweetness tempered by a colloquial vigour and directness – music and speech combined. Above all, the versification is *varied*: it gives an impression of ordered clarity without monotony. Chaucer's staple verse is the decasyllabic couplet, though in practice it has *more* or *fewer* than ten syllables. Chaucer had the advantage of being able to use or suppress as he needed the inflectional ending ('final *-e*') in words like *shoures, were, felawshipe*, etc. (*GP*, 1, 23, 26). Thus in *shoures* it is sounded, giving a two-syllabled word, in *were* it is dropped (but in 366 it is sounded), in *felawshipe* it is elided with the *a* of *and*, the next word. The best 'rule' to follow is the 'feel' of the poetry, though this has to be determined in part by a thorough grasp of the meaning of the words and sentences.

An excellent guide to reading Chaucer is the gramophone record of the *General Prologue* read by Nevill Coghill, Norman Davis and John Burrow (Argo).

Appendix II

Textual Notes

The text of the *Prologue* is based on the Ellesmere MS (El), one of the oldest and best MSS of the *Canterbury Tales* (dated *c.* 1400–10). What seem to be clear scribal errors are silently emended (e.g. 497, *afterward that* > *afterward*), usually by reference to the Hengwrt MS (Hg), of about the same date. A number of preferred readings are also incorporated from the latter. The text of the *Canon's Yeoman's Tale* is likewise based on El, corrected in some places from other MSS as in Robinson's edition (I accept all of Robinson's readings). Owing to the excellence of El, there are few serious changes to be made in any new edition, and the text given here is substantially the same as that of the standard editions. The following textual details are perhaps worth noticing:

The General Prologue

1. In 131–2 El's *brist: list* are replaced by *brest:lest* (I take it that *brest* determined the rhyme word and was the standard Chaucerian form); in 178 *ben* (the usual form) replaces *beth*. Both seem to have been variations due to the scribe who copied the MS. In 10 *eye* is emended to *ÿe* to make the rhyme clear.
2. The following Ellesmere readings are rejected because they give inferior sense or metre: 74, *weren* (omitting the *n* gives a smoother line); 140, *and to been* (same reason); 215, *And* (*Ful*); 217, *And*; 240, *al the*; 287, *And* (for *As*); 359, *and countour*; 396, *drawe*; 525, *waiteth*; in 604 El omits *ne* and in 660 *him*; in 686 *lay* is supplied from MS Harleian 7334. 782, *But if* (*But*); 783, *hond* (*hondes*); 858, *in this manere* (*as ye may here*).
3. The following are also rejected, though there seems little to choose between them and those adopted: 148, *any* (*oon*); *it* (*he*); 234, *yonge* (*faire*); 332, *heed* (*berd*); 340, *was he* (*he was*) (but El gives an ugly jingle: *he . . . contree*); 612, *gowne* (*cote*); 669, *was* (*rood*; El is weaker); 774, *the stoon* (*a stoon*); 822, *gan for* (*bigan*).
4. In l. 8 the reading of three lesser authorities is accepted against El, Hg, etc. because it improves the metre, but the *-e* of *halfe* is bracketed to indicate that it may be a scribal 'improvement'.
5. Four other readings deserve comment:
   line 60, for *armee* Hg has *aryve* ('disembarkation'), a reading

unusual enough to be genuine, but rejected because it could easily be a scribal misreading of *armee* and also because it makes less good sense than the latter.

line 179, for *recchelees*, MS Harley 7334 has *Cloysterlees*, which was adopted by older editors like Skeat and Pollard, and has something to be said for it. However I prefer the view that l. 181 would become tautological if the Ha reading were genuine to the view that 181 is 'explaining' *cloysterlees* as a strange, unfamiliar word.

lines 252a–252b; these lines (found in Hg, etc.) look genuine though they may have been cancelled later because they interrupt the flow of sense. It seems reasonable to compromise by keeping them in the text but making them parenthetical.

line 512, for *dwelte . . . kepte* El has *dwelleth . . . kepeth*; there is no objection on grounds of meaning, but El breaks the otherwise carefully observed tense-sequence in this portrait (however, cf. 524, and also 210, etc.).

The Canon's Yeoman's Tale

El divides the poem into a *Prologue* (1–167) and *two parts* (168–418, 419–end). These divisions may be Chaucer's own or due to the scribe who copied the MS. It is more helpful to the modern reader to break the tale into three parts: an *Introduction* (corresponding to El's Prologue), in which the Canon and his Yeoman arrive on the scene and the Canon departs; a *Prologue* (corresponding to El's First Part), in which the Yeoman describes his life with the Canon; and a *Tale* (El's Second Part), in which the Yeoman tells the story of the False Canon and the gullible priest.

As in the text of the *General Prologue* in this volume, the spelling has been normalized and simplified slightly; the punctuation is editorial.

166. *Prologue*; El has *Here endeth the Prologue of the Chanouns Yemannes Tale; Here biginneth the Chanouns Yeman his Tale.*

328. *brat*; there is little to choose between this and *bak* (many MSS).

418. *The Tale*: El has *Explicit prima pars. Et sequitur pars secunda.*

547. El: *Consumed and wasted han my reednesse*, a line where metrical awkwardness is not unavoidable. Assuming that Chaucer *would* have avoided it (even in a poem which other evidence suggests was left unrevised) I print Robinson's proposed emendation.